Novell® NetWare® Commands and Installation Made Easy

Novell® NetWare®
Commands and
Installation

Doug Weber

Osborne **McGraw-Hill**

Berkeley New York St. Louis San Francisco
Auckland Bogotá Hamburg London Madrid
Mexico City Milan Montreal New Delhi Panama City
Paris São Paulo Singapore Sydney
Tokyo Toronto

Osborne **McGraw-Hill**
2600 Tenth Street
Berkeley, California 94710
U.S.A.

For information on translations and book distributors outside of the
U.S.A., please write to Osborne **McGraw-Hill** at the above address.

A complete list of trademarks appears on page 459.

Novell® NetWare® Commands and Installation Made Easy

1234567890 DOC 99876543210

ISBN 0-07-881614-9

Acquisitions Editor: Jeff Pepper
Technical Reviewer: Nick DiMuria
Copy Editor: Valerie Robbins
Word Processor: Bonnie Bozorg
Composition: Bonnie Bozorg
Proofreaders: Julie Anjos, Barbara Conway
Cover Design: Bay Graphics Design, Inc.
Production Supervisor: Kevin Shafer

DEDICATION

To James Weber, father and son

CONTENTS
AT A GLANCE

TABLE OF CONTENTS

ACKNOWLEDGMENTS

A very special thanks must go to Sam Sanders and his staff at Diversified Contractors, Morristown, N.J. Sam, Dottie, Viki, the book could not been written without your cooperation.

Among numerous others the author must thank are:

My parents, who have always been understanding.

Venessa, who lent her good name to the effort, and for whom completion of the book is no doubt a reward in itself.

Friends who lent their encouragement, with the writing, and with my efforts over the years to tame my personal computer.

A special thanks to Stan, whose friendship is valued even more than the knowledge and experience he always so willing shared.

The editors and staff of Osborne/McGraw-Hill for allowing me the opportunity to put ideas to paper.

The ownership of Integrated Productivity System, for the time and other support they granted me.

To the developers of NetWare, and the educators at Novell who shared their knowledge, my warmest appreciation. Any errors of fact or omission in my discussion of NetWare is indeed my responsibility, not theirs.

INTRODUCTION

Ensuring users are able to conveniently access and use a local area network is the primary objective of this book. This is a most important objective. A network installation exists for the benefit of its users. While parts of the book discuss topics not addressed directly to users, each topic discussed is important to ultimate user satisfaction. And several sections of the book are of direct interest to users of a NetWare supported local area network.

A second objective is to take some of the agony and pain out of the job of managing and maintaining a local area network. NetWare as a product can make your job of LAN manager relatively easy. But to gain this benefit you must understand NetWare as an operating system and know how to use NetWare to good effect. The contents of this book will help you accomplish this objective.

How This Book Is Organized

This book is meant to be read from front to back. Each chapter provides information important to understanding material presented in later chapters. Experienced network managers and users will, however, find certain chapters of more interest than others.

Chapter 1 introduces you to the concepts of local and wide area networking. This is followed in Chapter 2 by an overview of the NetWare operating system. Both chapters contain introductory material important to your understanding the new environment you are entering when you chose to link together previously standalone personal computers. The actual process of software installation on the server is relegated to Chapter 10. This reflects a judgment that many readers are working on an already up and running NetWare installation.

Chapters 3 and 4 discuss basic NetWare security features and demonstrate how, through NetWare's SYSCON and FILER utilities, you create user accounts and new directories and subdirectories on a server. Step-by-step, hands-on instructions for accomplishing these tasks are provided. Also reviewed in Chapter 4 is what a "useful" directory structure looks like, and how NetWare establishes directory security in its self-created, required server directories.

Chapter 5 reviews application software packages (word processing, spreadsheet, database programs) and how they may function on a network. You do not have to be using the specific applications programs discussed in Chapter 5 to benefit from the contents of that chapter. Understanding the differences between network and standalone applications is important to effective server directory structure and security design. Users may also want to read this chapter to better understand both the opportunities and complications that go with using applications on a PC network.

Chapter 6 takes you step-by-step through a directory and security design exercise, using as a reference point the applications discussed in Chapter 5. Chapter 6 takes you full circle to the Chapter 4 topics of creating new users, user groups, and directories and subdirectories.

Chapters 7, 8, and 9 discuss NetWare workstation commands and menus that can be accessed by network users. Chapter 7 provides hands-on instruction on creating network and search drive mappings and also introduces you to NetWare login scripts. Along with custom designed menus, login scripts are an important tool for helping users take advantage of the network. (Appendix C provides an example of a NetWare custom menu and brief instructions on how to create and use such a menu.)

Chapter 8 focuses on file management in server hard disk directories and subdirectories. File management on a network transcends the issues of how you create directories and move files from one location to another. As important is who has the right to perform these tasks, and what NetWare rights are required to accomplish a task. While Chapter 8 is intended as a hands-on guide to accomplishing specific file and directory management tasks, it should be read in light of the directory design and security discussions contained in Chapters 4 through 6.

For many network users, printing is the penultimate network task. Network printing certainly can be one of the more complex and, if not properly approached, more vexing of network tasks. Chapter 9 will not answer all your questions or discuss all the network printing situations you will encounter. It does provide a useful foundation for understanding available NetWare print services and for managing network printing.

While Chapter 10 focuses primarily on NetWare software installation, at the server and the workstation, it also contains instruction on how to use several NetWare console commands to monitor and properly shut down server operations. You do *not* simply turn off the power switch to your server machine.

Chapter 2 provides a foundation for file server and network performance monitoring, though that topic is not discussed at length in this book. However, in Appendix D you will find illustrations of information available through the NetWare menu utility FCONSOLE.

FCONSOLE can assist you in monitoring network performance, including NetWare's hot fix and disk caching features (discussed in Chapter 2).

Conventions Used in This Book

For the most part, this book follows the typographical conventions set up in the NetWare manuals. To make things as simple as possible for the reader, the following conventions are observed:

- New terms and words or text that are important to emphasize are shown in *italic*.

- All user input is shown in **boldface** type.

- Key presses on the IBM keyboard are shown as keys (ENTER) in the text.

- Filenames, directory names, DOS commands, and NetWare commands are expressed in capital letters so that you can pick them out quickly.

ADDITIONAL HELP FROM OSBORNE/McGRAW-HILL

Osborne/McGraw-Hill provides top-quality books for computer users at every level of computing experience. To help you build your skills, we suggest that you look for the books in the following Osborne/M-H series that best address your needs.

The "Teach Yourself" Series is perfect for beginners who have never used a computer before or who want to gain confidence in using program basics. These books provide a simple, slow-paced introduction to the fundamental usage of popular software packages and programming languages. The mastery learning format ensures that concepts are learned thoroughly before progressing to new material. Plenty of exercises and examples (with answers at the back of the book) are used throughout the text.

The "Made Easy" Series is also for beginners or users who may need a refresher on the new features of an upgraded product. These in-depth introductions guide users step-by-step from the program basics to intermediate-level usage. Plenty of hands-on exercises and examples are used in every chapter.

The "Using" Series presents fast-paced guides that quickly cover beginning concepts and move on to intermediate-level techniques, and even some advanced topics. These books are written for users who are already familiar with computers and software, and who want to get up to speed fast with a certain product.

The "Advanced" Series assumes that the reader is already an experienced user who has reached at least an intermediate skill level and is ready to learn more sophisticated techniques and refinements.

"The Complete Reference" is a series of handy desktop references for popular software and programming languages that list every command, feature, and function of the product along with brief, detailed descriptions of how they are used. Books are fully indexed and often include tear-out command cards. "The Complete Reference" series is ideal for all users, beginners and pros.

"The Pocket Reference" is a pocket-sized, shorter version of "The Complete Reference" series and provides only the essential commands, features, and functions of software and programming languages for users who need a quick reminder of the most important commands. This series is also written for all users and every level of computing ability.

The "Secrets, Solutions, Shortcuts" Series is written for beginning users who are already somewhat familiar with the software and for experienced users at intermediate and advanced levels. This series gives clever tips and points out shortcuts for using the software to greater advantage. Traps to avoid are also mentioned.

Osborne/McGraw-Hill also publishes many fine books that are not included in the series described above. If you have questions about which Osborne book is right for you, ask the sales person at your local book or computer store, or call us toll-free at 1-800-262-4729.

OTHER OSBORNE/MCGRAW-HILL BOOKS OF INTEREST TO YOU

We hope that *Novell NetWare Commands and Installation Made Easy* will assist you in mastering this fine product, and will also peak your interest in learning more about other ways to better use your computer.

If you're interested in expanding your skills so you can be even more "computer efficient," be sure to take advantage of Osborne/M-H's large selection of top-quality computer books that cover all varieties of popular hardware, software, programming languages, and operating systems. While we cannot list every title here that may relate to NetWare and to your special computing needs, here's a book that complements *Novell NetWare Commands and Installation Made Easy*.

If you're looking for the best way to get started in telecommunications or to get more out of the on-line services available today, see *Dvorak's*

Guide to PC Telecommunications (ISBN: 0-07-881551-7). This book/disk package, written by the internationally recognized computer columnist John Dvorak with programming wiz Nick Anis, shows you how to instantly plug into the world of electronic databases, bulletin boards, and on-line services. The package includes an easy-to-read, comprehensive guide plus two diskettes loaded with oustanding free software and is of value to computer users at every skill level.

WHY THIS BOOK IS FOR YOU

This book is for you if

- You are a manager of a newly installed local area network and need to know how to manage NetWare security and directory structures.

- You are a new manager of an existing network who needs to document your existing network structure and to understand what you have inherited.

- You are considering purchasing network versions of a word processing, spreadsheet, or database package, and need to know more about what to look for in a LAN application package.

- You are a user of a NetWare network, and need to know how to manage files, directories, and drive pointers.

- You are planning to use, or currently are unsuccessful in using, your network printers.

- You are responsible for installing NetWare on a server, or for installing new network printers.

- You are considering the purchase and installation of NetWare to accommodate anticipated growth in your business or to allow you to effectively and efficiently use the PC investment you may have made already.

Learn More About NetWare

Here is another excellent Osborne/McGraw-Hill book on NetWare that will help you build your skills and maximize the power of the network software you have selected.

Novell NetWare: The Complete Reference, by Tom Sheldon, covers installation, configuration, and day-to-day use of the system for network administrators, advanced users, and end users. The author, a gold-level authorized installer and trainer, also provides a complete supervisor's guide to network planning and maintenance.

INTRODUCTION TO NOVELL NETWARE

What This Book Is About
Novell NetWare Versions
What This Book Is Not About
What Is a LAN?
NetWare Path Name Conventions
Summary

This introductory chapter includes

- an overview of what this book is about

- an overview of NetWare as a product

- a brief introduction to LANs and WANs

WHAT THIS BOOK IS ABOUT

This book is about installing, using, and managing day-to-day Novell NetWare. NetWare is a personal computer operating system designed to provide services to local area network (LAN) users. Developed by Novell, Incorporated of Provo, Utah, NetWare is the best-selling local area network management package on the market today.

This book is written for NetWare LAN managers who are responsible for

- setting up users on a network

- ensuring users are able to use the network conveniently

- maintaining data security

Although this book is written for NetWare LAN managers, it will also be of interest to any NetWare LAN user. Certain chapters can be used as a desk reference for users.

NOVELL NETWARE VERSIONS

Novell NetWare is a computer system that allows you and other users to access the services of a central computer. Until recently, this central computer was another personal computer, referred to as the *file server*. The type of PC most often used as a central file server is a brand of 286 or 386 PC. This book assumes that the LAN manager and users are operating under Advanced NetWare 286 (version 2.15) or SFT NetWare 286 (version 2.15). These versions of NetWare are optimized for 286 machines, but they can be run on some 386 machines.

Figure 1-1 summarizes the features found in the various versions of NetWare 286. Some of these features are required, while others may be optionally installed.

Hard Disk Support and Printer Support

Up to five hard disk channels

Up to 36 hard disk volumes in total; up to 16 volumes for any hard disk

Each hard disk volume may be up to 255MB in size, with up to 2GB of external hard disk storage recognized

Removable hard disk technology supported

COMPSURF utility included for hard disk preparation and installation

Up to five printers (three parallel and two serial) may be attached to the server for printer sharing

System Fault Tolerance

Duplicate file directory tables (FAT and DET) maintained

Hot Fix redirection after write/read verification

Uninterruptible power supply (UPS) monitoring

Disk duplexing (SFT NetWare only)

Disk mirroring (SFT NetWare only)

Transaction Tracking Service (TTS) (SFT NetWare only)

Server Support

Runs on many models of 286 and some 386 machines

Up to 15MB of RAM addressable

Directory caching, file caching, and directory hashing and elevator seeking used to speed hard disk data retrieval

Up to 100 simultaneous connections to a server

26 drive pointers available to each user

16 search drives may be defined

Server may be run in nondedicated mode, used as both a server and a DOS workstation (Advanced NetWare only)

Bridging and Remote Communications

Supports both internal and external bridging, with up to four different network interface cards (NICs) per server (for internal bridges) or workstation (for external bridges)

Remote communication supported

Message Handling Service (MHS) software available at no extra cost

Other Features

Menu software included for developing user menus

Supports Value Added Processes (VAPs) and Value Added Drivers (VADs), including TCP/IP

Includes a NetBios emulator for workstations

Compatible with a host of LAN topologies and network interface cards

Supports transfer and sharing of Apple Macintosh files (version 2.15 only)

Copy-protection eliminated, key card no longer required, but existing key card may be used for UPS monitoring

COMCHEK utility included for testing LAN connections

FIGURE 1-1.   Advanced NetWare 286 and SFT 286 features

WHAT THIS BOOK IS NOT ABOUT

Novell markets versions of NetWare other than Advanced Net-Ware 286 and SFT NetWare 286. This book is not intended as a guide to all these various NetWare versions.

This book does not, except in a general way, take account of NetWare 386, the latest PC version of NetWare, which is designed to take advantage of the 32-bit technology built into 386 PCs. Much of this book applies to NetWare 386, although certain limitations found in NetWare 286 do not exist in NetWare 386. For instance, the number of users who can be simultaneously logged into a NetWare 386 file server is not limited to 100, and the total amount of disk storage addressable under NetWare 386 is in excess of 4 gigabytes. However, this book should not be considered a specific guide to NetWare 386, nor used as a NetWare 386 supplement.

Novell is also developing versions of NetWare that will run on mini or mainframe computers. Generically referred to as portable NetWare, these versions of Netware will have the look and feel of NetWare as used on a PC central file server. Much of what is said in this book about how NetWare operates will apply to these various versions of portable NetWare. On the other hand, there are important differences. As a topic, portable NetWare goes well beyond the scope of this book.

This book is about versions of NetWare 286 installed and run on a PC central file server.

Before taking a closer look at the NetWare operating system, a brief note is in order on the subject of LANs.

WHAT IS A LAN?

A local area network, as pictured in Figure 1-2, consists of the following:

- Some type of cabling or communication media that links multiple PCs together, either directly or through some other hardware device (which may be, but does not have to be, another PC).

- A network interface card (NIC), which is a communications card inserted into each PC on the LAN and to which the cabling just mentioned is connected.

In a NetWare supported local area network, a specialized PC (the file server) runs the NetWare software package. The server

- Provides file and data management, printing, and communications services to users on the local area network.

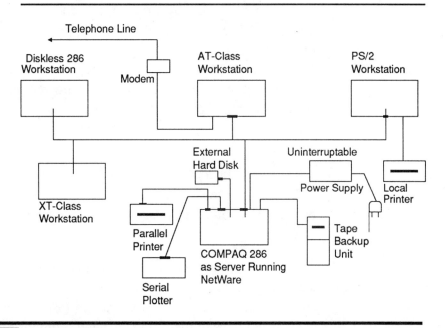

FIGURE 1-2.   A NetWare local area network

- May be attached to one or more printers or plotters to which any user on the network has controlled access.

  May be attached directly or indirectly to specialized communications devices, tape, or other file backup hardware, or other computer *peripherals*.

- May be interconnected through internal or external *bridges* to other general or special purpose file servers.

Before embarking on purchase of the equipment and software needed to set up such a LAN, you might well ask "Why bother with this additional, potentially complex, and probably expensive equipment and software purchase?" This is a good question.

Personal computers have been successful precisely because they are personal. You can power up your computer, load whatever software packages you choose to run, and print to your printer or plotter, unencumbered by other users, and independent of an organization's electronic data processing department rules, regulations, or personnel.

The great strength of the personal computer is the independence and freedom it provides. This personal character is also its weakness. Even in small business, educational, civic, or private organizations there are group requirements. For example:

- Data residing on a personal computer could be usefully shared, if the PC were not quite so personal; that is, if more than one person could simultaneously access the data files on that one machine.

- High-quality printer or plotter output is required, or preferred, and it is prohibitively expensive to purchase such devices for each individual PC in the organization (especially as your PC users spend most of their time on the PC composing or creating and relatively little of their total time printing or plotting).

- It is inconvenient or dangerous—from a data security perspective—to have different individuals all using the same PC (on which shared files reside or to which that high-quality printer or plotter is attached).

- Loss of data would result in significant negative consequences for the users or the business, and it is excessively time-consuming, costly, or inconvenient to perform frequent, daily data backups on all the separate PCs on which important data resides.

In short, you want to have your PC and the traditional benefits of centralized data processing operations at the same time. And that is precisely what the local area network is designed to provide: PC computing independence in a centralized file- and peripheral-sharing environment.

Before leaving the topic of LANs, a brief comment is in order about LAN *topologies* and the wider world of LANs, wide area networks or WANs.

Local Area Network (LAN) Topologies

Topology of a local area network usually means the cabling system that links the PCs (workstations and server) together. The network interface card (NIC) and other hardware to which cables are connected (active hubs, junction boxes, and so forth) and the software that allows for communication across the network are also, at times, included within the meaning of the term topology. Topology does not necessarily imply cabling. Communications may be over infrared light photo-links or other noncable media.

There is a great variety of LAN topologies on the market today; and a wide variety of wiring or cabling schemes, network interface cards, and associated communications protocols. Some typical topologies are illustrated in Figure 1-3.

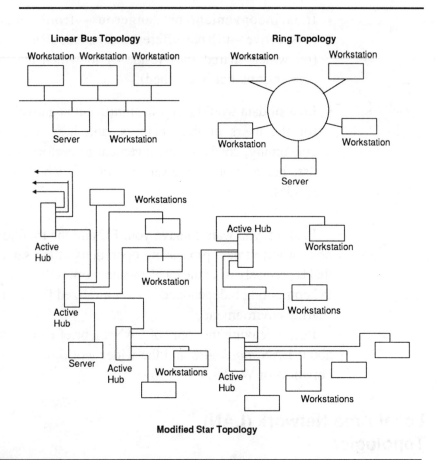

FIGURE 1-3.   Common LAN topologies

The relative strengths and weaknesses of each topology are not subjects for this book. Topology and NIC card selection are specialized topics, and difficult to discuss reliably in the rapidly advancing LAN technology market.

However, one point about the diversity of LAN topologies: NetWare allows you to interconnect many LAN topologies through NetWare bridging software. Bridging—in its internal and external forms—is discussed in later chapters. For now, note that NetWare allows for and encourages LAN interconnectivity.

Wide Area Networks (WANs) And Gateways

As they evolved early on, hardware and software to support personal computer interconnections had the limitation that the PCs had to be close together; that is, in local proximity to each other. Today the "local" in LAN is a misnomer. While PCs connected on a LAN may be proximately close, the definition of close is ever widening.

Improved remote communications technology and LAN topology bridging enable you to connect to a LAN in Berkeley, California (where the editor of this book works) and access services on another LAN in Merchantville, New Jersey (where the author resides). Formerly independent, geographically distant local area networks are increasingly interconnected, creating the existence of wide area networks (WANs).

Local area networks are not strictly networks of personal computers. You may find yourself working in an office with the personal computer on your desk running terminal-emulation software, allowing you to access data on one or more of the company's mini or mainframe computers. Hardware advances and gateway software provide the medium for PC interconnectivity to mini or mainframe computers.

It is reasonable to predict that many corporate **personal** computer users will in the near future be frequently interconnected to the company's "black boxes." Figure 1-4 hints at the possibilities contained within the wonderful world of wide area networks.

Just what might local area and wide area networking accomplish for you? Picture yourself on a warm evening viewing a Florida gulf coast sunset, while your individual, still personal computer is

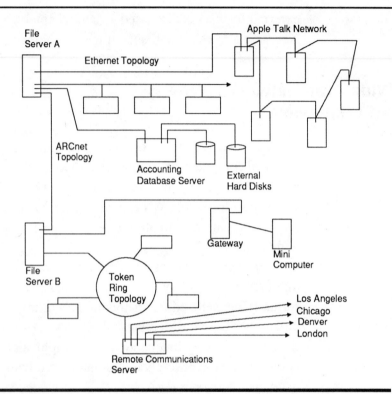

FIGURE 1-4.   Wide area network interconnectivity

connected by modem to a LAN anywhere in the world. Or, choose
Vale, Colorado, Costa del Sol, Spain, or almost any other location
as a place to live or vacation, because your personal computer is
connected to the world at large.

And whatever your LAN or WAN connection, the chances are
good that you will be using the services of Novell Netware.
NetWare has been and continues to be the largest-selling networking software application package on the market today.

NETWARE PATH NAME CONVENTIONS

On a LAN with multiple file servers, each with multiple data volumes created on one or more hard disks, finding your way around can be difficult. This is especially true as each file server running NetWare must have a volume named SYS. Under each SYS volume is a directory and subdirectory structure, and these will usually be similar on each file server. You need to be able to point to the correct SYS volume.

NetWare simplifies this process in a number of ways, the most important of which is inclusion of file server names, along with volume names, in what you know as the DOS path. In fact, network paths are not DOS paths, but that is not important for now. What is important is to understand NetWare's naming and path conventions. An example of a NetWare path is

FS1/SYS:PUBLIC

FS1 represents a file server named FS1. The file server name is separated by the delimiter / from the volume named SYS. A : delimiter is then used to separate the volume name from the directory PUBLIC.

In many instances, NetWare will allow you to use either a forward slash or a backslash as a delimiter or separator. However, the NetWare path definitions are generally recognizable by their use of the forward slash, /. The colon is always used as the delimiter between a volume name and a directory name.

If you work on a LAN with only one file server, the file server name can be dropped from the path. It is not necessary for locating the volume SYS, as there can be only one volume SYS on any one single file server. On an internetwork with multiple file servers, each file server must be uniquely named. While Novell in its documentation manuals uses FS1 as a file server name for illustration, it is strongly suggested you use a more meaningful, unique name. Company names may be used, for instance, 3M. Then again, a company with more than one file server interconnected will need additional information embedded in the filer server names for each to be unique. You could use 3M1, 3M2, and so on. You want file server names to be unique but brief and easily remembered. When you have to type the server name into a path definition, you will appreciate brevity and ease of recall and spelling.

Summary

This chapter included a brief introduction to the NetWare versions distributed by Novell. The organization plan for this book was reviewed. The concept and usefulness of local area and wide area networks were also discussed.

NetWare is a complex and robust operating system. Whether you have already purchased NetWare or are considering its use, it is hoped this book will help you make a quick start with understanding and using NetWare.

This book is only a beginning. The volumes of information packaged with your NetWare operating system software contain many nuggets of information worth mining, separate from or in conjunction with your explorations within the pages of this book.

NETWARE AS AN
OPERATING SYSTEM

A dvanced NetWare and SFT NetWare are unique operating systems. Both extend the standard personal computer operating system, DOS. An understanding of how NetWare is unique—in what ways it goes beyond DOS—is essential to successful LAN management. You need not be a hardware expert to successfully manage a LAN. It is important to understand what NetWare can do for you (often in the background).

This chapter reviews the NetWare operating system features that are standard in both Advanced NetWare 286 and SFT NetWare 286. Features unique to SFT NetWare are generally not reviewed in this book; for example, disk mirroring, disk duplexing and SFT Transaction Tracking Service (TTS).

NETWARE IS ITS OWN OPERATING SYSTEM

NetWare is its own operating system. The personal computer hardware on which you do your everyday work or recreation is controlled by its operating system software. Most probably, your computer is under the control of DOS, or *Disk Operating System*. Or perhaps you are using a new IBM PS/2 machine, running under OS/2, *Operating System Two*. Like DOS and OS/2, NetWare is the link between machine hardware and people who, like yourself, want to use that hardware for specific tasks. But NetWare is neither DOS nor OS/2. NetWare is a machine operating system with its own rules, architecture, and at times distinct hardware requirements.

NetWare is a popular success because it has the look and feel of DOS. What you know about DOS helps you to learn NetWare. Equally, what you know about the limits of DOS can, frequently, best be forgotten.

NetWare is also somewhat like OS/2. Through the server, NetWare does accomplish multitasking (or the illusion of multitasking) at the workstation. NetWare at the server is able to perform tasks for you (such as print job queueing and queue management) while you proceed to use your DOS or OS/2 workstation for other, separate tasks. And it is possible to install Advanced NetWare 286 on a server in nondedicated mode. In nondedicated mode, you can run one DOS session at the server—in the foreground, controlled through DOS keyboard commands—while NetWare runs in the background. And soon, Advanced NetWare 286 for OS/2 will allow you to run NetWare in the background on an IBM PS/2 machine with OS/2 in the foreground.

However, SFT NetWare cannot be run in nondedicated mode. And NetWare is not, strictly, a multitasking operating system. If you want to do true multitasking at your workstation, you will need to run OS/2, Concurrent DOS, or some other multitasking operating system at the workstation on the appropriate hardware platform (micro channel architecture, perhaps). But NetWare does free you from some of the limitations of DOS and moves you in the direction of multitasking. And NetWare can be run at the server with OS/2 for multitasking at the workstation. But it is in performing functions and services that neither DOS nor OS/2 perform that NetWare shines.

NETWARE: A MULTIUSER, MULTIPLE OPERATING SYSTEM WORLD

Unlike either DOS or OS/2, NetWare is a multiuser operating system. In this respect, Netware is like UNIX, another operating system designed for multiuser environments. Unlike UNIX, which has lacked consistency in its various versions, NetWare has maintained a high level of consistency in its user interface, while growing with the ever changing demands of the LAN industry.

Also unlike UNIX, NetWare was designed to interact with other operating systems, not to replace those systems. NetWare allows systems to interoperate. Tasks may be distributed across machines that are each running a unique operating system.

Perhaps the most fundamental point to remember is that NetWare interacts with, rather than replaces, your existing PC workstation operating system. Both the server and your workstation are smart machines. Each is capable of performing useful tasks or sharing responsibility for tasks. In short, you are operating in a *distributed operating environment*. How this environment influences installation and use of application packages is discussed in Chapters 5 and 6.

HOW INTEROPERABILITY IS ACCOMPLISHED

How is it possible for two distinct and quite different operating systems to work together? How is it possible for NetWare at the file server to talk to DOS or OS/2 at the workstation? In short, how is interoperability accomplished?

NetWare performs its interoperability magic by allowing you to place a part of itself, the NetWare *shell,* at the workstation. The NetWare shell is the gatekeeper that stands between your workstation operating system and NetWare at the server. Previously incorporated entirely in one of two programs (ANET2.COM or ANET3.COM), the shell is now configured as two separate programs, both of which must be loaded at the workstation for network communication between operating systems to occur. The first of these programs, IPX.COM, provides the *protocol,* or rules, for communicating across a particular LAN topology.

IPX.COM and NetWork Communications

IPX stands for Internetwork Packet Exchange. IPX is a subset of network communication protocols originated by Xerox called XNS, for Xerox Network Services. IPX.COM is loaded at the workstation prior to network communication being established.

IPX.COM directs information between workstations and the server (peer-to-host communications) and between workstations (peer-to-peer communications). NetWare, of course, is able to run on a number of different topologies: IBM Token Ring, ARCnet, and others. Because each of these topologies has its own rules for communication, IPX.COM must be customized for the topology and network interface card (NIC) of each workstation connected to the LAN.

NetWare provides a special program utility, *SHGEN* (Shell Generation), through which you customize IPX.COM. For more on SHGEN refer to Novell's *SFT/Advanced NetWare 286 Installation* manual. For those of you operating in an environment with workstations attached to more than one topology, it is essential to understand that IPX.COM for one topology will not work with IPX.COM for another topology. In fact, for some topologies, such as IBM Token Ring, certain files must be included on your boot disk and loaded before IPX.COM is loaded.

Therefore, it is essential that you

- clearly indicate on the workstation boot diskettes you generate the topology with which that diskette is to be used

- discourage users from passing boot diskettes around from machine to machine

If you do not take these precautions, users may end up using an incorrect IPX.COM for their workstations. The ability to customize IPX.COM actually is a strength of NetWare. Customizing helps keep the size of the IPX.COM file small. (But try to keep the IPX.COM customizing a secret.)

Just as IPX.COM allows for communication across the LAN topology, another program called a *redirector* is used at the workstation to allow you to talk to NetWare at the server. Actually, in the case of DOS, this program is one of three different programs: NET2.COM, NET3.COM, or NET4.COM. There is also a redirector for IBM PS/2 machines.

NET2.COM, NET3.COM, and NET4.COM

As developed and licensed for use by Microsoft Corporation, DOS is customized for particular hardware platforms. There is an IBM DOS, a Compaq DOS, and other hardware-specific versions of DOS. And DOS for any one hardware platform comes in various versions: IBM DOS versions 2.0, 3.0, 3.3, and 4.0, for example.

How does NetWare at the server remember which version of DOS is being run at the workstation? *It does not remember at all!* NetWare running at the server is running *NetWare*. Even in a nondedicated mode, the server runs DOS as an independent user session, allowing you to run DOS and DOS-based applications in the foreground while NetWare runs independently in the background.

The version of DOS you use at your workstation is important. NetWare requires that the workstation run a DOS version that is 2.0 or higher. And depending on the manufacturer and model of your workstation, a particular version of DOS may be recommended or required: IBM DOS version 2.2 or MS-DOS version 3.1, for example.

Unlike IPX.COM, the NET2.COM, NET3.COM, and NET4.COM programs do not have to be customized. However, the correct program must be used, which depends on the version of DOS you are running. It is important that the boot diskettes contain the version of these programs appropriate to the DOS version running at the workstation. Passing of boot diskettes from station to station should be discouraged.

How the DOS Redirector Works

The NetWare NETx.COM shell program is one more in a long list of Terminate-and-Stay-Resident (TSR) programs, SIDEKICK for the PC being one of the first and best-known TSR programs. When a TSR program is present on the workstation, keypresses are no longer passed directly to DOS for processing. Instead, requests for DOS services—recognized by the fact that a software interrupt call (21H) is generated—are first passed through a logic test. If, for instance, the NetWare shell programs are loaded and the keystroke combination is a NetWare command, DOS processes (word processing, spreadsheet, or database applications) running on the workstation are frozen in place, *terminated* but kept *resident*. Functional control is passed to the NetWare shell and appropriate messages are passed between the workstation and either the server or other workstations. Once the requested NetWare functions are completed, control is returned to DOS, its previous state is unfrozen, and whatever DOS tasks were processing continue uninterrupted.

An example of how this works is shown in Figure 2-1. **WHOAMI** is typed at the A:\> prompt followed by a press of the (ENTER) key. Since WHOAMI is a valid NetWare command, control is passed to the TSR portion of NetWare resident at the workstation, and DOS processing is suspended while WHOAMI is passed to the server for processing.

What if the command is neither a NetWare nor a DOS command? If the command issued was WHOAMI? followed by the (ENTER) key, the NetWare shell would not recognize this as a valid NetWare command and would pass it to the workstation's DOS processor for execution. Because WHOAMI? is also not a valid DOS command, the workstation would display the DOS response

Bad command or file name

This is one example of how NetWare works with your workstation's operating system. In this instance, DOS is allowed to send the "Bad command or file name" message when a command is neither a NetWare nor a DOS command.

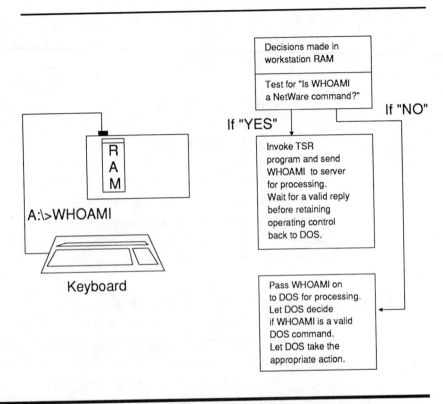

FIGURE 2-1.   WHOAMI command processing through the
NetWare shell

Netware is not the only LAN management software allowing
for interoperability. Other LAN management software packages
use this same approach to allow for server-workstation inter-
operability. The NetWare shell is, in this sense, one of a variety of
redirectors in use on LANs.

There are three advantages of the NetWare shell redirector:

- the Netware shell takes up only 60K of the 640K of RAM
  available on many PCs

- the shell can be configured to a great number of LAN topologies and shells are available for several workstation operating systems

- most important, the shell provides access to the very robust services of NetWare

The OS/2 Redirector
And Other Redirectors

Novell has developed and made available the OS/2 Redirector. This shell allows an IBM PS/2 workstation running the OS/2 operating system to interact with a NetWare server.

Also, perhaps available by the time this book is published, is an OS/2 version of Advanced NetWare 286. Just as Advanced NetWare 286 can be run in nondedicated mode—allowing a DOS session to run at the server—Advanced NetWare for OS/2 will allow an OS/2 session to be run simultaneously with NetWare on an IBM PS/2 server. Currently, an IBM PS/2 can be used only as a dedicated server.

Forthcoming from Novell will be some means of linking a NetWare server to UNIX workstations. One or more UNIX redirector shells may be used for this purpose. Such a possibility is by now no surprise to you.

USE OF THE DOS COMMAND
STRUCTURE LOOK AND FEEL

For the average network user, the distinction between DOS (or OS/2 or UNIX) commands and NetWare commands issued at the keyboard will be blurry at best. DOS commands can still be used and may even be required. Where NetWare commands are used, they have the look and feel of DOS.

DOS Commands on a NetWare LAN

Since DOS is being run at the workstation, it is possible and allowable to use DOS commands at the workstation. For instance, you can still use the DOS DIR command. Examples might be

```
A:\>DIR  Yourfile
K:\>DIR  Myfile
```

In the latter example the DOS DIR command is used to point to a NetWare server drive identified with a K: drive letter. NetWare recognizes DIR pointed toward the server as a valid command. However, you may find the NetWare NDIR command, discussed in Chapter 8, more to your liking.

Other commands, such as the DOS PATH command, may be used, but may not be as convenient, necessary, or flexible as NetWare commands and procedures. For instance, NetWare uses *search drives,* which are a welcome alternative to the PATH command. (More on this later.)

Some commands, such as CHKDISK, will function *only when directed at the workstation.* Unless necessary to workstation control, such commands should be avoided. A list of useable DOS commands is provided in Table 2-1.

Use of DOS Commands at the Server

DOS commands may be executed through the server keyboard only if the server is running in *nondedicated* mode *and* a user is toggled to the DOS session on the server. DOS commands issued while a nondedicated server is in NetWare Console mode will not be recognized as valid commands. And all DOS commands directed toward the server from a workstation must be passed through the NetWare shell and properly translated into NetWare server instructions.

Commands to Both the Server and Workstation	Commands for Use Only at the Workstation
DIR	CLS
TYPE	PRINT
MD or MKDIR	COPYCON
CD or CHDIR	VOL
DEL	FORMAT
RENAME	CHKDSK
RD or RMDIR	DATE
	TIME
	PROMPT
	VER
	ERASE
	SET
	VERIFY

TABLE 2-1.   Useable DOS Commands

DOS commands may be included in DOS batch files and in NetWare menu text files saved on the server. These files execute at the workstation. Where they are stored is irrelevant.

DOS Look and Feel to NetWare Commands

NetWare commands may be either server issued commands—which are referred to as *console commands*—or workstation commands—referred to as *command line* commands. Most users will not have occasion to issue console commands at the server. If issued by a user, console commands are invoked indirectly through a NetWare menu available at the workstation. In their pure form, console commands cannot be issued from a workstation. They must be issued through the server keyboard. (See Figure 2-2.)

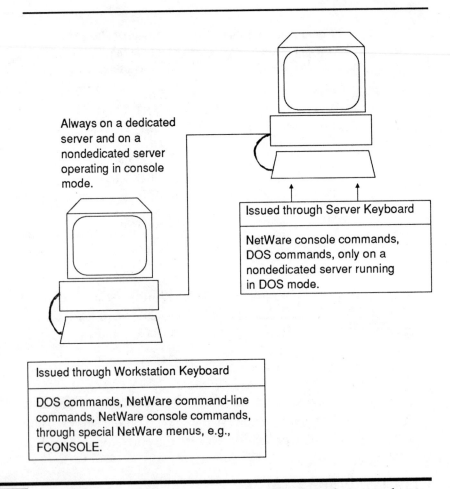

Always on a dedicated server and on a nondedicated server operating in console mode.

Issued through Server Keyboard

NetWare console commands, DOS commands, only on a nondedicated server running in DOS mode.

Issued through Workstation Keyboard

DOS commands, NetWare command-line commands, NetWare console commands, through special NetWare menus, e.g., FCONSOLE.

FIGURE 2-2.   Types of commands and where they may be issued

NetWare command line commands are invoked through the workstation keyboard, either from the DOS prompt (like DOS commands) or through a NetWare menu.

Like DOS commands, NetWare commands may be up to eight characters in length and may be followed, as appropriate, with a drive, path, and file specification. For instance, the NetWare equivalent of the DOS DIR command is NDIR. Issued from a prompt, the command might be

>NDIR K:Yourfile.*

The use of K: as a drive pointer will be explained later. For now, please accept on faith that you use K: to point to a subdirectory on the server named SUBDIR.

NetWare is consistent with DOS in allowing use of "*" or "?" as wildcards in filenames. As with DOS, NetWare commands may have options, or flags, that follow the basic command and modify it. NetWare flags, or command modifiers, provide functionality beyond DOS. For instance:

NDIR K:Yourfile.* SUB

This command instructs NetWare to search the current directory— pointed to with K:—for any files named Yourfile, disregarding their extensions: it then searches all subdirectories under the current directory. Thus, you might locate the following:

K:\SUBDIR\YOURFILE.NEW
K:\SUBDIR\YOURFILE.OLD
K:\SUBDIR\YOURFILE.NEW
K:\SUBDIR\YOURFILE.OLD
K:\SUBDIR\MARCH\YOURFILE
K:\SUBDIR\JANUARY\YOURFILE

Remember, you accepted on faith that K: was pointing to the SUBDIR subdirectory. In NetWare, K: is the same as K:\SUBDIR, once the \SUBDIR path has been assigned to K:. Again, this is NetWare, not DOS.

Clearly, NetWare is not only consistent with DOS, but it also adds functionality at the workstation and at the server. This added functionality is available at OS\2 workstations as well.

ADDED FUNCTIONALITY AT THE WORKSTATION

Once logged into the server, the workstation user may find that he or she has several powerful NetWare tools available for use. The word *may* is used because access to these tools is under the control of the LAN administrator or SUPERVISOR. An open system and security design is generally advisable. Through its good design, NetWare helps keep users out of trouble. And the more that users can do on their own, the less the NetWare administrator has to do for them. What are these features?

NetWare Menus

In designing NetWare, Novell has recognized that some users prefer to work at the DOS prompt from the command line, while others want help. This help comes in the form of a series of NetWare menus.

An example NetWare menu is shown in Figure 2-3. This menu is called from the DOS prompt by use of the MENU command. For now, it is the listed functions that are of interest. With the exception of number 9, Logout, each listed choice has an associated, specific NetWare menu. Each of these menus can be individually called by name from the DOS prompt. These are the named NetWare menus available from the prompt or from the Main menu:

1 Session
2 Filer
3 Volinfo
4 Syscon
5 Fconsole
6 Pconsole
7 Printcon
8 Printdef

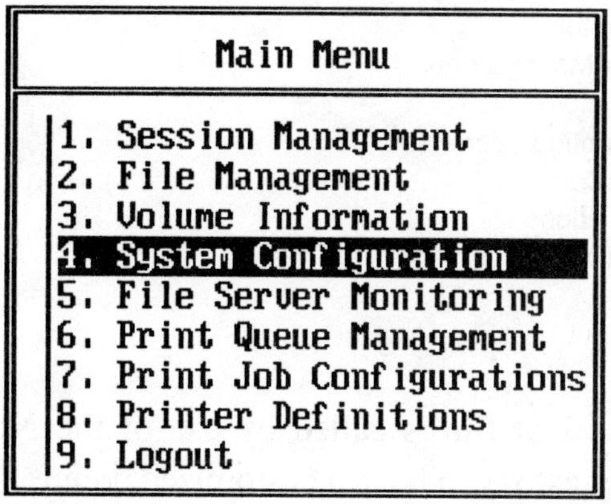

```
┌─────────────────────────────────────┐
│            Main Menu                 │
├─────────────────────────────────────┤
│ 1. Session Management                │
│ 2. File Management                   │
│ 3. Volume Information                │
│ 4. System Configuration             │
│ 5. File Server Monitoring            │
│ 6. Print Queue Management            │
│ 7. Print Job Configurations          │
│ 8. Printer Definitions               │
│ 9. Logout                            │
└─────────────────────────────────────┘
```

FIGURE 2-3.   NetWare's MAIN.MNU screen

Most of these menus are reviewed in later chapters. The menu shown in Figure 2-3 comes with NetWare, but it is a customizable menu—a menu you could create yourself. The ability to create custom menus for users, particularly novice users, is a feature of NetWare. Other menu systems can be installed at the server or at the workstation, but in many instances NetWare's basic menu features are adequate.

Custom Novell menus are created through a plain ASCII text file, following certain design requirements. The text file that defines MAIN is listed here:

```
%Main Menu,0,0,3
1. Session Management
        Session
2. File Management
        Filer
3. Volume Information
        VolInfo
4. System Configuration
        SysCon
```

5. File Server Monitoring
      FConsole
6. Print Queue Management
      PConsole
7. Print Job Configurations
      PrintCon
8. Printer Definitions
      PrintDef
9. Logout
      !Logout

When the text file is called by use of the NetWare MENU command, presto, you have a customized menu.

Quick File Access and Disk Space Sharing

Even though files stored at the server must be transmitted over the LAN to the workstation, you may perceive requested files being accessed more rapidly from the server than when called from your workstation's disk drives. This is not an illusion. NetWare uses four techniques to speed file access at the server:

- directory caching

- directory hashing

- file caching

- elevator seeking

Each of these techniques are server features and are discussed later in this chapter.

As important as quick file access is the ability of users to share files stored on the server hard disks. This sharing of files is a principle reason for installing a LAN. Because NetWare does not itself support sharing files stored at workstations, files must be stored on the server's storage media if they are to be shared. Does this mean that all files should be stored on the server? Not necessarily.

There are four arguments often expressed for storing files on a workstation's local disk drives.

- Local workstation hard disk drives provide added data security.

- If files are not stored at the local workstation, valuable and costly disk space goes unused.

- If the LAN goes down, the local workstation may still be usable and the files at the local workstation accessible.

- Locally stored files reduce the traffic the LAN must bear, helping ensure that the LAN is responsive.

If these arguments seem self-evident, they are equally in need of qualification. Yet these arguments all too often influence decisions involving thousands of dollars of expenditure for workstation hardware. For this reason alone, if not for what they reveal about NetWare as an operating system, these arguments are discussed here.

LOCAL DRIVE ADDED SECURITY   The notion that locally saved files are more secure than files saved at the server is false for at least three reasons:

- Local hard drives are usually accessible to anyone who turns on and boots the workstation.

- Tools and techniques for making local workstations secure are less than secure—unplugged keyboards can be replaced by other keyboards, locks can be picked, and hidden files or encrypted files can be unhidden or unencrypted.

• NetWare affords security to files stored at the file server beyond any security available at the workstation.

The notion of greater local security often rests on not understanding or not knowing the security features available through NetWare. Part of your job as a LAN manager or supervisor is to educate your users to the security they may gain from storing files at the server.

Of course, the notion of greater local file security may be based on the assumption that you, acting as the LAN manager or supervisor, will do a poor job of setting up and monitoring server file security. A good portion of this book is devoted to helping you establish and easily maintain file security on the network. In any event, you will not want to be an advocate of the greater file security at the local workstation position. In enunciating that proposition you are admitting that you are unable to provide a consistent, appropriate level of server file security.

COSTS REQUIRE UTILIZATION OF LOCAL DISK SPACE

If cost of local workstation disk space is truly a consideration, your organization may wish to consider two courses of action:

• Limiting future workstation acquisitions to diskless workstations, to workstations with only floppy drives, or to workstations with smaller (10 to 20MB) hard disk drives.

• Acquiring and installing software on the server (over NetWare) that allows any user on the network to access and utilize the hard disk space of any other hard disk on the network.

With diskless workstations, the reduced cost from not having disk drives is partially offset by the costs of Programmable Read Only Memory hardware, or PROM. A PROM must be installed in a diskless workstation in order to boot DOS and connect to the network.

Another disadvantage of the diskless workstation is that it is inoperable if the server or LAN is down. However, diskless workstations can be less expensive and they provide added file security. If the workstation lacks a local disk drive, server-resident files cannot be copied to diskettes at the workstation.

As mentioned earlier, NetWare does not allow users to share resources among workstations. To access a workstation hard disk, you must be logged in at that workstation. However, several software packages—developed to run on top of NetWare at the server—do allow users to share local resources (printers, hard disk space, and even workstation RAM). Such highly distributed resource sharing has advantages, particularly for sharing printers that for convenience are attached to a local workstation rather than to the server. But local hard disk space sharing across the network does pose complications, including the following:

- The ease, or difficulty, of backing up files from multiple hard disks spread over many diverse types of geographically separate workstations, and the extra time involved in such backups.

- Adequacy of file security for your files stored on someone else's workstation hard disk.

- Interpersonal or interoffice disputes about filling up other people's or office's hard disk space, and whether and how to "charge back" for use of this space.

- The reduced reliability of the LAN from the user's perspective. If the workstation on which you stored a file is not turned on, you will not be able to access the file from your workstation.

WORKSTATION INDEPENDENCE OF THE LAN   A justifiable reason for purchasing workstations with local disk drives, and storing files on local drives, is to allow the machines to be used independently of the server. Server independence may be desirable in the following cases:

- The LAN is down for extended periods of time (a less and less likely event).

- Machines are moved around, some on and others off the LAN.

- Machines are used on weekends when the file server is, perhaps, not running.

- Machines are taken out of the office for use, and it is deemed inconvenient or too costly to establish remote communications with the server.

In each of these situations, it makes sense to have at least one disk drive installed on every workstation. The workstation can be booted and used as a standalone machine, and files can be saved to the local disk storage medium. This is not, however, an argument for routinely storing files to local workstation drives.

USE OF LOCAL DISK STORAGE REDUCES LAN TRAFFIC

On a large LAN with a relatively slow topology (ARCnet, for instance), there may be benefits from storing files locally. For example, Paradox3, a database generator, recommends temporary, user-specific files be directed to a local workstation hard disk directory. Similarly, WordPerfect 5.0 allows for saving of temporary files at the workstation drives.

The benefit of locally stored temporary files is in direct proportion to the amount of LAN traffic. If word processing is the principle LAN activity, there will be little traffic across the LAN. Most work will occur at the workstations. Locating even temporary WordPerfect 5.0 files on the server is reasonable, and may ease the LAN manager's job of instructing users in the software.

In summary, there are instances in which access even to workstation hard disk space is useful. And there are occasions where data security or costs call for diskless workstations. In either instance, much of the benefit from your LAN will come from storing the vast majority of files at the server. Routinely storing files to local disk drives out of habit is a habit best broken.

Sharing Printers

NetWare allows up to five printers, plotters, or other print devices to be attached to the server for sharing by users. The limitation is that no more than three print devices may be parallel (LPT port) connected and no more than two serial (COM port) connected.

Printers are serviced by one or more *print queues*. Print queues are maintained by the network supervisor, and queues are assigned for servicing by particular printers. Access to printers can be limited to only those individuals defined as users of a particular print queue, or can be made available to all network users.

The print services of NetWare are becoming increasingly transparent to the user. When you are installing WordPerfect 5.0, you can define the existence and location of network printers. These network printers are included within WordPerfect 5.0 as among those available for use, taking advantage of NetWare print services features. But the user sees him or herself as working entirely within WordPerfect, which—for all intents and purposes—is the reality.

NetWare does not provide for users sharing printers or other peripherals attached to local workstations other than the workstation at which the user is logged into the network. However, NetWare is an *open* operating system. Novell encourages development of software that runs at the server and provides value-added processes or services such as workstation peripheral sharing. Numerous software packages exist that can be loaded on the server over NetWare, providing added LAN functionality.

ADDED FUNCTIONALITY
AT THE SERVER

The existence of NetWare at the server provides its own functionality, the print queue services just discussed being one such example. Other features and services of NetWare at the server are discussed here.

Multiple Topologies and Server Bridging

Today's LAN technology is well developed. A number of different wiring topologies and communications protocols exist, each with their distinct advantages, and the features and relative advantages are changing all the time. If you are a LAN manager you may prefer to use more than one topology in your organization, since no one topology is best for all situations. For instance, you may choose to link part of your organization into a high-speed, but more expensive, Token Ring topology. Another portion of your organization may use a less expensive ARCnet topology. NetWare accommodates linking diverse topologies together.

INTERNAL BRIDGES   Up to four different network interface cards (NICs) can be installed in a NetWare server, assuming sufficient expansion slots are available. NetWare at the server includes *internal bridging* software, which allows transparent communication across these disparate NICs (across what would otherwise be incompatible wiring and communications protocol schemes). For instance, without being aware of it, a user attached to the ARCnet topology can use the NetWare SEND command to send a brief message to another user or users who are attached to the Token Ring topology.

Multiple NICs installed at the server do not have to be different. NetWare also supports communication across NIC using the same topology. This option can help in a situation where LAN respon-

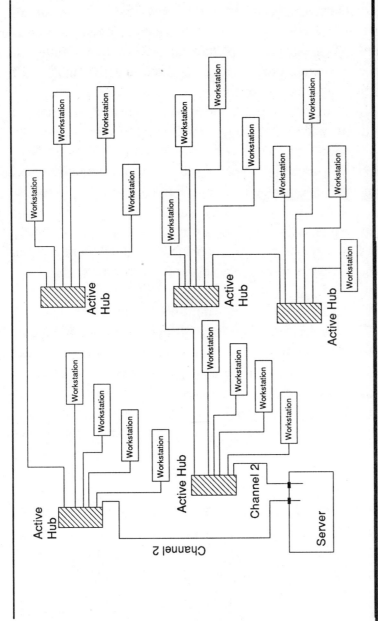

FIGURE 2-4. Use of internal bridging to provide multiple communication channels to the server

siveness is decreasing because too many workstations are simultaneously trying to access a single NIC channel into the server.

Figure 1-3 (in Chapter 1) pictures an ARCnet LAN with numerous workstations chained together through active hubs, all of them attached to the server through a single cable attached to a single NIC. You may improve server responsiveness by installing a second NIC and restructuring your cabling to split workstation communication with the server between the two installed NIC. Figure 2-4 illustrates this type of solution to the responsiveness problem and is another example of internal bridging.

 Lowered responsiveness may be for reasons other than too many stations simultaneously accessing one NIC channel. For example, it may be caused by insufficient server RAM for file caching.

Internal bridging also allows multiple servers to be interconnected. This is accomplished through placing the same type of NICs in each file server, with appropriate cabling, wiring, or other communications media (radio signals, microwaves) connecting to the NICs. In this instance, each server may have up to three other types of NICs installed. On such an internetwork you could support seven different topologies: the topology through which the two servers are connected and three other distinct topologies at each of the two servers.

EXTERNAL BRIDGES   It is not necessary that two servers be directly connected to each other. With NetWare, an external bridge may be established at a workstation through which other servers gain access to your LAN. This situation is illustrated in Figure 2-5.

The bridge workstation must be linked (cabled) to a server. And the workstation must be running specialized software—available with NetWare—which allows it to perform communication ser-

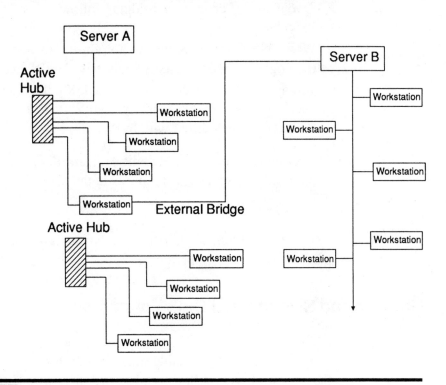

FIGURE 2-5.   External bridge LAN interconnection

vices across the LAN topologies connected to it. Because of the importance of both reliability and speed, a workstation serving as an external bridge is often run as a *dedicated* external bridge workstation. However, if you have sufficient memory in the workstation, and you wish to run the risk of the external bridge being slowed down or unintentionally crashed, NetWare allows the external bridged workstation to perform a dual role, as both a bridge and a DOS workstation.

Two words of caution on bridging follow:

- While NetWare is robust in its ability to support multiple topologies, the NICs selected must have NetWare drivers available for them to function properly. Ask before purchasing, or check your NetWare manuals or a NetWare dealer for advice on hardware compatibility with NetWare.

- Occasionally NetWare's ability to link diverse topologies is obviated by "advances" or quirks in the diverse hardware to be interconnected.

Ask a dealer or consult your NetWare manuals for guidance before purchasing expensive hardware.

Number and Size of Hard Disk Volumes

DOS allows you to attach multiple hard disks to a PC, and the hard disks may be of considerable size: 100MB, for instance. But until the advent of DOS 4.0, a 100MB hard disk installed under DOS had to be *partitioned* into multiple *volumes*. This was because DOS as an operating system could recognize or address hard disk space in no more than 32MB "chunks." Figure 2-6 illustrates how a 100MB hard disk might have been partitioned for use under earlier DOS versions.

DOS gives each partition a volume name and points to each volume with one of the available DOS drive pointers, A through E. While this allows you to use larger hard disks with DOS, there is one distinct limitation. You have to guess at how much space to assign to each partition. Pity the poor LAN supervisor who partitions the server hard disk as though it were a DOS disk and then finds the Accounting Department in need of more than the 20MB he or she allotted to the company's accounting database files. And

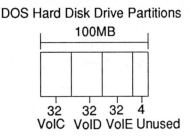

DOS Hard Disk Drive Partitions

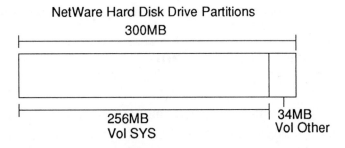

NetWare Hard Disk Drive Partitions

FIGURE 2-6.   How DOS and NetWare manage hard disk partitions

pity the supervisor responsible for supporting a company database that will not fit within 32MB, which is the total allowed for any one DOS volume (except under IBM-DOS 4.0).

Novell recognized that on a LAN, even more than on standalone PCs, the amount of contiguous addressable hard disk space needs to be substantial. Accordingly, NetWare allows up to 32 volumes per any one server, and each volume may be up to 255MB in size. Thus, a 500MB hard drive attached to a NetWare server could be partitioned into as few as two volumes (255MB and 245MB). This is possible because the disks are attached to the file server, which is running the NetWare operating system, not DOS.

It is strongly recommended—with the exception of a required DOS partition on a nondedicated server—that you never partition hard disks that are 255MB or less in size, and never set up a partition of less than 255MB, except for the last (residual) partition of a large hard drive. *Security is not enhanced by setting up separate hard disk partitions.* NetWare security rests at the directory level, which is one step down from the volume level. (The day you find yourself having to back up all your files on a hard disk, repartition the hard disk, and reinstall the files—because it seemed logical to set up different volumes for accounting, company policy, or sales—you will rue not having taken this advice to heart.)

Built-in Hard Disk System Fault Tolerance

With files shared among users, the need for hard disk reliability becomes critical. NetWare has built into it a number of *system fault tolerance* features. Fault tolerance is built on the assumption that all hardware will eventually fail, or crash. Especially critical are hard disk failures. Advanced NetWare 286 and SFT NetWare help avoid the most dire consequences of hard disk failure. This is achieved through the techniques discussed here.

DUPLICATE DIRECTORY ENTRY TABLES   With a hard disk, failure is not always sudden. Parts of the hard disk begin to fail, but the disk may continue to be usable, unless the portion that fails contains the disk's file allocation table.

Simplified, the *file allocation table* keeps track of where a file or portions of a file are located on the hard disk. NetWare disks have both a file allocation table (FAT) and a directory entry table (DET). The latter includes information about NetWare's user, group, and directory security. If information in either the FAT or DET is lost, the entire hard disk may be inaccessible or unsecured.

To avoid this unhappy turn of events, NetWare maintains on the hard disk both an original and a backup copy of both the DET and

FAT. If any sectors containing DET or FAT information in the original tables goes bad, NetWare *tolerates* this *fault* by

- going to the backup copies of the DET and FAT for the required information

- rewriting the lost information to an alternative location on the hard disk

- including the defective sector of the original table as a *bad block* in the hard disk's *bad block table*

Figure 2-7 illustrates the concept. DET and FAT duplication enhances server hard disk reliability.

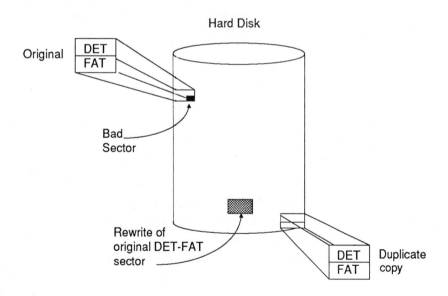

FIGURE 2-7.   Duplicate DET and FAT tables

Before leaving the topic of directory entry tables, a brief note is in order about what constitutes a directory entry. NetWare creates one entry in a directory entry table for each of the following:

- every named directory

- every named subdirectory

- every named file

- every five trustee assignments

A hard disk with 200 files in 5 subdirectories of 1 main directory to which 50 trustee assignments are associated has 216 directory entries in its directory entry table as follows:

$$
\begin{array}{rl}
200 \text{ files} = 200 & \text{directory entries} \\
5 \text{ subdirectories} = 5 & \text{directory entries} \\
1 \text{ main directory} = 1 & \text{directory entry} \\
50 \text{ trustee assignments} = 10 & \text{directory entries (50/5)} \\
\text{Total Entries} \quad 216 &
\end{array}
$$

If the maximum allowed entries in your directory entry table is exceeded, your hard disk is virtually full, regardless of how much unused space actually exists. NetWare will establish a default size for your directory entry table based on the total size of your hard disk. It is not usually necessary to estimate or instruct NetWare on the amount of space to set aside for recording of DET entries. However, this decision is under your control at hard disk config-uration and installation time, if you so choose.

READ-AFTER-WRITE VERIFICATION AND AUTOMATIC HOT FIX
Rewriting of lost DET and FAT information to a new hard disk sector is a special case of a system fault tolerance

technique termed *Hot Fix*. NetWare ensures that information written to the hard disk is always written to a good sector where, at that moment at least, the information is retrievable. This occurs on the fly while the system power is on, that is, while the system is "hot."

Hot Fix is accomplished as follows. Information written from server RAM to the hard disk is first buffered, that is, placed in a temporary storage area in the memory of the server. NetWare then writes the information to sector(s) of the hard disk. Before releasing information from the server's memory buffer, NetWare reads the written sectors to determine if the information is retrievable. This is *read-after-write verification*. If the information is not retrievable, NetWare does the following:

1. Marks the bad sectors from which information was not retrievable in the disk's bad sector table.

2. Rewrites the information from the buffer to the disk's defined *Hot Fix Redirection Area*.

3. Then, and only then, releases the information from the buffer.

The Hot Fix Redirection Area is a section of the hard disk set aside for recording information written to bad sectors and represents about 2% of the total hard disk space.

The reason for writing to the Hot Fix Redirection Area, rather than to any open, good sectors of the hard disk, is to allow monitoring of the mechanical and electronic integrity of the entire disk. Experience and testing demonstrate that if more than 2% of your hard disk has bad sectors, the probability of a general hard disk failure is considerable. If the 2% Hot Fix Redirection Area is nearly full, it is time to back up your data and install a new hard disk system. The probability of your hard disk failing is reaching 100%.

UPS MONITORING   Hard disks, and other pieces of computer equipment, function only so long as power is available to them. Sudden, unexpected loss of power can cause damage to hardware and loss of data. In the case of a database, entire files may be corrupted and data made nonrecoverable.

Therefore, maintenance of a continual power supply can be critical. One option is to purchase a battery backup system that kicks in whenever the power to the server is interrupted. However, batteries last only so long. NetWare, through a feature called *UPS monitoring,* is able to detect when a backup power supply is being used and can signal users to log out of the network or risk losing their data. After a defined period of time, NetWare properly brings down the server, helping ensure the integrity of the data and the system.

Hard Disk Information Access Speeds

Accessing files located at the server may appear faster to users than accessing the same files from a local workstation hard disk. This assumes, of course, that users are paying attention and comparing on this feature. As with many LAN amenities, it is slowness of access, rather than speed of access, that users will notice.

If NetWare cannot ensure that you, as the LAN manager, receive "Ataboys," it does ensure that files are accessed as speedily as possible from your server hard disks. NetWare helps ensure that you do not lose any "Ataboys" you have accumulated. It does this through four techniques:

- directory caching

- directory hashing

- file caching

- elevator seeking

These techniques are discussed here. Each technique is designed to reduce the time normally associated with *mechanical* retrieval of electronically recorded information on the hard disk.

DIRECTORY CACHING   Directory caching involves reading a copy of the hard disk's directory entry table and file allocation table into the server's RAM. When you call for a file, NetWare looks to the *RAM-resident copy* of the DET and FAT tables for direction on where the file, or portions of the file, are located on the hard disk. Normally, this information would have to be read *at mechanical speed* from the DET and FAT tables on the hard disk itself. By looking to the RAM-resident copy, the required DET and FAT information is retrieved at RAM electronic speed. The time savings is perceptible. Security information contained in the DET is also frequently used, and caching of the DET ensures that this information is always readily available at electronic speed.

With the exception of the SYS volume, directory entry table caching is not mandatory, but directory caching is highly recommended. If your server's RAM is too small to accommodate directory caching on volumes other than SYS, an additional investment in server RAM will usually be worthwhile.

DIRECTORY HASHING   The DET and FAT are like shoe boxes full of unsorted index cards, each card containing information about a particular file. When a new file is created, a new card is added to the shoe box. This new card is placed randomly among the other cards already in the shoe box. If you want to find a new card you must search sequentially through the shoe box until you come to it.

Directory hashing is analogous to taking the cards in the shoe box and placing them in alphabetical order. Directory hashing creates an index of the DET information. When information about the location of a file is requested, NetWare can check an index (an alphabetical listing) to quickly locate the correct file card for the file requested. *New card* would be found among the N's. Directory hashing is automatic.

FILE CACHING   DET and FAT information is essential for retrieving files. However, the reads and writes associated with actual file retrieval and storage presents the greatest potential for slow LAN responsiveness. NetWare assists with this through *file caching*.

The first time a file is requested, it is located on and read from the hard disk. The requested file is read into the server's RAM, and then passed along to the workstation from which the file request originated. Local workstations do not directly access a server's hard disk.

Once placed in the server RAM, the file may continue to reside there. If a second user requests the same file, NetWare is able to pass along a copy of the file as it exists in RAM, rather than having to go to the hard disk. Thus, files that are cached are retrieved at electronic speed, rather than at mechanical, hard disk speed.

On an active LAN, it may not be possible to cache all files in RAM. Once the RAM space available for file caching is full, NetWare uses a "last request, most often requested" algorithm to place newly requested files into RAM. A request for a file not cached will always cause that file to be cached. However, files removed from the cache will be those having the least total requests. This helps ensure cached files will likely be the ones users most often require.

You do not have to set aside a part of the server RAM for file caching. NetWare automatically uses available RAM for file caching. How much RAM do you need to allow for an acceptable level of file caching? Enough to make your LAN reasonably responsive to users.

If your users are doing word processing, with few requests to the server for files, an occasional lengthy wait for the server to respond may be tolerable. If your users are sharing database files that require frequent updating from the server, substantially more server RAM may be necessary, both to accommodate the size of database files and to ensure that all frequently used database files are retained in RAM.

FILE, DET, AND FAT CACHING AND BUFFERING IN REVERSE

Thus far, read requests from the hard disk have been the focus of discussion. This section discusses how NetWare handles writing to the hard disk.

When you create a new file and save it to a server hard disk, NetWare first creates the file in the RAM of the server. The RAM-resident copy of the file is then written through server buffers to the hard disk. Once the file is in RAM, you continue working at the workstation just as though the file had been already saved to the hard disk. The processes of read-after-write verification, Hot Fix, and duplicate DET and FAT creation and maintenance are handled in the background from the user's perspective.

When you are making changes to a file that is already cached in RAM, NetWare further speeds its own hard disk write operations by writing only those portions of the file that have changed. Changed portions of a file are often referred to as *dirty blocks*. Writing only dirty blocks to the hard disk reduces the overall disk writing load of the server, again helping ensure that the server keeps up with the service demands of network users.

ELEVATOR SEEKING

Eventually, NetWare must read from or write to the hard disk. When performing this task, NetWare employs a technique called *elevator seeking*. Imagine that your hard disk sectors are floors of a 20-story building. The first floor is the lobby, through which all files must pass. On the first floor is a listing of where each file is located throughout the rest of the building. On your server hard disk building, this list is NetWare's directory entry and file allocation tables.

If a file is large, portions of the file are stored on separate floors. As parts of the file are added, deleted, or changed (dirty blocks updated), it is necessary to move parts of the file from one floor of your hard disk building to other floors (other hard disk sectors).

Other files are also competing for floor space. The hard disk manager allows files, or parts of files, to be stored on any floor where open space exists. Before long, parts of a single file reside on many different floors, along with pieces of other files. After a while, parts of a file (A, B, C, D, and so forth) are no longer in alphabetical (sequential) order throughout the building. Figure 2-8 shows what this storage situation might look like. Of course, the file pieces can be located, because the directory entry table and file allocation table are keeping track of where parts of the file are located throughout the building.

If you go into the building to retrieve your file, in sequential (A, B, C) order, the directory entry and file allocation tables tell you to go first to floor 4, then up to 7 and 15, down to 11, up to 12, on up to 19, and then down to 9. This is how your hard disk read-write heads would normally behave, moving back and forth across the hard disk's platters any number of times until all pieces of a file are sequentially located and retrieved.

But, you say, an elevator has a control panel. You can select at once all the floors at which you need to stop to retrieve all the pieces of your file. And the elevator will need to make only one trip up (or down) the building for you to retrieve the entire file. This is elevator seeking logic.

Using the elevator's logic, you minimize trips up and down the building to retrieve files, saving both time and wear and tear on the building's elevator. NetWare's elevator seeking algorithm for accessing hard disks works in the same way. Rather than retrieving parts of a file in file part sequence, it reorders the retrieval sequence to minimize passes of the hard disk's read-write heads across the surface of the hard disk platters, saving time and wear and tear on your hard disk.

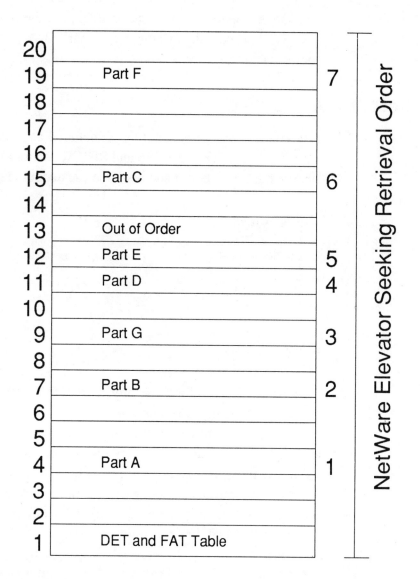

FIGURE 2-8. Elevator seeking

With elevator seeking, when the hard disk must be accessed, the process is made as speedy as possible. And the life of your hard disk is also extended (though any hard disk may fail at any moment).

Resource Accounting

Automatic resource accounting is included as a software option with Advanced NetWare 286 and SFT NetWare. Items for which charge rates may be set and resource use accounted are

- blocks read

- blocks written

- connect time

- disk storage

- service requests

Whether to account for use of any or all of these resources is under your control as the LAN manager.

NetWare is neutral in its unit of management. Charge rates are defined by you, and a unit of charge represents no specific, assumed monetary value. That is, a charge of 1 divided by 10 equals one tenth of one. But whether one represents one dollar (in which case 10 cents is being charged) or 100 dollars (with one tenth representing 10 dollars) is arbitrary.

You can think in terms of NetWare accumulating *units* or *beans,* or multiples or fractions of beans. You assign the monetary value of a unit —the value of "1"—a meaning outside of NetWare. One unit or bean is just a unit or bean, until and if you decide to call it a dollar, a peso, a ruble, or whatever.

While NetWare is universal and flexible in its unit or bean accounting, only those resources just listed can be accounted through NetWare. Each of these resources are server resources. NetWare accounting does not accumulate beans for local workstation device usage (local hard disk space, local printer usage, or local RAM usage).

If it is critical to know how much total local disk space is being written to by members of the organization, some additional resource accounting mechanism is required. This mechanism can be additional resource accounting software, installed at either the workstations or at the server.

If the NetWare resource accounting seems rudimentary or incomplete, it is. But this is consistent with Novell's approach to developing and marketing its product. Features found in NetWare are often suggestive of what can be done through the server. Novell encourages third parties to extend the basic features contained in NetWare through development of NetWare-compatible, server-based software packages that run over NetWare.

This Novell marketing strategy has helped create a market where you can choose the software package that best meets your organization's particular needs from among a variety of server add-on software.

Until additional software is available and affordable, you more often than not will find NetWare features quite serviceable. If your organization is doing no LAN resource accounting, the NetWare accounting is a good, adequate tool with which to begin, learn, and gain the experience necessary to make an informed decision about which add-on resource accounting package best meets your needs.

Directory Structure

NetWare, as a distinct operating system, manages the hard disk's directory structure differently than DOS. This allows NetWare to provide security and other useful directory and file-management services not found under DOS. Three of these features are discussed here.

DRIVE POINTERS "A" TO "Z"   In a DOS environment, files may be located in numerous user-defined directories and subdirectories. Unless you are using DOS 4.0 or some additional software DOS shell to assist you, you must know the correct spelling and logical sequence of the directory and subdirectory *paths* to locate and use a file. Life is simpler under NetWare.

With NetWare, drive letters "A" through "Z" may be used to point to specific subdirectories. Referred to as *drive mappings,* these network paths can be accessed simply by typing the associated drive letter at the prompt (or even from within some application packages).

If you forget what letters are associated with what paths or mappings, the NetWare MAP command lists this information for you. Just type **MAP** and press (ENTER) at the prompt.

An example of NetWare mappings is shown below. To point to location FS1/SYS1:DATA/USERS on your file server, type **K:** and press (ENTER). Job done.

```
Drive A:   maps to a local disk.
Drive B:   maps to a local disk.
Drive F: = FS1/SYS:LOGIN
Drive H: = FS1/SYS1:DATA/USERS/VENESSA
Drive I: = FS1/SYS1:
Drive J: = FS1/SYS1:OSAS/DATA
Drive K: = FS1/SYS1:DATA/USERS
Drive L: = FS1/SYS1:DATA
Drive M: = FS1/SYS:
Drive P: = FS1/SYS1:DATA/PROJDATA
Drive R: = FS1/SYS1:DATA/SHARED/READONLY
Drive S: = FS1/SYS1:DATA/SHARED/READWRIT
       ========
SEARCH1: = Z:, [FS1/SYS:PUBLIC]
SEARCH2: = Y:, [FS1/SYS:PUBLIC/ACER/IBM_PC/V3.3]
SEARCH3: = X:, [FS1/SYS:APPS/LOTUS]
SEARCH4: = W:, [FS1/SYS:APPS/WORD]
SEARCH5: = V:, [FS1/SYS:APPS/PROJECTS]
SEARCH6: = U:, [FS1/SYS:PUBLIC/MESSAGES]
SEARCH7: = T:, [FS1/SYS:MTN_TAPE]
SEARCH8: = Q:, [FS1/SYS:SYSTEM]
```

To point to the subdirectory VENESSA, which is under FS1/SYS1:DATA/USERS, type **H:** and press (ENTER).

By convention, NetWare assumes that the first letters of the alphabet are reserved as local workstation drive pointers. Depending on what version of DOS you are using, A:, B:, and C: or A: through E: will be reserved by NetWare as local workstation drive pointers. However, you can use the DOS LASTDRIVE command to reserve additional drive letters (F: through H:, for instance) for use as local drive pointers. As a normal practice this is unnecessary and is not recommended.

For illustration, assume you are using a recent version of DOS and that drive letters "A" through "E" are reserved by NetWare for use as local drive pointers. Letters "F" through "Z" are reserved for use as network, or internetwork, drive pointers. "F" through "Z" pointers are unique to each user at each workstation. You can be pointing to one location on the network with F: while other users are pointing to entirely different locations with F:. Or they may not even use F: as a drive pointer.

As a user, you can decide which drive pointer letter to use. You may choose to use H: to point to your home user directory SYS1:DATA/USERS/VENESSA. Or, as illustrated in Chapter 7, you can use G:. It is under your control to determine where each letter points.

Drive mappings are established using variants of the MAP command, or through the NetWare SESSION menu. SESSION and the MAP command are discussed in detail in Chapter 7.

SIXTEEN SEARCH DRIVES   Of the 24 drive pointers "F" through "Z," up to 16 may be defined as search drives. The letters associated with a search drive are not under your direct control but are assigned by NetWare, beginning from the bottom of the alphabet and working upward through unused drive letters.

If the letter "Z" is already in use as a network drive pointer, the first search you create (referred to here as S1, for search drive one) is assigned the letter "Y" (if "Y" is not also already in use).

The benefit of search drives comes from NetWare's assistance in locating executable, command, and batch files—files identified by the extensions .EXE, .COM, and .BAT. Under plain-vanilla operating procedures of either DOS or NetWare, .EXE, .COM., and .BAT files can be accessed only when the user is pointing to the subdirectory in which the requested file is located. To use the file YOURFILE.BAT located in C:\YOURDIR, you have to make C:YOURDIR your current (default) directory, or at least include the C:\YOURDIR path definition in your request for the file. The same is true of plain NetWare network drives.

If MYFILE.BAT is in F:FS1/SYS:USERDIRS/MYSUBDIR, you must be pointing to that location to use MYFILE.BAT. The process of changing directory pointers is simplified: just type **F:** and press (ENTER) to change to the FS1/SYS:USERDIRS/MYS-UBDIR mapping. But the entire path definition must be known for NetWare to locate MYFILE.BAT in the MYSUBDIR subdirectory.

DOS gets around this inconvenience through the DOS PATH command. The PATH command can point to one or more alternative locations to which DOS looks to find .EXE, .COM, and .BAT files, when the named file is not located in the user's current default directory. A typical DOS PATH command is

PATH C:\DOS;C:\WP;C:\LOTUS123;D:\BATFILES

If it is not in the current directory, DOS searches for YOUR-FILE.BAT in the DOS, WP, LOTUS123, and BATFILES subdirectories, the latter residing in a volume or disk identified with the pointer D:\. Of course, DOS searches for any file named YOURFILE.BAT and executes the first occurrence of that named file. Place YOURFILE.BAT in C:\DOS, and it will execute from there, even if another version of YOURFILE.BAT, so named, is located in D:\BATFILES.

NetWare search drives function nearly the same as the PATH command, but with fewer limitations. With the DOS PATH command

- You must retype the entire list of named subdirectories when you add a subdirectory to the path definitions.

- You are limited by DOS in the number of characters the path can contain, somewhat less than the length of an entire line.

This latter limitation would be especially restrictive on an internetwork, where the server and volume names must be included as part of any path or map definition.

By allowing you to define sixteen different search drives, NetWare is, in essence, allowing you to point to up to sixteen unique subdirectories as alternate locations from which to execute a named .EXE, .COM, or .BAT file. This is equivalent to having sixteen different locations defined within a single DOS PATH command.

NetWare also allows other types of executable files to be found and executed from search drives (other than .COM, .EXE, and .BAT files). These "other" files may need to be called with a NetWare command. For instance, the NetWare MENU command looks for a named file that has the extension .MNU. If the named file MAIN.MNU, for instance, is not in the current directory but is in a directory identified as a search drive, the MAIN.MNU file in the search drive directory will be located and the MENU MAIN.FILE command executed.

Similarly, in WordPerfect 5.0 you can define a named macro to which WordPerfect 5.0 appends the extension .WPM. If a file named ADDRESS.WPM is not in your current directory but is in a NetWare search drive, the macro will execute from within WordPerfect 5.0. If you have ADDRESS.WPM in more than one search drive (in search drives 2 and 9, for instance), NetWare will execute the first encountered occurrence of the named macro (from search drive 2 in this example). In practice WordPerfect and NetWare can combine to create an even more dynamic work environment, as discussed later in Chapters 5 and 6.

Search drives are a powerful tool. NetWare even allows you to use search drives to point to local workstation drives. If you feel the need to define a DOS PATH, you should issue the PATH command only *after* all required NetWare search drives are defined. If the DOS PATH command is issued prior to NetWare search drive definition, NetWare may override the PATH command, confounding you and your users. You may want to dispense altogether with use of the PATH command and just use NetWare search drives.

EFFECTIVE SECURITY   NetWare security rests at the directory level. As the network manager—or, in certain instances, as a user—you may limit access to a directory or subdirectory to a single user. Or you may allow only selected rights to be exercised by a user or user group in a particular directory or subdirectory.

Table 2-2 contains a summary of the effective rights that are definable and controllable at the directory or subdirectory level through the services of NetWare. The topic of directory security is discussed extensively in following chapters.

Print Management

NetWare allows for sharing of multiple print devices attached to the file server. Recent versions of NetWare provide new tools to manage network printing. The PCONSOLE menu utility provides advanced print queue definition and management features.

The PRINTDEF menu utility allows you to define *forms, print devices,* and *modes* for printing to server attached printers. And you may copy these special print definitions to or from other

Effective Right	Operating Rights Conveyed
SEARCH	Allows a search of the directory entry table (DET) for file and directory or subdirectory names and file and directory attributes
OPEN	Allows files to be opened for use
READ	Allows reading from open files
WRITE	Allows writing to open files
CREATE	Allows for writing a new file (carries with it an implied open)
DELETE	Allows files and directories or subdirectories to be deleted
PARENTAL	Allows for creating and erasing of directories and subdirectories; also required for setting or changing trustee and directory rights in any directory or subdirectory
MODIFY	Allows file attributes to be modified and directories and subdirectories to be renamed

TABLE 2-2.   NetWare Effective Rights

servers on an internetwork. You may even access the file NET$PRN.DAT—and the print device and mode definitions contained therein—on a server other than the server to which you are currently logged in.

A third menu utility, PRINTCON, allows you to set up configurations for print jobs, using the definitions set up through PRINTDEF. Such print configurations may be made specific for each user on the network.

Use of PCONSOLE is important to print management on even the simplest of LAN installations and is a utility you will want to make available to many of your users. (PCONSOLE is discussed in Chapter 9.) PRINTCON and PRINTDEF are advanced utilities that are not required for successful use of NetWare, and with which ineffective use may create unexpected, and apparently unexplainable, network printing difficulties. Thus, only a brief discussion of PRINTCON and PRINTDEF is provided (in Chapter 9).

Message Handling Services (MHS)

Local area networks allow establishment of electronic mail services. Linking of electronic mail systems across local area networks (and across wide area networks) presents a problem because the protocols used to communicate within one LAN or WAN may be different from those used in another LAN or WAN. With the purchase of NetWare, you may have received special Message Handling Services (MHS) software. MHS is Novell's attempt to allow communication across disparate communications protocols. Message Handling Services is important software that you may well want to support on your server.

ADDITIONAL NETWARE FAULT TOLERANCE FEATURES

Thus far, the discussion of NetWare features applies equally to both Advanced NetWare 286 and SFT NetWare 286, and to most versions of those software packages. However, there are several features that are available only with SFT NetWare. These extended features all represent, in one fashion or another, opportunities to make your LAN more system fault tolerant. These extended system fault tolerant (or SFT) features include

- TTS (Transaction Tracking Services)

- disk mirroring

- disk duplexing

These topics are not discussed in this book. To learn more about each of these system fault tolerance features, refer to Novell's *SFT/Advanced NetWare 286 Installation* manual.

Summary

This chapter provided an overview of NetWare features available at the workstation and at the server. The objective was to provide you with an understanding of how NetWare operates as a system separate from and free from the limitations of DOS, as well as how, through the NetWare shell files, NetWare and DOS are able to coexist.

USER ACCESS
TO THE NETWORK

Users may encounter numerous obstacles on a PC network. If you are a LAN manager, your job is to remove or lower as many of these obstacles as possible, while maintaining the advantages of a LAN—security of data, accounting for LAN resource usage, network printing availability, and scheduled file backups, among others. Users gain these advantages, while they retain a sense of PC autonomy and independence.

Some trade-offs are necessary. Users give up some freedoms when using the network.

- They must log in as a named user, and in the process overcome any other primary access barriers you place in their way, including login password, workstation, or time restrictions.

- They must accept the restrictions and limitations on accessing files—placed on them by you as the network manager or by other users given directory or file-security management rights.

This chapter takes you step by step through the process of setting up users on your server. You are introduced to the login-password security features available in NetWare, each of which is under your control as the network manager. As manager, you may share some of this security responsibility with your users. Or you may retain a high degree of centralized control over server login-password security.

However, most users come from the world of PC independence, a world they like, prefer, and will be reluctant to forgo. One strength of NetWare is that it gives you discretion in applying the security features. If there is a bias in this chapter it is toward minimal security and shared responsibility with users for security.

CONNECTING THE WORKSTATION TO THE NETWORK

The first obstacle to overcome is physical connection of the workstation to the physical network. To accomplish this, you need

- correct network interface card (NIC) address and interrupt settings

- proper NIC to cable connections

- to boot the workstation and load properly configured NetWare shell files

The NIC Address

The NIC is the primary interface between any network node—a workstation or the server—and the LAN cable (or other LAN communication medium). NICs are specific to topologies, but for any one topology there are multiple NIC manufacturers and NIC models. You may have NICs of different models or manufacturers installed at different workstations, as long as each NIC is designed for the same topology.

However, each NIC installed must have a unique address on the network. On a small LAN with one server and one topology (one

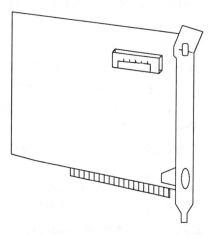

FIGURE 3-1. NIC hardware address settings

cabling scheme), the workstation is uniquely identified through the NIC *node address*. Figure 3-1 illustrates how toggle switches are set to define a NIC's node address. You should consult your NIC documentation for guidance on how to set the switches to define a particular address setting.

If two workstation NICs on the same cabling system have the same node address, information cannot be reliably delivered, as the workstations cannot be distinguished one from the other. Because of the importance of unique addresses, you will want to maintain a list of NIC addresses in use on the network. When a new workstation is installed, you can refer to the list and select an unused NIC address setting.

Note the following:

- Some cards build an address into the card itself. You will need to purchase cards with unique *firmware* addresses, or run a software program that adjusts the firmware address setting (if such a program is available).

- NICs for IBM PS/2 machines allow the address to be set through software contained on the IBM PS/2 REFERENCE diskette.

The NIC installed at the server must also have an address setting unique from those at the workstations. If you do internal bridging through the server—with up to four NICs installed in the server— each NIC must have a unique node address.

The NICs installed in a server also have associated with them a *network address*. Unlike the node address, which resides physically on the NIC, the network address is defined through NetWare system generation software procedures (part of NetWare's NETGEN program routines). The network address number, associated with a particular NIC installed at the server, applies to the entire cabling system to which that server NIC is attached.

In summary, each workstation NIC, and each of up to four server NICs, are uniquely identified through a combination of NIC node addresses and NetWare defined network addresses. Figure 3-2 illustrates how network and node addresses might be used on a LAN that includes two servers and three cabling topologies.

In Figure 3-2 Server_X is linked (through three separate NICs) to one Token Ring and two ARCnet topologies. Each topology is assigned its own network address: 1, 2, or 3, in this example. Because Server_X and Server_Y share the same Token Ring topology, the network address for Server_Y is also set at 1, through the NetWare system generation (NETGEN) process. (For more on NETGEN, refer to Chapter 10 and Novell's *SFT/Advanced Net-Ware 286 Installation* and *SFT/Advanced NetWare 286 Maintenance* manuals.) While sharing the same network address, Server_X and Server_Y are uniquely identified on the Token Ring network through the unique node address settings on the NICs installed in each server (as well as through their unique server names).

Because NetWare uses a combination of network address and NIC node address to identify a workstation, on the internetwork pictured in Figure 3-2, workstation A's NIC may use the same node address as the NIC installed in workstation C. These two workstations are connected to Server_X through separate server NICs, each with its own associated network address, and so are uniquely identified. And because Token Ring NICs will not function on an ARCnet topology—and vice versa—there is no risk that workstation A will be moved to the ARCnet topology nor workstation C to the Token Ring topology (though if both machines are switched, each would still be uniquely identified).

Workstations C and F could, technically, share the same NIC node setting, since each workstation is cabled to the server through separate server NICs, each with its own assigned, unique network address. However, workstation C and F share the same topology, if not currently the same physical network cabling system. If workstation C were moved to the same cabling system to which workstation F is cabled—a simple matter of unhooking and rehooking a cable at the back of workstation C—these two workstations would be sharing the same NIC node and server NIC

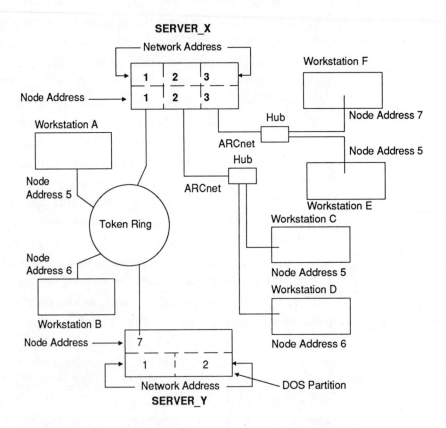

FIGURE 3-2. Network and node addresses on internally bridged servers

network address, and would therefore no longer be uniquely identified.

As a rule, NICs sharing the same cabling topology should be set with unique NIC addresses, especially if they are connected to the same server—even if they are not currently connected to the same physical cabling system.

NIC IRQ Settings

On DOS-based machines, hardware components such as serial ports, parallel ports, and disk coprocessor boards are accessible through *interrupt request* settings, or IRQs. IRQs are channels, or lines, used between a computer's central processing unit (CPU) and other computer hardware to transmit requests to begin or end tasks. If a workstation (or server) is not to become confused in its attempts to communicate with parts of itself, care must be taken in how IRQs are set on hardware devices such as network interface cards.

NIC cards generally come with a factory default IRQ line setting. *Change the setting at your own risk.* The NetWare LAN drivers, used in configuring NetWare shell files, contain assumed information about the IRQ line settings used on NICs. If you change the NIC's IRQ from the factory default, you may have to generate custom NetWare shell files for the workstation in which the NIC is installed. Most manufacturers try to use an IRQ setting that is unused in standard AT, XT, or PS/2 style machines, so the manufacturer's IRQ setting will usually work. Any changes you make can create conflicts with other parts of the workstation's hardware. If in doubt, refer to the manufacturer's NIC documentation.

Change the IRQ setting as a last resort, when all other attempts to establish network communication have failed.

Cable Connections and COMCHEK

Cable connections can be simple to complex, depending on the topology adopted and the intermediate connecting devices used, if any. After installation, most cable problems are easy to resolve, as when a cable has come loose from the connector joining it to the NIC (or to an intermediate junction box, for example, an ARCnet active hub). Or what you believe is a cable problem may turn out to be something else, as when the power is not on at an intermediate cable junction box or hub.

For difficult to detect problems, such as a break or short in a length of cable, special hardware and software diagnostic tools are available. Whether investment in such tools is advisable depends on your topology. On an ARCnet topology, using active hubs, it is easy to determine whether a length of cable is faulty. Test the integrity of a suspected length of cable by using it in a location where communications are functioning. If the cable works there, the cable is not the problem. For other topologies, more sophisticated line diagnostic tools may be beneficial.

NetWare provides a simple utility for testing for faulty LAN cable and NIC connections: COMCHEK. COMCHEK is a peer-to-peer communications checking program. NetWare need not be running at the server for you to use COMCHEK at workstations.

To use COMCHEK:

1. Boot your workstation with DOS (or the appropriate operating system).

2. Load the IPX.COM file configured for that workstation's NIC address and IRQ. (At the prompt type **IPX** and press (ENTER).)

3. Locate your NetWare 286 DIAGNOSTICS diskette, on which the COMCHEK.COM file resides.

4. Place the DIAGNOSTICS diskette, or another diskette to which COMCHEK.COM has been copied, in a local workstation drive. (Or map your workstation to a server directory and copy COMCHEK.COM to that server directory. See Chapter 7 for instructions on using the MAP command and Chapter 8 for instruction on using NCOPY.)

5. Change your current on-screen default drive to the local or network drive that points to COMCHEK.COM, type **COM-CHEK** at the prompt, and press (ENTER).

6. When unique user information is requested from within the NetWare Communication Check screen, type some identification to uniquely identify the workstation, such as **WORKSTA-TION1** or **DON'S WORKSTATION**, and press (ENTER).

After a brief delay, COMCHEK should display on screen this first workstation's network and node address and the unique workstation/user ID you provided.

Leave Workstation1 running COMCHEK and proceed to run COMCHEK at each and every other workstation on the same cabling system. As you proceed through COMCHEK trials, information for all workstations thus far checked will appear on all screens of workstations running COMCHEK (at which point it will become clear why you provided a verbal identification for each workstation to supplement the workstation network and node address identifications).

Figure 3-3 shows a listing from two workstations running COMCHEK. Each workstation is left running COMCHEK in order to check for duplicate NIC node addresses. Unfortunately, if duplicate node addresses exist, COMCHEK will fail to create its workstation listing. The same will be true if a cable is bad, or disconnected, or power not turned on at an intermediate device

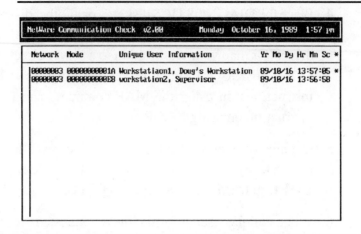

```
┌─────────────────────────────────────────────────────────────┐
│ NetWare Communication Check  v2.00       Monday  October 16, 1989  1:57 pm │
└─────────────────────────────────────────────────────────────┘

   Network  Node         Unique User Information        Yr Mo Dy Hr Mn Sc *

  │00000003 00000000001A Workstatiaon1, Doug's Workstation  89/10/16 13:57:05 *
  │00000003 0000000000E8 workstation2, Supervisor           89/10/16 13:56:58
```

FIGURE 3-3.   Two-station COMCHECK check

(such as an ARCnet active hub). Thus, while COMCHEK can tell
you what is working, you will have to identify and resolve the
problems when they exist.

If a workstation running COMCHEK fails to list itself on the
screen, check first to see if the physical cable connections are
secure. Next, check that the NIC is seated well in the workstation
and that its connectors are not dirty or damaged. Finally, check the
physical address set on the NIC. If it is a duplicate address to a
workstation already communicating on the network, that is probably the problem. Change the address and try again.

USER BOOTING
OF THE WORKSTATION

For users to gain access to the network from a DOS workstation,
they must do the following:

1. Load or boot DOS.

2. Load IPX.COM, configured for the user's workstation.

3. Load either NET2.COM, NET3.COM, or NET4.COM, depending on which version of DOS is running at the workstation.

Users may also want to issue the following DOS prompt command:

```
a:\>PROMPT $P$G
```

This version of the prompt command tells DOS to display entire path names at the on-screen DOS prompt. This is especially useful on a network, where path names may be lengthy, and will be invaluable in learning NetWare.

At this point you are attached to *a server* on the LAN and may proceed to log in to a *specific server*.

The process of booting the workstation and initiating user login can be automated through a DOS AUTOEXEC.BAT file. An example is shown here:

```
IPX.COM
NET3.COM
PROMPT $P$G
F:
LOGIN
```

Note that some topologies require additional files be loaded at the workstation prior to IPX.COM. If your NIC documentation calls for this procedure, do as follows:

1. Place the necessary files on your boot diskette.

2. Insert in your AUTOEXEC.BAT file, preceding the IPX.COM command, the additional commands required to load those files.

USER LOGIN AND PASSWORD SECURITY

You are attached to a server on the network when you issue the IPX command and the appropriate NET command. On a network with multiple servers, your attachment is to a server that is closest and available to you at that moment.

You do not have to be a defined user on the server to which you are automatically attached. The connection is a restrictive attachment, only allowing you to issue the NetWare LOGIN command. You will not be able to access files resident on a particular server's hard disks or otherwise take advantage of server print or other services until you log in as a specific user.

On your workstation screen, change to the first available NetWare network drive pointer. At the prompt type **F:** (or **D:** if you booted your workstation with an earlier version of DOS) and press (ENTER). (Refer back to the end of Chapter 1 and portions of Chapter 2 if you are unfamiliar with the concept of network drive pointers and paths.)

This first available network drive pointer (F: or D:) automatically points you to the directory called LOGIN on the server to which you are provisionally attached. The path to which F: is pointing may also include a volume or server name if you have more than one server on an internetwork or more than one volume on your single server. NetWare automatically drops server or volume names if they are not needed to define unique paths. (If your workstation screen is not displaying a netware path, type **PROMPTPG** and press (ENTER).)

In the examples that follow, it is assumed you have only one server on your network and that it is named FS1. Refer to Chapter 7 for further direction on logging in and attaching to multiple servers on an internetwork.

You are now ready to issue the LOGIN command. Type **LOGIN** along with the user name **GEORGIO** and press (ENTER). If, as in the AUTOEXEC.BAT file listed in the previous section, LOGIN is issued without a user name parameter, you are prompted for a user name, at which point enter **GEORGIO** and again press (ENTER).

Your screen may display a prompt asking for a password. If it does, provide a password, any password, and press (ENTER). Your screen will now look something like the following:

```
F:\LOGIN>LOGIN GEORGIO
Enter your password:
Access to server denied.
You are attached to server FS1.
```

You were denied access to server FS1 (or to whatever server you happen to be attached) because you provided either an invalid user name, GEORGIO, or an invalid password. One of the most basic security features of NetWare is that it does not tell you which you got wrong. In this case, both user name and password are probably incorrect.

Or, it could be that the name and passwords you provided were correct but known to a server other than the server to which you are currently attached. That problem could be remedied by referencing as part of the LOGIN command the server to which you really want to log in. For example:

```
F:\LOGIN>LOGIN FS2 GEORGIO
```

Which brings up the question, how do user names and passwords become known to the server?

Required User Name

Any user logging into a Novell server must provide a valid user name, a name known to the server to which the user is logging in. User names must be unique and can be up to 47 characters in length.

Users should be distinguished from *groups*. Each user name represents, in effect, an account name. In theory, you could allow everyone in your organization to log in with the same login name, to the same account. In practice, you will want individuals to have unique names, and possibly unique passwords.

Unlike user names, which are used in logging in and for which server resource usage may be accounted, *group names* are nominal categories used only to make security management easier. If you are a named user and a member of a named group (ESTIMATORS, for example) you cannot log in with the group name. However, as a member of the group ESTIMATORS, you will have whatever rights the group ESTIMATORS has, once you are logged in under your own user name.

Using the Same User Name
On Different Interconnected Servers

If yours is an internetwork environment with multiple servers, you may choose to create a particular user on more than one server, perhaps on all servers on the network.

Unlike Banyan Vines, another popular networking software package, NetWare does not have any facility to automatically propagate user names and associated rights from one server to other servers. Whether this feature, which in Vines is known as Street Talk, is especially beneficial is a matter for debate. The point is, if you want GEORGIO created on servers FS1, FS2, FS3, and FS4, you will need to take the time to do the setup four times.

Here are some notes on setting up users on multiple NetWare servers:

- A user does not have to be created on all servers to gain access to programs or services of other servers. An ATTACH feature allows you to be attached to numerous servers simultaneously.

- You may attach to another server as the user GUEST, or as any other user created on the server you are attaching to, if you know and provide the correct user password (if required).

- If you choose to create an identical user on more than one server, the MAKEUSER utility, which comes with NetWare, may help make the setup task easier, particularly if you have a large number of users to create.

- If a user is set up on more than one server and has identical user names on more than one server, the user may, at your option, change the password on one server and have that password synchronized on all other servers on the network that know of the user name.

If a GEORGIO user account exists on servers FS1, FS2, and FS3, a user logged in as GEORGIO can issue the SETPASS command at the screen prompt and automatically change the GEORGIO account password on all three servers under these conditions:

- the GEORGIO account password is the same on all three servers

- users on these three servers are allowed to change passwords

- all three servers are on and functioning

If any of the GEORGIO server accounts has a password that differs from the password logged in with, that account's password will not be synchronized. NetWare assumes that accounts with different passwords are completely separate user accounts.

While user names and associated restrictions may be created through the MAKEUSER program, you will probably find yourself using NetWare's SYSCON (System Configuration) menu utility. Later in this chapter you are taken step by step through setting up a user via the SYSCON menu utility. But first, a note about two very special users: SUPERVISOR and GUEST.

THE USER SUPERVISOR   SUPERVISOR is an all-powerful user who is able to do almost anything on the network, including the following:

- Create new users and define security arrangements for those users.

- Create group categories, define the security associated with those categories, and make users members of a named group.

- Delete users from a list of group members, or delete a user account.

- Create print queues and determine which users are allowed to act as *queue operators*.

- Designate users as *console operators*.

- Create SUPERVISOR equivalents—users who have all the rights of a SUPERVISOR, including those listed here.

The user SUPERVISOR cannot be deleted from the known users of a server. But because SUPERVISOR is such an all-powerful figure, you will want to establish a confidential password that must be provided by anyone logging in as SUPERVISOR. (Any supervisor equivalents should also have passwords.)

It is while logged in as SUPERVISOR that you perform SYSCON network-management responsibilities.

THE USER GUEST   The user GUEST is created by NetWare to make it convenient for users on one server—FS1, perhaps—to have access to some or all of the files and services of other servers —FS2, for instance. Users may log in to a server by using the name GUEST. Or, once logged into one server under their own account name, a user may simultaneously ATTACH to other servers as the user GUEST. The role of GUEST will be discussed in more detail in Chapter 6. For now, be reassured that NetWare sets the rights of the user GUEST on a server such that anyone logging in or attaching as GUEST is quite restricted, unless *you* make a server's GUEST rights less restrictive.

The ATTACH command is reviewed in Chapter 7. However, a question to consider here is "Should the user GUEST have a password, and what effect does this have on use of the ATTACH command?"

Because GUEST exists for the convenience of using multiple servers in an internetwork environment, you normally will not want the GUEST account password protected. If you restrict GUEST's rights on a particular server to only those server directories or services to which you want anyone to have access, there is no need to assign a password to the user GUEST.

If you establish a password for the GUEST user account, the password will need to be provided whenever a user logs in or attaches to the server as GUEST. You can restrict access to the GUEST user account.

Optional or Required Password

It is up to you as the user SUPERVISOR to determine whether passwords will be required, and whether passwords can be changed. The default setting in NetWare is the least restrictive: no password is required, but a user may at any time establish a password for his or her user name and then change that password at any time.

However, as user SUPERVISOR you may at your discretion do any of the following:

- require users to have a password

- require passwords to be of some minimum number of characters

- require passwords to be unique, with no two users having the same password

- require passwords to be changed periodically

- reserve to yourself the responsibility of setting passwords for users

These restrictions are not inclusive. You may, for instance, require users to have passwords that must be changed periodically, without having any restriction on length or uniqueness of passwords. You can place on the users the responsibility for setting and changing passwords.

You may establish a password for GUEST, in which case attachments or logins as GUEST must be accompanied by the established password. It is possible to

- Require passwords, but leave the GUEST user account without password protection (as long as no one logs in as GUEST, at which point they will have to create a password for GUEST).

- ATTACH as GUEST, with a password not required (because it does not yet exist).

If this is an anomaly, it is an appropriate anomaly. The purpose of the GUEST account is to allow easy but controlled access to a server's files or services by persons not set up as users on that server.

Grace Logins

Another feature, Limit Grace Logins, allows you as the user SUPERVISOR to limit the number of times a user may log in with an expired password before being forced to change that password. This feature applies only if a periodic change of password is required.

Should you require passwords, and if so how restrictive should you be? The key is to understand that when a person logs in as a particular user, he or she has all the rights, privileges, and responsibilities of that named user. Requiring passwords helps ensure that individuals do not inadvertently damage or delete other users' files, and also ensures that confidential data is not accessible simply through knowing, or even guessing at, someone's network user name: SUE, JOHN, or WHOMEVER.

But for individuals who are used to independent PCs, requiring a password is a psychological barrier to using a network. A rule of thumb: allow users to set their own passwords, but do not place any restrictions on length, uniqueness, or expiration dates for passwords, at least initially. Once users become comfortable with the network, and better understand the importance of their password for protecting their own data from other users, then consider minimum length, uniqueness, and periodic password change requirements.

Other Login Security Features

NetWare allows you as the user SUPERVISOR to further restrict user login in three ways: concurrent connections, time restrictions, and intruder lockout.

CONCURRENT CONNECTIONS   In theory, a user could log in to a particular server up to 100 times, which is the maximum number of login connections that NetWare 286 and SFT NetWare can keep track of at any one time. If you choose, you can limit the number of *concurrent connections* for any user to one connection. This not only prevents any user from tying up a server, but it also forces that user to log out of one workstation before going to another part of the building to use a second workstation. If a user must first log out, his or her account cannot be used by someone else in his or her absence.

In a small, friendly office, limiting concurrent connections may not be necessary. Or you may want some of your users, if not all of them, to be able to have two or three concurrent login connections. For instance:

- A user manning a help desk for the network will find it convenient to be able to log in as the user he or she is assisting. However, there are other Value Added Processes you can load on a server to allow a help desk person to capture another person's screen for the purpose of diagnosing difficulties or for instructional purposes.

- You may want to keep your machine running one task while you log in to another workstation to accomplish a second task (a crude form of multitasking).

You are not required to limit concurrent connections. It is an option.

TIME RESTRICTIONS   Another option is to limit times of the day, for selected days of the week, during which a user is allowed to log in. This is useful if you want to be sure users do not log in during a file backup, for instance, or if you want to prevent use of the network on weekends.

Time restrictions are specific to users and can be defined differently for different users. There is a global time restriction screen you can define, but the restrictions become effective only for new users created on the network after you create the restrictions, and even then you can modify the time restrictions for particular users.

Time restrictions are an option only. Consider carefully whether invoking this restriction is a real necessity for your organization. If not, do nothing. NetWare will assume no login time restriction unless you, as the user SUPERVISOR, tell it differently.

INTRUDER LOCKOUT   A feature you may want to invoke is *intruder lockout*. This feature, if invoked, applies equally to all users on the server.

If an intruder wished to log into a user account, it would be easy enough to guess at or read from the user's screen the user's login name. You may have noticed, however, that passwords are not displayed on the screen when typed at the prompt. Unless he or she is a keyboard reader—and there are people who can do this—your intruder would have to guess at the user's password, and would likely be incorrect at least for the first few guesses.

Intruder lockout keeps track of the number of times an incorrect password is used when a user attempts to log in. Once some number of successive attempts is exceeded without a valid password being provided (the default is seven attempts), the account is locked and all further attempts to log in are summarily rejected for a period of time. You choose for how long an account is locked. The default is fifteen minutes, but may be set at any combination of days, hours, and minutes. However, if a user successfully logs in prior to the incorrect login attempt threshold being reached, the count of unsuccessful attempts is set back to zero.

As with other features, intruder detection is an optional feature with no intruder detection as the default setting. If your users have passwords, and if you want to invoke intruder detection, the NetWare default values are reasonable, although a threshold of four incorrect login attempts, with both the bad login count retention time and the length of account lockout set at fifteen minutes is recommended. This results in intruders being detected and accounts locked more quickly, but with users who are poor typists being able to try again after fifteen minutes.

You must balance the risk of intruders logging into your network against the frustration of users who want and need to get onto the server finding themselves locked out.

 A user will be locked out even if it is someone else who provides the wrong password.

If you use intruder lockout, consider also allowing users to change their own passwords. Then, if they get it wrong, it is their password that they forgot, not one you imposed on them.

The exception might be on a large internetwork where you could, on separate servers, have identical user account names—three Johns, four Sues—and to maintain these as unique accounts on the internetwork you must have a unique password for each of these identical user account names. In this instance, as network manager, you may choose to retain responsibility for setting user passwords.

FUNCTIONAL USERS AND GROUPS

Keeping track of the security rights and other responsibilities of 30, 60, or 100 users can become a LAN administrator's nightmare. NetWare simplifies this management problem by allowing you to create groups and functional users who by definition have certain rights and responsibilities.

Console Operators

One special functional user is the *console operator*. Any named user may be made a console operator. Console operators have special rights within the NetWare menu FCONSOLE. Most importantly, they are able to shut down the server.

Print Queue Managers

Printing on the network is one of the more important tasks, and one needing the most monitoring and day-to-day management. NetWare allows you, as SUPERVISOR, to designate any user a *queue operator*. While all users are able to manage their own print jobs, queue operators are responsible for all jobs in the print queue for which they are an operator. (See Chapter 9 for further details.)

Nominal User Groups

You may choose to define groups, or categories of users, for your network. Groups might be defined by job function or by the computer applications used. For instance:

Defined by Job Function	Defined by Application Used
Accounting	Accounts_Payable
	Accounts_Receivable
Clerical	Word_Perfect
	Word
Sales	dBaseIV
	Paradox3

If you take this listing and draw lines between items on the left that go with items on the right, you might have a lot of lines. Sales, for instance, may use all of the applications listed on the right.

This really is no problem. You can define as many groups as you wish. The real questions are these:

- What security rights should be afforded each of these groups?

- Who should be made a member of each group, thereby acquiring the security rights of the group?

If you are working now on planning your network security, plan to use groups extensively. The ability to establish and maintain security through groups is a major strength of NetWare. This will become more apparent as you plan your security using the information in Chapters 4 and 6.

USING GROUPS TO CONSERVE DIRECTORY ENTRIES

A not so obvious benefit of using groups to establish security is conservation of *trustee assignments*. You may not yet know what a trustee assignment is, but you do know that you use up one directory entry in your hard disk's directory entry table for each five trustee assignments you make. However, five trustee assignments to the group ACCOUNTANTS equals one directory entry, regardless of how many users are included as members of the group ACCOUNTANTS.

THE EVERYONE GROUP   One group is established at the time you install NetWare: the group *EVERYONE*. To this group are attached those trustee assignments and effective rights that you want every user on the server to have. Any user you create on the network is automatically made a member of the group EVERYONE. While you can delete users from this group, you will seldom want to do so. In Chapter 4 you will see just how NetWare manages EVERYONE's effective rights.

EVERYONE becomes an important group for shortcutting in security management. If you want all users to have access to WordPerfect, simply assign to the group EVERYONE the rights necessary to effectively use WordPerfect. All users will be able to use that package without further action being required, because they are members of the group EVERYONE.

LOGGING IN AS SUPERVISOR

The time has come to use your server. You are the system SUPER-VISOR. It is your responsibility to create user accounts and network security. To do so, you must either log in as the user SUPERVISOR or log in as a user who is equivalent to SUPERVI-SOR. On a newly installed server, there will be no users equivalent to SUPERVISOR, until you make them equivalent.

Boot your workstation and log in as SUPERVISOR:

F:\>LOGIN SUPERVISOR

If you are working at a nondedicated server, you may need to type **DOS** and press (ENTER) to switch from server Console mode to DOS mode prior to issuing the LOGIN command.

If you are logging into a newly installed NetWare server, you will not be prompted for a password for the user SUPERVISOR.

On an existing network you will, hopefully, have to provide a password to log in as SUPERVISOR. Otherwise, your server is not secure: any person can log in as SUPERVISOR without having to provide a valid account password.

If you are able to log in without being required to provide a valid password, the first action you should take is to establish a password for SUPERVISOR.

Using SETPASS to Set
The SUPERVISOR's Password

Having logged in as SUPERVISOR, at the prompt type

F:\>SETPASS

Press (ENTER) and you are prompted for a password. Type in a *memorable* password and press (ENTER).

You are asked to retype the password you just entered. Since passwords are not displayed on the screen during their entry, you cannot tell if you made a typing error the first time you entered your new password. The retyped password is compared to your first typing. If they match, you have created a password. If they do not match, you will have to reissue the SETPASS command and try again.

USING SYSCON TO CREATE
NEW USERS AND USER GROUPS

In this section you are guided through the process of using the menu SYSCON to create new users and user groups. You also will create a backup supervisor and establish a password for this supervisor-equivalent user.

To access SYSCON from the prompt, either type **SYSCON** and press (ENTER), or type **MENU MAIN** and press (ENTER). The MENU MAIN command calls NetWare's Main menu utility. Highlight **4. System Configuration** and press (ENTER). The SYS-CON menu shown in Figure 3-4 should appear on your screen.

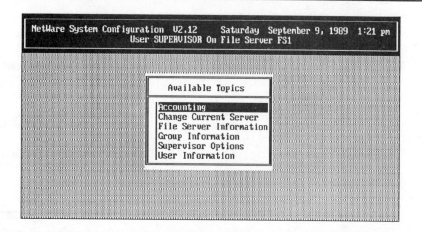

```
NetWare System Configuration  V2.12     Saturday  September 9, 1989  1:21 pm
                        User SUPERVISOR On File Server FS1

                              ┌─────────────────────────┐
                              │     Available Topics     │
                              ├─────────────────────────┤
                              │ Accounting             · │
                              │ Change Current Server    │
                              │ File Server Information  │
                              │ Group Information        │
                              │ Supervisor Options       │
                              │ User Information         │
                              └─────────────────────────┘
```

FIGURE 3-4. SYSCON Available Topics screen

About NetWare Menus

Within any NetWare menu, you can make a selection either by using the (UP) and (DOWN) cursor keys to highlight an option or by typing the first letter. If two or more items on the menu start with the same letter, you must type the first, the second, and any additional letters of an option title until the highlight bar is over the selection you desire. Press (ENTER) to invoke a highlighted selection, and you are shown one the following:

- additional information

- another menu of options from which to make a choice

- a list, such as a Group Members list, to add or delete listed items

```
┌─────────────────────────────────────────────────────────────────────────┐
│ The function key assignments on your machine are:                         │
│                                                                           │
│ ESCAPE          Esc             Back up to the previous level.            │
│ EXIT            Alt F10         Exit the program.                         │
│ CANCEL          F7              Cancel markings or edit changes.          │
│ BACKSPACE       Backspace       Delete the character to the left of       │
│                                 the cursor.                               │
│ INSERT          Ins             Insert a new item.                        │
│ DELETE          Del             Delete an item.                           │
│ MODIFY          F3              Rename/modify/edit the item.              │
│ SELECT          Enter           Accept information entered or select      │
│                                 the item.                                 │
│ HELP            F1              Provide on-line help.                      │
│ MARK            F5              Toggle marking for current item.           │
│ CYCLE           Tab             Cycle through menus or screens.            │
│ MODE            F9              Change Modes.                              │
│ UP              Up arrow        Move up one line.                         │
│ DOWN            Down arrow      Move down one line.                       │
│ LEFT            Left arrow      Move left one position.                   │
└─────────────────────────────────────────────────────────────────────────┘
```

FIGURE 3-5.   NetWare menu help screen

Having more than one item start with the same letter within a menu is one of the few design flaws in NetWare. When you develop custom menus, you will want to avoid this problem. Novell has maintained consistency in its menu choices from version to version of NetWare. Having created an inconvenience, they have not gone on to create confusion.

You can at any time get help on what function and other keys to use within NetWare menus. In a NetWare menu, simply press (F1) twice. NetWare will display the help menu shown in Figure 3-5. Press (ESC) twice to return to the SYSCON Available Topics screen.

 Any menu or submenu with a double line around it is one in which you can *do something*. That is, you can highlight a choice, press (ENTER), and something more happens.

A single-bordered menu is for *information only*. There will be nothing more you can do at that point except take note of the information provided, and press (ESC) to move back up to a previous menu level.

NetWare menus are *tiled* menus. Like pieces of tile, they can each have their own pattern and one submenu placed on the screen over other menu tiles. However, a screen header is always visible. The NetWare screen header displays your NetWare version, the date, the time, and user name information. (See Figure 3-4.)

In this chapter tiled SYSCON menus are generally displayed in their overlaid form. In later chapters, submenus are not always displayed in their tiled form, and the NetWare screen header is seldom displayed. This is a concession to space in the book.

Setting Up Template Global Restrictions

NetWare allows you to define certain global defaults that apply to *new users*. Specifically, while logged in as SUPERVISOR, you may set default

- login time restrictions

- intruder detection restrictions

These defaults automatically become the restrictions for new users you subsequently create, but they do not apply to users already set up on the server. To save time later, set default restrictions as you want them set for *most* of your users before creating any new users. You can then loosen or tighten the restrictions for particular users.

Or, you can change defaults and then create users who need those default settings, and then again change the defaults and create another set of users, *ad infinitum*.

SETTING LOGIN TIME RESTRICTIONS   In order for you to set global login time restriction defaults, highlight **Supervisor Options** and press (ENTER). You will see a list of supervisor options as shown in Figure 3-6.

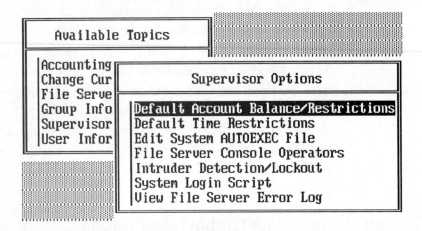

```
┌──────────────────────────┐
│    Available Topics      │
├──────────────────────────┤
│Accounting┌────────────────────────────────────┐
│Change Cur│        Supervisor Options          │
│File Serve├────────────────────────────────────┤
│Group Info│ Default Account Balance/Restrictions│
│Supervisor│ Default Time Restrictions           │
│User Infor│ Edit System AUTOEXEC File           │
└──────────│ File Server Console Operators       │
           │ Intruder Detection/Lockout          │
           │ System Login Script                 │
           │ View File Server Error Log          │
           └────────────────────────────────────┘
```

FIGURE 3-6.   SYSCON SUPERVISOR options

Select **Default Time Restrictions** and press (ENTER). A screen with days of the week across the top and half hours of the day down the left column appears, with an asterisk in each intersecting cell (see Figure 3-7). An asterisk indicates that login *is* allowed for that half-hour period. Use the arrow keys to move around the screen without altering the asterisked cells.

To delete an asterisk, press the (SPACEBAR). To replace an asterisk, press (INSERT). If you want to change a *block* of time, press the (F5) (Mark) key. Pressing (F5) anchors the cursor. Now use the arrow keys to move around the screen—or use the (HOME), (END), or (PGUP), and (PGDN) keys—to highlight a section of the screen. When you now press the (SPACEBAR), an entire section of asterisks is removed from the screen. (Or, blocking an area, (INSERT) places an asterisk in all the marked blank cells.)

There is a shortcut to exiting NetWare menus, which you do not want to use at this point. To leave SYSCON and return to DOS, press (ALT-F10). An **Exit SYSCON** option appears with the highlight bar over **Yes**. Do not press (ENTER) now.

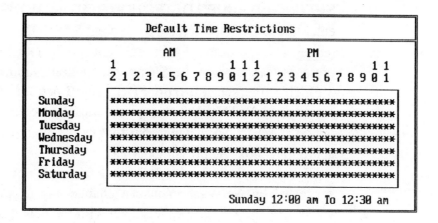

FIGURE 3-7.   Login Time Restrictions screen

If you use (ALT-F10) to quick exit, you will lose any edits not previously saved.

In this case, you are still viewing—and to NetWare still editing—the Login Time Defaults screen. If you quick exit, you lose these edits (as explained in a help screen if you press (F1) at this point). To avoid losing your global default setup changes, at the **Exit SYSCON** prompt, either press (ESC) or select **No** and press (ENTER).

Now you can press (ALT-F10) and (ENTER) to quickly exit from SYSCON and not lose your edits. This works from within any NetWare menu, including custom menus you design.

The global default time restrictions you set take effect, but do not apply to existing user accounts, only to users you create after this point. For instance, if you want the user GUEST to have the default login restrictions you just developed, you will have to either delete and recreate the user GUEST or change GUEST's user account time restrictions screen (see Other User Information Options later in this chapter).

SETTING INTRUDER DETECTION RESTRICTIONS   You re-enter the SYSCON screen by typing SYSCON and pressing (ENTER) at the prompt. Again highlight **Supervisor Options** and press (ENTER) to view the Supervisor Options submenu (Figure 3-6). This time, select **Intruder Detection/Lockout**. If you are on a newly installed NetWare server, the Intruder Detection/Lockout option is set to **No**. Change **No** to **Yes** by typing **Yes** into the appropriate box and pressing (ENTER).

Global intruder detection/lockout defaults are now in effect, as suggested by NetWare. You can change any of these default values. Figure 3-8 shows the screen with the new default values set. Change any of the defaults you wish, and then press (ESC) twice to return to the SYSCON Main menu.

As with global time restrictions, global intruder detection/lock-out values have no effect on existing users on the network. These values apply only to new users created after this point.

```
┌──────────────────────────────────────────────────────────┐
│                Intruder Detection/Lockout                  │
├──────────────────────────────────────────────────────────┤
│Detect Intruders:                Yes                         │
│                                                            │
│Intruder Detection Threshold                                │
│Incorrect Login Attempts:        7                           │
│Bad Login Count Retention Time: 0  Days   0  Hours   30 Minutes│
│                                                            │
│Lock Account After Detection:    Yes                         │
│   Length Of Account Lockout:    0 Days   0  Hours   15 Minutes│
└──────────────────────────────────────────────────────────┘
```

FIGURE 3-8.   Intruder detection and lockout defaults

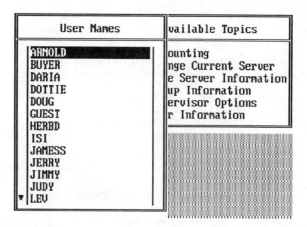

FIGURE 3-9.   SYSCON User Names screen

Defining New Users

You are now ready to create new user accounts on the network. From the SYSCON Available Topics menu, select **User Information**. You will see a list of current server-defined users as shown in Figure 3-9.

On a newly installed NetWare server, only two users are listed: GUEST and SUPERVISOR. On an existing network, there may be a long list of existing user account names, probably more than will display in the User Names screen box. You can move the cursor through the entire list of user names by using the (UP) and (DOWN) arrow keys. Or, by typing the first letter of a valid user name, you will skip down the list to the corresponding alphabetical point in the listing. If you hear a beep, try a different letter of the alphabet. If you use the typing method of moving through the list, you will have to press (ESC) before you can go back up the list.

To add a new user account to the current list, press (INSERT). (INSERT) is consistently used in NetWare menus to add items to a

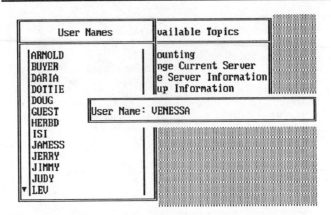

FIGURE 3-10.   User VENESSA typed into User Name box

list. You will see a box in which to type a user name. Type the user name VENESSA (see Figure 3-10) and press (ENTER).

If there is not already a VENESSA user account on your server, VENESSA will be added in appropriate alphabetical placement within your list of user accounts, as shown in Figure 3-11.

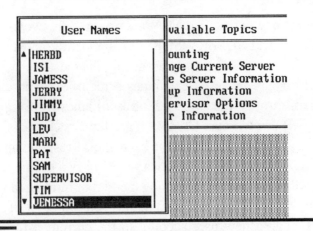

FIGURE 3-11.   User VENESSA added to User Names list

Anyone can now log in to the server using the user name VENESSA. VANESSA will not be recognized as a user name, unless you have VANESSA (spelled with two a's) set up as a separate user account. Before proceeding further, press (ESC) to return to the SYSCON Available Topics menu.

A Caution About User Names

A word of caution is in order. While NetWare allows user names greater than eight character in length (greater than the allowed length of a DOS filename), you may want to keep your user names to eight characters or less. The reason has to do with automatic tape backup systems. To understand the problem, you need to know that you will probably want to create a subdirectory for each user on the network, and the name of the subdirectory will be spelled exactly the same as the name of the user.

The problem encountered with some tape backup systems is outlined here. While a system may say that it is fully NetWare compatible, meaning that it can back up files from any NetWare server directory or subdirectory, in practice some tape backup software can recognize only subdirectories that conform to DOS standards. That is, some software will recognize as valid only a subdirectory name that is eight or less characters in length. If your user name is DOUGLASLEE, NetWare will recognize the name and allow you to place files in that subdirectory. However, your tape backup software may not back up files in the DOUGLASLEE subdirectory (or in any subdirectory that comes alphabetically after DOUGLASLEE), because it cannot recognize DOUGLASLEE as a valid subdirectory name. Unless you know that the tape backup software you are using or plan to use is really 100% NetWare compatible, keep your user names to eight characters or less. The same advice goes for volume and server names.

Creating Passwords Through SYSCON

Earlier in this chapter you set a password for the user SUPERVI-
SOR by issuing the SETPASS command at the screen prompt. You
can also control passwords through SYSCON.

CREATING A NEW PASSWORD FOR VENESSA   To set
or change a user's password, follow these steps:

1. From the SYSCON Available Topics menu, select **User Information**.

2. Highlight the user VENESSA and press (ENTER).

To move quickly through the list of users to VENESSA, use the
typing method.

   A User Information submenu, as shown in Figure 3-12, should
now be on your screen. Place the highlight bar over **Change
Password** and press (ENTER).

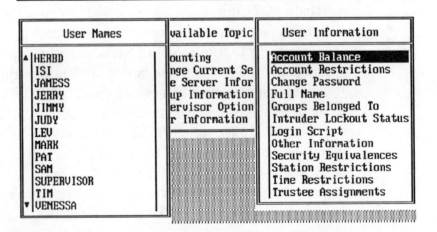

FIGURE 3-12.   SYSCON User Information screen

```
┌─────────────────────────────────────────────────────┐
║  Enter New Password:                                  ║
└─────────────────────────────────────────────────────┘
```

FIGURE 3-13.   SYSCON New Password Prompt

You will see a space in which to type a new password (see Figure 3-13). Type the password **WILEY**. As you type, your keystrokes are not shown on the screen.

After you press (ENTER), you are prompted to retype the password. If you fail to type the password the same way twice, you are informed of your error (see Figure 3-14). Press (ESC) and try again.

Wiley should now be VENESSA's password. To verify this, exit SYSCON (press (ALT-F10)) and log in as VENESSA.

CHANGING AN EXISTING PASSWORD   Once a password is created, it can be changed only if you are logged in as one of the following:

- the user SUPERVISOR

- a supervisor-equivalent user

- the named user whose password you are changing

```
┌─────────────────────────────────────────────┐
│  New Password Not Retyped Correctly,         │
│       <Press ESCAPE to continue>             │
└─────────────────────────────────────────────┘
```

FIGURE 3-14.   SYSCON New Password Not Retyped
Correctly Screen

For the named user to change his or her own password, he or she must first correctly type the old password. (This is true whether you are changing the password through SYSCON or by way of the SETPASS command.) Requiring a user to type the old password in changing to a new password makes sense. It prevents someone else from changing your password while you are logged into but away from your workstation.

Using either the SETPASS command from the prompt or the SYSCON menu, change VENESSA's password from Wiley to Cagey. If you wish, this is a good point at which to take a break.

Other User Information Options

Before proceeding, log back in as SUPERVISOR and call up the SYSCON menu. Highlight **VENESSA**, select **User Information**, and press (ENTER). You will see a number of User Information items from which to chose (refer back to Figure 3-12). You must be logged in as a SUPERVISOR or supervisor-equivalent to have some of these items listed. A user entering SYSCON would not see the Intruder Lockout Status choice, and would only be able to view security settings you created as SUPERVISOR, not to change them.

You have already learned how to change a password. Security Equivalences is discussed at the end of this chapter. The other listed items are as follows:

• **Account Balance**   If you have initiated server accounting, as SUPERVISOR, you can use this choice to establish an account balance for a user account—an amount of beans with which the user can operate.

• **Account Restrictions**   This option allows the SUPERVISOR to disable an account or set an expiration date for a user account.

- **Full Name**   This option allows the SUPERVISOR to indicate more clearly than a user login name just who is the user in question: John Jones, as opposed to JOHN. The information provided is for documentation only and has no effect on server operations.

- **Groups Belonged To**   Users can select this item to view, but not change, the groups of which they are a member. A newly created user is a member of the group EVERYONE. As SUPERVISOR, you can add a user to other groups set up on the network.

- **Intruder Lockout Status**   This option displays the default intruder lockout status inherited by the user from the global system defaults at the time that user was created on the server. As SUPERVISOR, you can change these user defaults. The changes here have no effect on the global, system intruder lockout status default.

- **Login Script**   NetWare's *user login script* is analogous to a DOS AUTOEXEC.BAT file. Any user can create and change their own user login script. As SUPERVISOR, you can create or change the user login script for any user account. See Chapter 7 for further details.

- **Other Information**   This information is for viewing only and includes a user identification code through which the server keeps track of user information, including naming of a user network mail box.

- **Station Restrictions**   Through this option, as SUPERVISOR, you can define the workstations to which a user can log in, and in this way restrict stations from use by a user.

- **Time Restrictions**   This option allows you, as SUPERVISOR, to customize login time restrictions for a user. This option works identically to the global time restrictions screen reviewed earlier in this chapter.

- **Trustee Assignments**   It is through this option—along with Groups Belonged To and Security Equivalences—that you establish directory and file security for users. The Trustee Assignments option is reviewed in detail in Chapter 4.

You must be logged in as SUPERVISOR (or supervisor-equivalent user) to create or modify trustee assignments through SYSCON. As you will learn in Chapter 4, in certain instances users can themselves create or alter trustee assignments to other users, without being a supervisor-equivalent.

Creating New Groups on the Network

You may now want to create some group categories on your network, again using SYSCON. From the SYSCON Available Topics menu, highlight **Group Information** and press (ENTER). A Group Names submenu will appear, such as that shown in Figure 3-15.

The group names in your list will be different from those shown here. If you are on a newly installed server, only the group EVERYONE will appear in the list. The group EVERYONE is explored more fully in the next chapter.

To create a new user group, follow these steps:

1. Press (INSERT) to display the Group Names entry box.

2. Type the group name **EXECUTIVE**.

3. Press (ENTER).

If you were logged in as the user SUPERVISOR, or as a supervisor-equivalent, you created a new group. For security, users

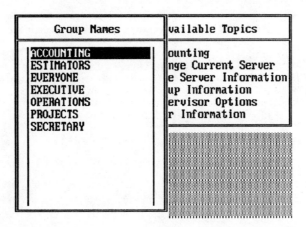

FIGURE 3-15.   SYSCON Group Names screen

must always have SUPERVISOR rights to create or modify a server group.

The next step is to complete the group EXECUTIVE picture. Place the highlight bar over the group **EXECUTIVE** and press (ENTER). A Group Information submenu appears as shown in Figure 3-16. Each of these items will be briefly explored in turn.

FULL NAME   With the highlight bar over **Full Name**, press (ENTER). You will see a space in which to provide a full name for the group EXECUTIVE. This can be anything you want, within the space provided. One useful option is to provide a telephone number or extension for the individual responsible for organizing or maintaining this group on the network. If someone thinks they should be a member of the group EXECUTIVE, whom do they call? Full Name will give them the number.

As with Full Name under the User Information submenu, a group Full Name is used strictly for documentation.

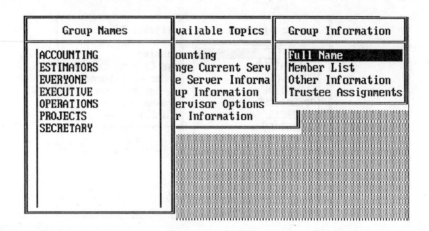

Group Names	vailable Topics	Group Information
ACCOUNTING	ounting	Full Name
ESTIMATORS	nge Current Serv	Member List
EVERYONE	e Server Informa	Other Information
EXECUTIVE	up Information	Trustee Assignments
OPERATIONS	ervisor Options	
PROJECTS	r Information	
SECRETARY		

FIGURE 3-16.   SYSCON Group Information screen

MEMBER LIST   Highlight the **Member List** option and press
(ENTER). Initially, no users are members of the EXECUTIVE group.
Users are automatically added only to the group EVERYONE.
You should see a blank Group Names list.

To add members to the Group Members list, press (INSERT) to
call up a Not Group Members list. At this point, Not Group
Members includes all users thus far set up on your network.

Highlight the user you created previously, **VENESSA**, and
press (ENTER). This adds VENESSA to the EXECUTIVE Group
Members list. To add another user, again press (INSERT) to reveal
the Not Group Members screen. This time highlight **SUPERVI-
SOR** and press (ENTER).

To add multiple users to a Group Members list simultaneously:

1. Press (INSERT) to reveal the Not Group Members screen.

2. Highlight a user and press the (F5) (Mark) key.

3. Move the cursor down or up to another user and again press the
   (F5) (Mark) key.

4. Press (ENTER).

Both individual users you highlighted are added to the EXECU-
TIVE Group Members list.

You may have noticed that listed choices marked with (F5) are
displayed in a different color from unmarked items. You also may
have noticed that the highlight bar blinks on and off when sitting
over a marked choice. If you mark an incorrect choice, pressing
(F5) again will turn off the blinking cursor and unmark a selection.
This (F5) (Mark) key feature works in all NetWare menus where
you are allowed to mark items for inclusion in, or deletion from, a
list.

You may continue to add individual users to the group EXEC-
UTIVE. On the server from which examples for this book were
taken, six users are members of the group EXECUTIVE (see
Figure 3-17).

In practice, one user never needs to be made a member of the
EXECUTIVE group. This is the user SUPERVISOR who, by
default, has all rights to all directories on the network. SUPERVI-

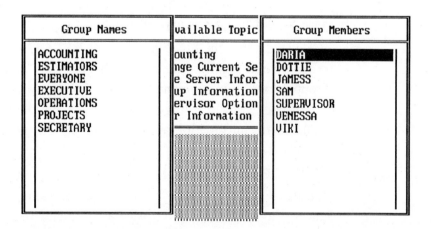

FIGURE 3-17. The group EXECUTIVE's Group Members
screen

SOR gains no additional rights by being a member of the group EXECUTIVE. Having SUPERVISOR in the list does no harm, but it is redundant. Follow these steps to remove SUPERVISOR from the EXECUTIVE Group Members list:

1. If Group Members is not the current submenu selection on the screen, get to that point. From the SYSCON Available Topics menu select **Group Information** and press (ENTER).

2. Select **EXECUTIVE** and press (ENTER).

3. In the Group Members list, highlight **SUPERVISOR**.

4. Press the (DELETE) key. You will be asked to confirm that you want to delete this user from the Group Members list.

5. To delete the user (or a group of marked users) keep the highlight bar over **Yes** and press (ENTER).

You should now have removed SUPERVISOR from the Group Members list for the group EXECUTIVE. Press (ESC) to move back to the Group Names menu.

OTHER INFORMATION   To learn more about the group EX-ECUTIVE, place the highlight bar over **EXECUTIVE** and press (ENTER). Next, highlight the **Other Information** choice from the Group Information submenu and press (ENTER).

This is one of those single-line screens mentioned earlier. The display is for information only (see Figure 3-18).

TRUSTEE ASSIGNMENTS   Finally, highlight **Trustee Assignments** and press (ENTER). You will notice that for groups this space is initially blank. No trustee assignments have been made. Groups you define on the network initially have no effective rights: new groups have no rights to any directory or file on the network,

```
Last Login:
File Server Console Operator:
Disk Space In Use:
User ID:
```

FIGURE 3-18.   User Other Information

regardless of how many individual users have been included among the Group Members list.

The exception to this is the group EVERYONE, which is automatically created when you install NetWare and for which certain trustee assignments are standard with NetWare. The next chapter will explore in more depth NetWare effective rights and the role of both trustee assignments and directory masks in determining effective rights.

DELETING USERS OR GROUPS FROM THE SERVER

Deleting either a user or a group from your server setup is quite simple. However, do not undo what you have just completed if you plan to follow along with later examples in the book.

To delete a group or user, follow these steps:

1. Enter **SYSCON**.

2. Go to either the **Group Information** or **User Information** selection and press (ENTER).

3. Highlight the group or user you want to delete.

4. Press (DELETE).

5. To cancel the deletion process, press (ESC) or place the highlight bar over **No** and press (ENTER).

6. If you really want to delete the selected group or user from the server setup, keep the highlight bar over **Yes** and press (ENTER).

Adding or deleting users or groups involves the same process as adding or deleting items from any other NetWare menu listing.

SECURITY EQUIVALENTS AND THE BACKUP SUPERVISOR

You can create trustee assignments for a user or group within SYSCON. Before proceeding to the topics of Chapter 4, this section briefly notes one more way you can manage user security through SYSCON. In the process you will establish VENESSA as a *backup* supervisor-equivalent.

Security Equivalents

NetWare allows you to make any user equivalent to any other user or user group on the network. To see how this is accomplished within SYSCON, go to **User Information** and within the User Names screen highlight the user **VENESSA**. Press (ENTER) to reveal the User Information submenu.

Next, highlight **Security Equivalents**, as shown in Figure 3-19, and press (ENTER). You will see a Security Equivalences listing, with the group EVERYONE listed (see Figure 3-20).

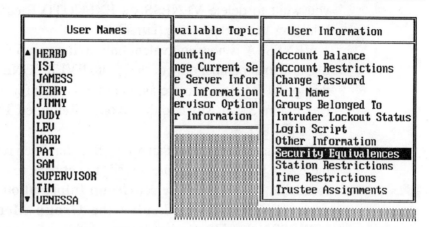

User Names	vailable Topic	User Information
▲ HERBD	ounting	Account Balance
ISI	nge Current Se	Account Restrictions
JAMESS	e Server Infor	Change Password
JERRY	up Information	Full Name
JIMMY	ervisor Option	Groups Belonged To
JUDY	r Information	Intruder Lockout Status
LEV		Login Script
MARK		Other Information
PAT		Security Equivalences
SAM		Station Restrictions
SUPERVISOR		Time Restrictions
TIM		Trustee Assignments
▼ VENESSA		

FIGURE 3-19.   SYSCON User Information, Security
Equivalents screen

NetWare uses the term *security equivalent* in two somewhat
inconsistent ways:

- to refer to one user being equivalent to another user

- to refer to the security equivalent rights conveyed through
  membership in a NetWare group

In this instance, VENESSA is shown as equivalent to the group
EVERYONE and to the group EXECUTIVE. A user can gain
membership in, and equivalent rights of, any group *either* by being
made a member of the group or through this Security Equivalences
menu. The effects are identical.

You can also revoke a user's rights through this menu. In this
instance, remove VENESSA from the EXECUTIVE group by
deleting her security equivalency. From the Security Equivalences
screen, highlight **EXECUTIVE** and press (DELETE). Confirm that

you want to delete VENESSA's EXECUTIVE equivalence by selecting **Yes** and pressing (ENTER).

VENESSA is now equivalent only to the group EVERYONE. She is also a member only of the group EVERYONE. To confirm this, press (ESC) so you are again at the User Information screen (see Figure 3-12). Move to the **Groups Belonged To** option and press (ENTER).

If you are still in doubt that VENESSA has been removed from the EXECUTIVE group, press (ESC) to get back to the SYSCON Available Topics menu, select **Group Information** and, for the group EXECUTIVE, display the **Group Members** list. VENESSA should no longer be included.

The Backup SUPERVISOR

It is advisable to create a user who is equivalent to the user SUPERVISOR. While you can never delete the user SUPERVISOR, you may forget SUPERVISOR's password. Having a backup, equivalent supervisor, with a different password (kept

```
  Other Users And Groups          e      Security Equivalences

ACCOUNTING          (Group)            EVERYONE          (Group)
ARNOLD              (User)      r
BUYER               (User)      r
DARIA               (User)      r
DOTTIE              (User)
DOUG                (User)      m
ESTIMATORS          (Group)     =
EXECUTIVE           (Group)
GUEST               (User)
HERBD               (User)
ISI                 (User)
JAMESS              (User)
JERRY               (User)
```

FIGURE 3-20.   SYSCON Other Users and Groups listing for selecting security equivalents

confidential) is one way to help ensure that you can still do SUPERVISOR activities on your server, including changing the SUPERVISOR's password to one you remember, without having to reinstall NetWare.

Of course, you will want to make this backup supervisor a fictitious user. You are ill-advised to make a regular user a supervisor-equivalent. Even if *you* routinely log in to the server as SUPERVISOR for the purpose of setting up users and maintaining security, you should set yourself up as a regular user and log in under that user name for the purposes of doing your everyday work. If you do everyday work while logged in as SUPERVISOR, it is easy to forget you have supervisor rights, and all too easy to delete users or otherwise inadvertently wreak havoc on the security arrangements you have established.

If your boss insists on having SUPERVISOR rights, set him or her up twice as two different users: one for when he or she logs in as a supervisor-equivalent and one for doing work. In fact, if your boss often logs in as SUPERVISOR, you need to rethink your setup of the boss's normal work user account name. All of this applies equally if you are the boss.

For now, make VENESSA a supervisor-equivalent. From SYS-CON, go into **User Information**, **VENESSA**, and **Security Equivalences**. Press (INSERT) and you will see a list of all groups and users currently set up on the server, including SUPERVISOR (see Figure 3-20). Move the cursor or type your way down to the point where the highlight bar is over the user name **SUPERVI-SOR**. Press (ENTER). SUPERVISOR now appears in VENESSA's security equivalency listing.

Summary

This chapter introduced you to your responsibilities as a LAN manager or server SUPERVISOR with regard to setting up new users and user groups on the network.

Guidance was provided on linking workstations to the network, on logging in to the server, and on the login and password security options open to you.

You also learned how, while logged in as the user SUPERVISOR or as a supervisor-equivalent, you can use SYSCON to create new users and user groups, make users members of a group, or make one user equivalent to other users.

Other features of SYSCON, such as invoking resources accounting, are explored in later chapters.

EFFECTIVE RIGHTS
AND A USEFUL
DIRECTORY STRUCTURE

This chapter introduces you to planning NetWare directory security, a topic given additional attention in Chapter 6. You are introduced to the NetWare required directory structure and to how directory security is established through management of trustee assignment rights and directory mask rights.

A useful addition to the required directory structure is offered and you are walked through the process of creating portions of this directory structure. Both FILER and SYSCON are used to create directories and trustee assignments.

NETWARE EFFECTIVE RIGHTS

NetWare's primary file security rests at the directory and subdirectory levels. You need to understand clearly and unequivocally how NetWare helps you establish and manage effective user rights in directories.

An *effective user right* allows a user to do something in a directory or subdirectory. As Table 4-1 shows, a user may need a combination of effective rights to actually accomplish a task. To read a file from the server to the workstation RAM, a user needs a minimum of Search, Open, and Read rights in the directory in which the requested file is located. (This is true regardless of whether that file is currently cached in server RAM.)

NETWARE'S REQUIRED DIRECTORY STRUCTURE

Your decisions about server directory structure are the most important decisions you will make. The security of your data, the ease of file backups or archiving, and the success in using applications on the network will all hinge on your server directory structure decisions. NetWare gives you a start with this.

Action in a Directory	Minimum Rights Required
Create a file with a new name	CW
Read a file from the server to a workstation's RAM	SOR
Write a file obtained from directory A (with SOR rights) to directory B, where the filename already exists in directory B	SOW (in B)
Copy a file from directory A into directory B, where the filename is not in use in directory B	CWD (in B)
List files using DIR or NDIR command	S
Rename a file in a directory	SRWM
Delete a file	D
Change a file's flags	SM
Create a directory or subdirectory	CP
Remove a directory, a subdirectory, and all files in both directories.	SDMP
Change directory mask rights	P
Make a trustee assignment to another user to your own home directory	P

TABLE 4-1.   Effective Rights Required to Accomplish Tasks

As generally discussed at the end of Chapter 1, NetWare organizes information stored at the server as follows:

- **Server name**   Distinguishes one server from another on an internetwork.

- **Volume name**   Distinguishes each hard disk attached to the server, or a portion of a hard disk.

- **Directory**   Identifies the first level of hard disk organization beneath volumes.

- **Subdirectory**   One or more subdivisions beneath the directory level.

The NetWare operating system is maintained on the server in a hard disk volume named SYS. Beneath the required volume SYS, NetWare automatically creates—at the time of server software installation—four required directories and a related subdirectory structure. If you operate with a nondedicated server, a DOS volume is also created.

Figure 4-1 illustrates NetWare's required directory structure and summarizes the effective rights that users have in each directory.

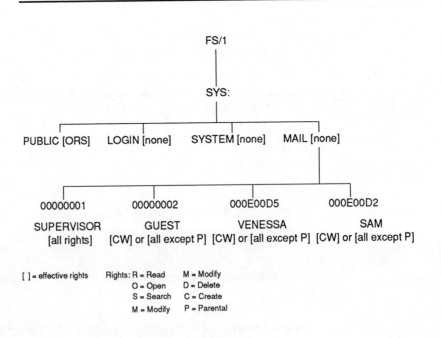

FIGURE 4-1.   NetWare's required directory structure and user effective rights

The four required directories branching off the root volume SYS are LOGIN, MAIL, PUBLIC, and SYSTEM. The subdirectory structure under MAIL is created as users are added to the server.

You can leave the security arrangement for these directories unchanged, but you will want to know the contents of these directories and what users can and cannot do within them. Table 2-2 in Chapter 2 and Table 4-1 provide guidance about the functional opportunities conveyed to users through each NetWare effective right, or combination of effective rights. How these effective rights are established is discussed after a brief review of the four required directories and the effective rights that users have in them.

LOGIN

The directory LOGIN exists for the convenience of users logging into a server. As illustrated in Figure 4-1, users receive no effective rights to the LOGIN directory, although they are able to ATTACH to a server through LOGIN directory services. LOGIN exists for the purpose of assisting users to access the network. Beyond that function, users have no access rights to the LOGIN directory. Not having search rights, they cannot even see a listing of the files contained in LOGIN.

SYSTEM

The directory SYSTEM contains files necessary for server operations and for management of the network by you as the user SUPERVISOR. Included here are NetWare Console commands.

As with LOGIN, users have no effective rights in SYSTEM and so no direct access to files in SYSTEM. As SUPERVISOR you can access files in this directory, with all rights, including the right

Row	Column 1	Column 2	Column 3	Column 4	Column 5	Column 6	Column 7	Column 8
1	Directory Rights < >	<CDMOPRSW>	<CDMOPRSW>	<CDMOPRSW>	<CDMOPRSW>	<CDMOPRSW>	<CDMOPRSW>	<CDMOPRSW>
2	DIRECTORY\ SUBDIRECTORY	LOGIN/	SYSTEM/	PUBLIC/	PUBLIC/ DOS/	PUBLIC/ DOS/ V2.0	PUBLIC/ DOS/ V3.0	PUBLIC/ DOS/ V4.0
	GROUPS and USERS Trustee Assignment( )							
	Effective Rights [ ]							
3 G	EVERYONE (TA)	( )	( )	(_ O _ RS _)	( )	( )	( )	( )
4 R	[ER]	[none]	[none]	[_ O _ RS _]	[_ O _ RS _]	[_ O _ RS _]	[_ O _ RS _]	[_ O _ RS _]
5 U	(TA)	( )	( )	( )	( )	( )	( )	( )
6 P	[ER]	[ ]	[ ]	[ ]	[ ]	[ ]	[ ]	[ ]
7	(TA)	( )	( )	( )	( )	( )	( )	( )
8	[ER]	[ ]	[ ]	[ ]	[ ]	[ ]	[ ]	[ ]
9 U	GUEST (TA)	( )	( )	( )	( )	( )	( )	( )
10 E	[ER]	[none]	[none]	[_ O _ RS _]	[_ O _ RS _]	[_ O _ RS _]	[_ O _ RS _]	[_ O _ RS _]
11 R S	VENESSA (TA)	( )	( )	( )	( )	( )	( )	( )
12	[ER]	[none]	[none]	[_ O _ RS _]	[_ O _ RS _]	[_ O _ RS _]	[_ O _ RS _]	[_ O _ RS _]
13	SAM (TA)	( )	( )	( )	( )	( )	( )	( )
14	[ER]	[none]	[none]	[_ O _ RS _]	[_ O _ RS _]	[_ O _ RS _]	[_ O _ RS _]	[_ O _ RS _]

TABLE 4-2.   Directory Security Plan for NetWare Required Directories

Row	Column 1		Column 9	Column 10	Column 11	Column 12	Column 13	Column 14	Column 15
1	Directory Rights < >		<CDMOPRSW>	<CDMO RSW>	<CDMO RSW>	<CDMO RSW>	<CDMOPRSW>	<CDMOPRSW>	<CDMOPRSW>
2	DIRECTORY\ SUBDIRECTORY		MAIL/	MAIL/ 00000002	MAIL/ 000E000D5	MAIL/ 00000007			
	GROUPS and USERS Trustee Assignment ( ) Effective Rights [ ]								
3	EVERYONE	(TA)	(C____W)	✓	✓	✓	✓	✓	✓
4		[ER]	[C____W]	[C____W]	[C____W]	[C____W]	[ ]	[ ]	[ ]
5		(TA)	✓	✓	✓	✓	✓	✓	✓
6		[ER]	[ ]	[ ]	[ ]	[ ]	[ ]	[ ]	[ ]
7		(TA)	✓	✓	✓	✓	✓	✓	✓
8		[ER]	[ ]	[ ]	[ ]	[ ]	[ ]	[ ]	[ ]
9	GUEST	(TA)	(W)	(CDMO_RSW)	✓	✓	✓	✓	✓
10		[ER]	[C____W]	[CDMO_RSW]	[C____W]	[C____W]	[ ]	[ ]	[ ]
11	VENESSA	(TA)	✓	(CDMO_RSW)	(CDMO_RSW)	✓	✓	✓	✓
12		[ER]	[C____W]	[CDMO_RSW]	[CDMO_RSW]	[C____W]	[ ]	[ ]	[ ]
13	SAM	(TA)	✓	✓	✓	(CDMO_RSW)	✓	✓	✓
14		[ER]	[C____W]	[C____W]	[C____W]	[CDMO_RSW]	[ ]	[ ]	[ ]

TABLE 4-2. Directory Security Plan for NetWare Required Directories (*continued*)

to delete files. To avoid accidental deletion of SYSTEM files consider the following:

- Not routinely mapping (pointing) SUPERVISOR to the directory SYSTEM.

- Doing routine daily work under a LOGIN name other than SUPERVISOR (under a user account name that has no rights to SYSTEM).

- Flagging files in SYSTEM as Readonly, meaning that a file can be accessed, but not overwritten.

File flagging is a NetWare security feature discussed at the end of this chapter.

PUBLIC

The directory PUBLIC contains those NetWare commands and executable files used by all users. NetWare's Command-Line commands are in PUBLIC. NetWare gives users only those minimum rights necessary to use PUBLIC files: Search, Open, and Read. Unless you are logged in as SUPERVISOR or a supervisor-equivalent user, you can neither delete nor modify PUBLIC files.

You should leave unaltered the PUBLIC security structure as defined by NetWare. If you are considering placing additional files in PUBLIC for which users will require effective rights beyond Search, Open, or Read, a better alternative is to create a separate directory for these files, outside the NetWare required directory structure. An example of this is discussed here and in Chapter 6.

MAIL and User Subdirectory Mail Boxes

The final required directory is MAIL and, beneath MAIL, user-specific MAIL subdirectories. MAIL subdirectories are named with the alphanumeric code corresponding to a user's server ID code. See Figure 3-18 in the previous chapter for user VENESSA's server ID code.

Users have limited rights in the MAIL directory and all sub-directories, except for their own subdirectory mailbox beneath MAIL. MAIL is, in a sense, a place holder in the directory structure and will usually remain an empty directory, except for subdirectory definitions. The purposes of the MAIL directory are

- to point to a subdirectory structure

- to serve as an aid in creating effective security arrangements in the MAIL subdirectories

In a user's personal MAIL subdirectory—in his or her own mailbox—the user has all rights except the Parental right. Exclusion of Parental prevents users from creating subdirectories under their mailbox subdirectory or changing the security arrangements for this directory. A user can Search for files, Open a file, Read its contents to a workstation, Delete a file, Create and Write a new or revised file, and Modify file flags, but only in his or her own mailbox subdirectory.

In every other subdirectory under MAIL—in other users' mail-boxes—a user is limited to Create and Write rights. Create and Write effective rights enable you to send electronic mail to another user's subdirectory mailbox under a new filename. But with only Create and Write rights, you cannot view mail in the other user's mailbox, nor list the names of files in those mailbox subdirectories.

How NetWare creates the MAIL security arrangements is discussed here. You will want to keep this MAIL directory and subdirectory structure in place and unaltered. While Novell no longer bundles an electronic mail package with NetWare (it did with version 2.0a), this structure is used by some third-party electronic mail packages. Also, it is in MAIL subdirectories that NetWare places, and knows to look for, a user-specific user login script (a topic discussed in Chapter 7).

Confirming Required Directory Rights With the RIGHTS Command

To confirm effective rights in the NetWare required directories, log in as the user GUEST (or as some other user who is not a supervisor-equivalent). Type **MAP** at the prompt and press (ENTER) to display your current drive mappings. You should see a mapping to the directory PUBLIC, probably with drive Z:\ used as the drive pointer.

Switch to the PUBLIC drive pointer (type **Z:** and press (ENTER)) and then issue the RIGHTS command (type **RIGHTS** and press (ENTER)). Or, issue the RIGHTS command with an associated drive pointer; for example, type **RIGHTS Z:** and press (ENTER). You will see the following listing on the screen:

```
Z:\PUBLIC>RIGHTS
FS1/SYS:PUBLIC
Your effective rights are [R O  S ]
    You may Read from Files.        (R)
    You may Open existing Files.    (O)
    You may Search the Directory.   (S)
```

NetWare displays any type of right within brackets: directory mask rights, trustee rights, or effective rights. In this instance, the capital letters contained in brackets represent effective rights. In figures and tables developed exclusively for this book, brackets [ ] are consistently used to display effective rights, with < > used to display directory rights and ( ) used to display trustee assignment rights. However, this handy convention is not used by NetWare. You must exercise caution when you are looking at NetWare's rights information on screen or you may be fooled into believing a displayed right is an effective right, when it is not.

Next map yourself to SYSTEM, LOGIN, or MAIL, and issue the RIGHTS command to check your effective rights in those directories. In the case of SYSTEM and LOGIN, you will see this message:

```
Your Effective Rights are [            ]:
   You have NO RIGHTS to this directory area.
```

Alternatively, you may view your effective rights through either the NetWare SESSION or FILER menu (see Chapters 7 and 8 for assistance).

If you have more effective rights than discussed here, you are working on a server where NetWare required directory security has been altered for your user account. This may be a matter for concern. Along with this chapter, Chapters 5 and 6 will help you decide whether any correction to your existing server security is advisable.

HOW NETWARE EFFECTIVE RIGHTS ARE CREATED

An effective right exists when a user has acquired, within a specific directory, both a directory mask right and a corresponding trustee assignment right. At a concrete level, directory mask and trustee assignment rights represent information contained in

- each server hard disk volume's directory entry table (DET)

- NetWare's bindery files (NET$DIND.SYS and NET$BVAL)

The directory entry table was discussed in Chapter 2. The *bindery files* are the repository for information about NetWare defined users and groups. Because of the importance of this information for effective server operation and for directory-level security, the bindery files are located in the SYSTEM directory as hidden files.

Further details about the content of either directory entry tables or bindery files is not critical information, unless you are programming directly to the NetWare operating system. What is required is an understanding of the directory mask rights and trustee assignment rights concepts and how you manage both to create user effective rights.

Each of the eight NetWare rights—Search, Open, Read, Write, Create, Delete, Modify, and Parental—may be included within a directory mask or a trustee assignment. The key point to remember is that for a right to be effective for a user, that right must be contained in both a directory mask and a trustee assignment.

To view the directory mask rights and trustee assignments created by NetWare, log in as the user SUPERVISOR, and follow along with the hands-on instructions that accompany the following discussion of directory mask and trustee assignments.

The Directory Mask

A *directory mask* is information that attaches to a specific directory or subdirectory. Rights defined in a directory mask are always specific and unique to that directory or subdirectory. And each directory mask is unrelated to and independent of the masks of other directories up or down the directory tree structure.

The directory masks of each NetWare required directory are shown across the top line of Table 4-2. You may confirm the contents of these directory masks through the FILER menu utility (as illustrated later in this chapter). Or, while pointing to the root volume SYS, you may issue the LISTDIR command with an appropriate command flag. The latter approach is used here.

Type **MAP** and press (ENTER) to view your current directory mappings. If you have a pointer to SYS, simply change drive pointers by typing the drive letter and pressing (ENTER). Alternatively, map yourself to SYS and then change to the associated drive pointer. Type the following command-line statements and press (ENTER) to use this second approach to seeing directory mask rights.

```
MAP Q:=(servername)/SYS:
Q:
LISTDIR/A
```

You will see information like the following listed on the screen:

```
LOGIN        7-03-89   5:51p   [RWOCDPSM]
MAIL         7-03-89   5:52p   [RWOCDPSM]
 00000001    7-03-89   5:55p   [RWOCD SM]
 00000002    7-03-89   5:55p   [RWOCD SM]
 000E00D2    7-15-89   2:12p   [RWOCD SM]
 000E00D5   11-15-89   9:35a   [RWOCD SM]
PUBLIC       7-03-89   5:52p   [RWOCDPSM]
SYSTEM       7-03-89   5:50p   [RWOCDPSM]
```

The capital letters enclosed within brackets represent directory mask rights, not effective rights. As mentioned earlier, NetWare does not use separate symbols to distinguish one type of right from another. You just have to know that LISTDIR displays directory mask rights (unlike the RIGHTS command, which displays effective rights).

Each directory mask is unrelated to every other directory mask. Having a directory mask for the MAIL directory that includes all rights (row 1, column 9 of Table 4-2) does not foreclose a less inclusive directory mask for mail subdirectories (row 1, columns 10 through 12 of Table 4-2).

Remember that directory mask rights do not represent effective rights, unless they are accompanied by a complimentary trustee assignment. The directory mask rights for PUBLIC includes all rights (Table 4-2, row 1, column 4). But as a user you have only

Search, Open, and Read effective rights (row 4, column 4). Similarly, the SYSTEM and LOGIN directory masks contain all rights (columns 2 and 3, row 1 of Table 4-2), but no user effective rights (columns 2 and 3, rows 10, 12, and 14).

A third point to remember is that the directory mask applies equally to all users (except SUPERVISOR or supervisor-equivalent users). By removing the Parental right from each MAIL subdirectory mask (row 1, columns 10, 11, and 12 of Table 4-2), NetWare ensures that no user can ever change the trustee assignments of any of the MAIL subdirectories.

If you remove all but a Search right from a directory mask, users in that directory can never do more than see a listing of filenames.

All rights are included in a directory mask when you first create the directory or subdirectory. If you plan your directory structure properly, you will usually leave the directory mask unchanged, with all rights in it. By itself, the directory mask conveys no effective rights. In advising you to leave the directory mask unchanged, it is implied that you will manage directory security through trustee assignments.

Trustee Assignments

Trustee assignment rights attach to either an individual user or to a group. An individual acquires trustee assignment rights in these ways:

- directly, through a trustee assignment made to his or her own user account

- indirectly, by being made a member of a group to whom a trustee assignment is made

- indirectly, by being made equivalent to another user

Trustee assignments rights are ultimately user specific. You must personally acquire trustee assignment rights to gain effective rights, even if you do acquire those trustee rights indirectly through membership in a group or through being made equal (equivalent to) one or more other users to whom trustee assignment rights have already been made.

The trustee assignments created by NetWare may be viewed from within the SYSCON menu. You must be logged in as the user SUPERVISOR (or a supervisor-equivalent user) to have this information display on screen. Log in as the user SUPERVISOR. At the prompt type **SYSCON** and press (ENTER) to call up the SYSCON Available Topics menu.

NETWARE'S TRUSTEE ASSIGNMENTS TO PUBLIC AND MAIL

The first trustee assignments NetWare creates are to the group EVERYONE. These trustee assignments are created at the time you install the NetWare software on the server.

From the SYSCON Available Topics menu, select **Group Information** and press (ENTER). Move the cursor down to the group **EVERYONE** and press (ENTER). Now move the cursor to **Trustee Assignments** and press (ENTER).

At a minimum you will see two trustee assignments:

• a Read, Open, and Search trustee assignment to the directory PUBLIC

• a Write and Create trustee assignment to the directory MAIL

On a newly established server, these will be the only trustee assignments to EVERYONE and your screen should look like Figure 4-2.

The effect of these trustee assignments is shown in Table 4-2 and will be discussed momentarily. For now, note that the PUBLIC

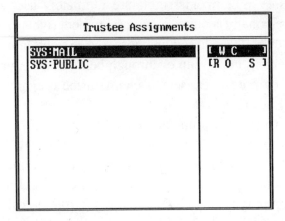

```
┌──────────────────────────────────────────────────┐
│               Trustee Assignments                 │
├────────────────────────────┬───────────────────────┤
│ SYS:MAIL                   │ [ W C      ]          │
│ SYS:PUBLIC                 │ [R O     S ]          │
│                            │                       │
│                            │                       │
│                            │                       │
│                            │                       │
│                            │                       │
│                            │                       │
└────────────────────────────┴───────────────────────┘
```

FIGURE 4-2.   NetWare's trustee assignments to EVERYONE

trustee assignment has been entered into column 4, row 3 of Table 4-2 and the MAIL trustee assignment into column 9, row 3.

NETWARE'S TRUSTEE ASSIGNMENT TO NEW USERS

As each new user is created on the server, NetWare creates

- a new, user-specific subdirectory under the required directory MAIL

- a trustee assignment for the user to the newly created MAIL subdirectory

To view this MAIL subdirectory trustee assignment, press (ESC) to get back to the SYSCON Available Topics menu, select **User Information** and press (ENTER). Highlight the user **GUEST** and press (ENTER). Next, select **Trustee Assignments** and press (ENTER). You will see a trustee assignment like that shown in Figure 4-3. On a server with NetWare newly installed, this trustee assignment will be the only trustee assignment to GUEST. On an established

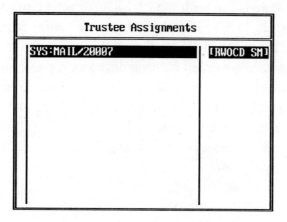

FIGURE 4-3.   NetWare's trustee assignment to new users

server, additional trustee assignments may exist (whether rightly or wrongly you may decide later).

The trustee assignment to GUEST is displayed in Table 4-2 in column 10, row 9. Following the same procedure you used to see GUEST's trustee assignment, you may confirm the existence of a similar trustee assignment to every other user, in their own uniquely identified MAIL subdirectory.

The Elegance of NetWare Security Management

An elegant formula or solution is one which says or does a lot in few words or with little effort. $E=MC^2$ is an elegant formula, to those in the know about such matters. It says a lot, quite succinctly. In a similar, if not quite as powerful a manner, NetWare security is elegant. Only a few trustee assignments are required to manage security for the entire required NetWare directory structure.

In combination with the PUBLIC directory mask, one trustee assignment to EVERYONE creates the entire required security arrangements for PUBLIC. User rights within the MAIL directory structure are governed by each directory's mask and two trustee assignments, one to the group EVERYONE (aimed at the directory MAIL) and one to the individual user (aimed at his or her own mailbox subdirectory beneath MAIL). The resulting security arrangement is elaborate, as you are about to see, but the means to achieving that arrangement is easy.

EFFECTIVE RIGHTS ELABORATED

To understand how NetWare's elegant, frugal security assignments support an elaborate directory structure, it is necessary to understand two more features of NetWare trustee assignments:

- Unlike directory mask rights, which are specific to one directory, trustee assignment rights fall through the directory structure.

- Unlike directory masks, for which there is only one per directory, several different trustee assignments may in combination determine a user's effective rights in a particular directory or subdirectory.

The first principle is illustrated by considering what additional security arrangements are needed to establish security for DOS subdirectories placed beneath NetWare's PUBLIC directory. The question of why you would want one or more versions of DOS supported through the server is discussed later in this chapter.

DOS Security on the Server

Figure 4-4 summarizes how NetWare creates directory rights through directory mask and trustee assignment manipulations in the required NetWare directories, as well as in any DOS directories you might create under the PUBLIC directory.

Users have Search, Open, and Read rights in the required directory PUBLIC because:

- The PUBLIC directory mask includes Search, Open, and Read rights.

- Users have Search, Open, and Read trustee rights in PUBLIC (through a trustee assignment to the group EVERYONE).

With DOS subdirectories placed beneath PUBLIC, what additional security actions must you initiate? The answer is *none*. By placing DOS under PUBLIC, users automatically have Search, Open, and Read rights in the DOS subdirectory to which they are eventually mapped. (For guidance on creating directories and copying files, see Chapter 8, as well as the latter portions of this chapter.) No additional security actions are required for these reasons:

- When you create a directory or subdirectory, the directory mask automatically contains all rights (see Table 4-2, row 1, columns 6, 7, and 8).

- Trustee assignments flow downward through a directory structure, so an implied Read, Open, and Search trustee assignment already exists for the group EVERYONE in each of the DOS subdirectories beneath PUBLIC (by virtue of the

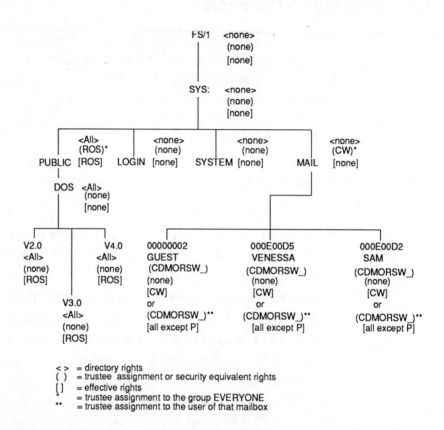

FIGURE 4-4. VENNESA's effective user rights in NetWare's required directory structure

EVERYONE trustee assignment falling down through the PUBLIC subdirectory structure).

- The implied trustee assignment combines with the the directory mask to yield effective rights to the group EVERYONE of Read, Search, and Open (as shown in row 4, columns 6, 7, and 8 of Table 4-2).

Because new users are automatically made members of the group EVERYONE, they also acquire Read, Open, and Search rights in PUBLIC and in each of the DOS directories beneath PUBLIC (illustrated on lines 10, 12, and 14, columns 4 through 8 of Table 4-2).

As already mentioned, NetWare security management is elegant: simple, powerful, and to the point. One trustee assignment accomplishes a lot.

A second example of flow-through trustee assignments is found in the MAIL subdirectory. Also illustrated there is how multiple trustee assignments feed each other to add rights back into a lower level directory.

MAIL Subdirectory Security

As you saw earlier in SYSCON, and as illustrated in Table 4-2 (column 9, row 3), a trustee assignment of Write and Create is made to the group EVERYONE in the directory MAIL. If the directory mask rights for MAIL did *not* also include Create and Write rights, the group EVERYONE would *not* have those effective rights. Because *both* the MAIL directory mask **and** the MAIL trustee assignment include Create and Write rights, these rights are effective rights (and are listed as such in Column 9, row 4 of Table 4-2).

Because each user set up on the server is automatically made a member of the group EVERYONE, the users GUEST, VENESSA, and SAM also acquire an effective Create and Write right in the MAIL directory (Column 9, Rows 10, 12, and 14 of Table 4-2) without any additional trustee assignment needing to be made to them.

Look again at the group EVERYONE. Because trustee assignments fall through the directory structure, Table 4-2, row 4, columns 10 through 12 show the group EVERYONE having Create and Write effective rights in each mailbox subdirectory beneath MAIL. Again, no additional trustee assignment is required.

Not only does the group EVERYONE have Create and Write rights in every MAIL subdirectory mailbox, so does each new user set up on the server. As row 18 of Table 4-2 illustrates, VENESSA has Create and Write rights in the user GUEST's 00000002 mailbox (column 10) and in SAM's 00000007 subdirectory mailbox (column 12). Similarly, SAM has Create and Write rights (row 14 of Table 4-2) to GUEST's and VENESSA's subdirectory mailboxes: 00000002 (column 10) and 000E00D5 (column 11). No additional trustee assignments are required to create this Create and Write security arrangement.

However, if you are wondering why users seem to have more than just Create and Write rights in some of the subdirectories under MAIL, you are on to another important, and last, complication regarding NetWare directory level security. But before tackling this extra complication be sure you understand the preceding discussion. If you are at all confused, and most of us are the first time we try to understand how directory mask rights and trustee assignments combine to yield effective rights, a rereading of this chapter to this point is in order.

Adding Rights Back into A User's Own Mailbox Subdirectory

Trustee assignment rights are made to a user or group at a directory or subdirectory level and filter downward from that point through the subdirectory structure. When combined with a particular directory or subdirectory rights mask, actual or implied trustee rights result in effective rights in that directory.

Less obvious is that users can gain rights through combinations of trustee assignments. Using a directory rights planning form, such as Table 4-2, helps sort through how multiple trustee assignments contribute to effective security arrangements. Figure 4-5

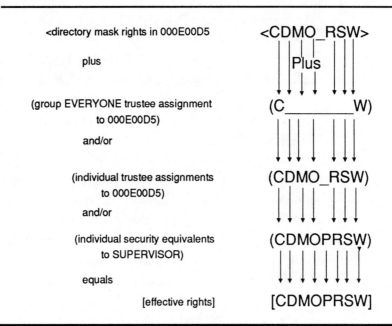

<directory mask rights in 000E00D5	<CDMO_RSW>
plus	Plus
(group EVERYONE trustee assignment to 000E00D5)	(C_____W)
and/or	
(individual trustee assignments to 000E00D5)	(CDMO_RSW)
and/or	
(individual security equivalents to SUPERVISOR)	(CDMOPRSW)
equals	
[effective rights]	[CDMOPRSW]

FIGURE 4-5.   Adding up effective rights

illustrates how multiple trustee assignments jointly contribute to establishment of effective rights in a directory.

As illustrated in Figure 4-5, the MAIL subdirectory assigned to VENESSA has a directory mask with all rights except Parental. Therefore, neither VENESSA nor any other user can exercise Parental right activities in subdirectory 000E00D5. But none of the remaining directory mask rights become effective until combined with trustee assignment rights.

The group EVERYONE has a Create and Write trustee assignment to the MAIL directory (column 9, row 3 of Table 4-2), which falls through to the MAIL subdirectories. Because VENESSA is a member of the group EVERYONE, she acquires Create and Write rights in subdirectory 000E00D5 (see Figure 4-5). But these two effective rights are inadequate to VENESSA managing her mailbox subdirectory files. Accordingly, NetWare makes an additional trustee assignment to VENESSA to her own mailbox subdirectory. The trustee assignment is for all rights except the Parental right. (This trustee assignment to VENESSA is illustrated in Figure 4-5 and in Table 4-2, column 11, row 11.) When combined with the directory mask rights for the MAIL subdirectories, VENESSA gains all the effective rights she needs to effectively manage her MAIL subdirectory files.

This would be the end of the story, and VENESSA would have all rights except Parental in her MAIL subdirectory mailbox (as illustrated in Table 4-2, column 11, row 12), except for one factor not taken into account in Table 4-2 but illustrated in Figure 4-5. In a previous chapter you made VENESSA equivalent to the user SUPERVISOR. Technically, Table 4-2 correctly expresses VENESSA's current effective rights. With the Parental right removed from her 000E00D5 subdirectory, she does *not* have an effective Parental right. However, the bottom line of Figure 4-5 shows VENESSA having all effective rights, including the Parental right, and in a narrow sense Figure 4-5 is also correct. How can both illustrations be correct?

On the one hand, removal of the Parental right from the directory mask means that any user, including SUPERVISOR, has no Parental right in that directory or subdirectory. On the other hand, exclusion of the Parental right does not prevent SUPERVISOR or a supervisor-equivalent user adding the Parental right back into the directory mask, thereby creating an effective Parental right in that directory. It is only SUPERVISOR or a supervisor-equivalent user who can alter a directory mask in the absence of an effective Parental right in that directory or subdirectory.

In summary:

• Through a trustee assignment you can add rights back into a subdirectory, but you can never take trustee rights away. Once a trustee right exists for a user at a higher level in the directory structure (Write and Create in MAIL), that trustee right exists at all lower regions of that branch of the directory tree (the MAIL subdirectories).

- You can limit effective rights in a lower level subdirectory by taking a right out of a directory mask (as illustrated in the MAIL subdirectory masks), but the revoked right is revoked for all users, even the user SUPERVISOR. However, SUPERVISOR or a supervisor-equivalent user can add rights back into a directory mask.

A SUGGESTED DIRECTORY STRUCTURE

With some understanding of how NetWare allows you to manage directory security, you can turn your attention to the question of how you might design your overall directory structure. Specifically, what should you look for in a good directory structure, and what might a good directory structure look like?

The directory structure shown in Figure 4-6 is a structure for a single-server hard disk that maximizes the criteria for a good structure. To the four required directories of NetWare are added three DOS subdirectories beneath a PUBLIC/DOS subdirectory. Beneath a second server volume, named SYS1, an APPS and DATA directory structure is created.

APPS and DATA could have been created under the volume SYS. Placing them under a separate server volume is done only to illustrate what you might encounter if you are working on a server with multiple hard disk volumes.

Criteria for a Good Directory Structure

Before considering the directory security you might establish for the proposed directory structure, take a moment to consider what

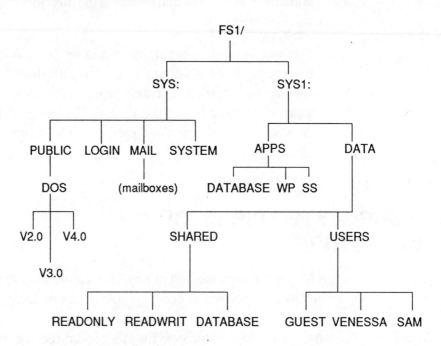

FIGURE 4-6.   A suggested directory structure

a good directory structure looks like. It is against these criteria that you will judge an existing or proposed structure to be good or bad. A good directory structure has these features:

- ensures server data is secure

- makes easy the job of managing server security

- allows users freedom to accomplish their jobs, today and tomorrow

- ensures installed applications—word processing, database, spreadsheets—operate reliably and flexibly

- allows for convenient, timely (at least daily) backup of data files

- does not have the limitations you are used to living within the DOS world

As you will see, the proposed directory structure performs well against these criteria.

Why Place DOS on the Server?

You may want to create DOS subdirectories at the server for at least three reasons:

- If you are using diskless workstations, those workstations must look to the server for DOS commands.

- Through the use of a NetWare search drive, external DOS commands, such as EDLIN, can be made easily and always available to users.

- Placing DOS at the server can help ensure that a correct version of COMMAND.COM is loaded at a workstation.

The third reason requires some further elaboration. COMMAND.COM is a DOS command that must be loaded at the workstation each time you leave a DOS application program—WordPerfect, Lotus 1-2-3, and so forth. The version of COMMAND.COM loaded must be a correct version for the workstation hardware platform on which you are working.

On standalone PCs with a hard disk, the usual way of ensuring that COMMAND.COM is reloaded (in its correct version) is to use the DOS PATH command to create a DOS path to COM-MAND.COM on the local hard disk. But use of NetWare search drives can confound the workings of the DOS PATH command. Moreover, you may not have a hard disk at your local workstation. If not, and if you are pointing to a floppy disk in a local drive that does not have COMMAND.COM, your DOS workstation will hang up when you exit an application. (Your workstation may also hang up or malfunction if the floppy disk contains an incorrect version of COMMAND.COM for that workstation's hardware.)

Place DOS on your server (or a version of DOS appropriate for each type of hardware platform on you network) and you can ensure that a correct version of COMMAND.COM is reloaded to a workstation, and at the same time make the external DOS commands (those not available when you first boot your workstation with DOS) available to your users.

Two NetWare login script tools are available to help you manage DOS on the server. The first is a series of NetWare identifier variables (%MACHINE, %OS, and %OS_VERSION), which automatically map a user to the correct version of DOS at the server for the workstation on which the user logs in. You will normally use these identifier variables within a NetWare search drive MAP definition. The second tool is the COMSPEC command, which tells your workstation where to look for COMMAND.COM. Both of these tools are discussed in a later chapter under the topic of NetWare login scripts.

You are not required to have your workstation use DOS from the server. But it is a definite convenience.

The APPS and DATA Directories

Why should you create separate APPS and DATA directories? For three reasons:

- protection of program files (executable and command files) from accidental deletion or corruption

- convenience of file archiving (file backup)

- ease (elegance) of server directory security management

PROTECTION OF PROGRAM FILES   If you mix program (executable and command) files with data files, you run the risk of users deleting or otherwise destroying the program files, if they have either Delete or Write rights in the data directories where program files also reside. (And more often than not some users will need Write or Delete rights.) Since the rights required to load program executable and command files are only Search, Open, and Read, why would you (except for habits developed from the standalone PC world) place program files in a directory that includes Write, Delete, or even Modify effective rights?

EASE OF FILE ARCHIVING   A common standalone PC directory design is to place data files in a subdirectory below a program directory: word processing files in a subdirectory beneath a word processing program directory, spreadsheet files in a sub-directory beneath the spreadsheet program files, and so forth. This strategy could be used and program files protected from accidental deletion. But placing data files in subdirectories beneath application file directories unnecessarily complicates file archiving.

NetWare's LARCHIVE and NARCHIVE commands allow you to point to a single directory to initiate a file archiving session and to then archive all files in that directory and in all subdirectories beneath the directory at which archiving was initiated.

With data directories placed beneath program directories, you must do one of the following:

- Begin archiving at the SYS1 volume, and backup your program files along with your data files (a waste of time and storage media, since program files seldom change).

- Go through three archiving sessions: one for APPS/DATA-BASE/DATA, one for APPS/WP/DATA, and one for APPS/SS/DATA (an inconvenience at best).

Program files seldom have to be backed up: when a new application or an updated version of an application is installed is usually often enough. Data files need to be backed up daily, or more often. A separate DATA directory and subdirectory structure serves as a convenient place to begin a NetWare archiving session. You can point to DATA, initiate an archiving session, and know that all your data files (in subdirectories beneath DATA) will be backed up.

With program files in a separate subdirectory structure (beneath APPS) your archiving session is more efficient, saving time and storage media space in bypassing application program files. (You will, of course, back up any new application programs you install on your server, even if the installation falls before your normal scheduled date for archiving APPS directory structure files.)

EASE OF SECURITY MANAGEMENT   Security is also more easily managed with the arrangement shown in Figure 4-6. As few as three trustee assignments could establish the bulk of the security required for the APPS and DATA directories (although in Table 4-3, more are suggested).

The PUBLIC directory security arrangement is instructive on how to manage application program directory security. Following the PUBLIC example, you can make one trustee assignment for the group EVERYONE of Read, Open, and Search to the directory APPS, and in that one step create much of the required APPS directory security. Just such a trustee assignment is illustrated in column 2, row 3 of Table 4-3.

With each application directory mask containing all rights (row 1, columns 2 through 5 of Table 4-3), the trustee assignment to EVERYONE in APPS (row 3, column 2) falls through the directory structure and applies to all users of the server who are

Row	Column 1	Column 2	Column 3	Column 4	Column 5	Column 6	Column 7	Column 8
1	Directory Rights < >	<CDMOPRSW>	<CDMOPRSW>	<CDMOPRSW>	<CDMOPRSW>	<CDMOPRSW>	<CDMOPRSW>	<CDMOPRSW>
2	DIRECTORY\ SUBDIRECTORY	APPS/	APPS/ DATABASE	APPS/ WP	APPS/ SS			
	GROUPS and USERS Trustee Assignment ( )							
	Effective Rights [ ]							
3	G EVERYONE (TA)	(___O_RS_)	( )	( )	( )	( )	( )	( )
4	R [ER]	[___O_RS_]	[ ]	[ ]	[ ]	[ ]	[ ]	[ ]
5	O (TA)	( )	( )	( )	( )	( )	( )	( )
6	P [ER]	[ ]	[ ]	[ ]	[ ]	[ ]	[ ]	[ ]
7	S (TA)	( )	( )	( )	( )	( )	( )	( )
8	[ER]	[ ]	[ ]	[ ]	[ ]	[ ]	[ ]	[ ]
9	U GUEST (TA)	( )	( )	( )	( )	( )	( )	( )
10	E [ER]	[___O_RS_]	[___O_RS_]	[___O_RS_]	[___O_RS_]	[ ]	[ ]	[ ]
11	S VENESSA (TA)	( )	( )	( )	( )	( )	( )	( )
12	R [ER]	[___O_RS_]	[___O_RS_]	[___O_RS_]	[___O_RS_]	[ ]	[ ]	[ ]
13	S SAM (TA)	( )	( )	( )	( )	( )	( )	( )
14	[ER]	[___O_RS_]	[___O_RS_]	[___O_RS_]	[___O_RS_]	[ ]	[ ]	[ ]

TABLE 4-3.   Security Plan for the Suggested Directory Structure

Row	Column 1		Column 9	Column 10	Column 11	Column 12	Column 13	Column 14	Column 15
1	Directory Rights < >		<CDMOPRSW>	<CDMOPRSW>	<CDMOPRSW>	<CDMOPRSW>	<CDMOPRSW>	<CDMOPRSW>	<CDMOPRSW>
2	DIRECTORY\ SUBDIRECTORY		DATA/	DATA/ SHARED/	DATA/ SHARED/ READONLY	DATA/ SHARED/ READWRIT	DATA/ SHARED/ DATABASE		
	GROUPS and USERS Trustee Assignment ( ) Effective Rights [ ]								
3	EVERYONE	(TA)	( )	( )	(__O_RS_)	(CD_O_RSW)	( )	( )	( )
4		[ER]	[NONE]	[NONE]	[_O_RS_]	[CD_O_RSW]	[NONE]	[ ]	[ ]
5	DATABASE	(TA)	( )	( )	( )	( )	(CD_O_RSW)	( )	( )
6	USERS	[ER]	[ ]	[ ]	[ ]	[ ]	[CD_O_RSW]	[ ]	[ ]
7		(TA)	( )	( )	( )	( )	( )	( )	( )
8		[ER]	[ ]	[ ]	[ ]	[ ]	[ ]	[ ]	[ ]
9	GUEST	(TA)	( )	( )	(_O_RS_)	[CD_O_RSW]	[NONE]	( )	( )
10		[ER]	[NONE]	[NONE]	[_O_RS_]	[CD_O_RSW]	[NONE]	[ ]	[ ]
11	VENESSA *	(TA)	( )	( )	( )	( )	[CD_O_RSW]	( )	( )
12		[ER]	[NONE]	[NONE]	[_O_RS_]	[CD_O_RSW]	[CD_O_RSW]	[ ]	[ ]
13	SAM *	(TA)	( )	( )	( )	( )	[CD_O_RSW]	( )	( )
14		[ER]	[NONE]	[NONE]	[_O_RS_]	[CD_O_RSW]	[CD_O_RSW]	[ ]	[ ]

GROUPS and USERS rows labeled: G R O U P S (rows 3–6), U S E R S (rows 9–12)

* member of group DATABASE-USERS

TABLE 4-3.   Security Plan for the Suggested Directory Structure (*continued*)

	Column 1	Column 16	Column 17	Column 18	Column 19	Column 20	Column 21	Column 22
Row								
1	Directory Rights < >	<CDMOPRSW>	<CDMOPRSW>	<CDMOPRSW>	<CDMOPRSW>	<CDMOPRSW>	<CDMOPRSW>	<CDMOPRSW>
2	DIRECTORY\ SUBDIRECTORY	DATA/ USERS/	DATA/ USERS/ GUEST	DATA/ USERS/ VENESSA	DATA/ USERS/ SAM			
	GROUPS and USERS Trustee Assignment ( )							
	Effective Rights [ ]							

Row	GROUPS / USERS		Column 16	Column 17	Column 18	Column 19	Column 20	Column 21	Column 22
3	EVERYONE	(TA)	(>	(>	(>	(>	(>	(>	(>
4		[ER]	[ ]	[ ]	[ ]	[ ]	[ ]	[ ]	[ ]
5		(TA)	(>	(>	(>	(>	(>	(>	(>
6		[ER]	[ ]	[ ]	[ ]	[ ]	[ ]	[ ]	[ ]
7		(TA)	(>	(>	(>	(>	(>	(>	(>
8		[ER]	[ ]	[ ]	[ ]	[ ]	[ ]	[ ]	[ ]
9	GUEST	(TA)	(>	(CDMO_RSW]	(>	(>	(>	(>	(>
10		[ER]	[ ]	[CDMO_RSW]	[ ]	[ ]	[ ]	[ ]	[ ]
11	VENESSA	(TA)	(>	(>	(CDMO_RSW]	(>	(>	(>	(>
12		[ER]	[ ]	[ ]	[CDMO_RSW]	[ ]	[ ]	[ ]	[ ]
13	SAM	(TA)	(>	(>	(>	(CDMO_RSW)	(>	(>	(>
14		[ER]	[ ]	[ ]	[ ]	[CDMO_RSW]	[ ]	[ ]	[ ]

TABLE 4-3.   Security Plan for the Suggested Directory Structure *(continued)*

members of the group EVERYONE. Compare columns 2 through 5 of Table 4-3 to columns 4 through 8 of Table 4-2 to see just how similar is this approach to managing APPS directory structure security to management of PUBLIC directory structure security.

If you do not want a user using a particular application program, do not map him or her to the application program subdirectory in question. Effective rights are useless in the absence of supporting NetWare drive mappings.

A suggested security arrangement to go with the directory structure proposed in Figure 4-6 is summarized in Table 4-3 and will be implemented later in this chapter. But first, you need to create the directory structure.

USING FILER TO CREATE THE DIRECTORY STRUCTURE

In this section you will set up the APPS and DATA directories. If you are on a newly installed server, you may create DATA and APPS beneath the SYS root volume. On an established server, proceed with extreme caution. Do not attempt to change your server's existing security or directory structure until you thoroughly understand it.

If your server volume SYS already has an APPS or DATA directory, leave them in place, unaltered. Instead of altering them you can do one of the following:

- Read about, but do not actually do the activities suggested in the remainder of this chapter.

- Use other directory names in place of APPS and DATA (perhaps PROGRAMS and WORK).

- Place APPS and DATA in a volume other than SYS.

The latter is possible only if you are supporting multiple volumes on your server, and all the cautions about working in the SYS volume apply equally to other server volumes.

In an effort to assist as many readers as possible, the discussion that follows places APPS and DATA beneath a volume named SYS1. In other words, the examples assume multiple volumes are supported on your server (though the additional volume name may be different from SYS1). Again, the suggested structure to be set up is summarized in Figure 4-6.

Begin by logging into the server as the user SUPERVISOR (or as a supervisor-equivalent user). At the prompt, type **FILER** and press (ENTER). You will see the FILER Available Topics menu shown in Figure 4-7.

You are pointing in FILER at the same directory to which you were pointing when you typed the FILER command. You will be taken back to that same directory when you exit FILER.

While you are in FILER you can temporarily change to other directories. The directory to which you are pointing while working in FILER is always shown in the NetWare FILER menu header. On your screen, it may say something like this:

FS1/SYS:LOGIN.

The first thing to do is to point to the location under which you are going to create APPS and DATA.

Changing the Current Directory Path

Move the cursor to the **Select Current Directory** option and press (ENTER). You will see a Current Directory Path box with a current directory path corresponding to your current path (as shown in the FILER header).

```
╔══════════════════════════════════════════════╗
║          Available Topics                      ║
╠══════════════════════════════════════════════╣
║ ┌────────────────────────────────────────────┐║
║ │ Current Directory Information              │║
║ │ File Information                            │║
║ │ Select Current Directory                   │║
║ │ Set Filer Options                          │║
║ │ Subdirectory Information                    │║
║ │ Volume Information                          │║
║ └────────────────────────────────────────────┘║
╚══════════════════════════════════════════════╝
```

FIGURE 4-7.   FILER Available Topics menu

Delete the entire current path or mapping by backspacing over the existing path definition. You now want to place a new path in this field. You may do so through either

- A Typing method, which is the same as typing a path at the prompt.

- An Insert mode of NetWare, which allows you to "pick off" the path from lists of information.

The Insert method will be demonstrated later. For now, use the Typing method. In the space provided, type the file server and volume name on which you wish to install the APPS and DATA directories. Be sure to separate the file server and volume names with a slash, and follow the volume name with a colon. Your entry should look something like Figure 4-8. On a new server you may be pointing to (servername)/SYS:, instead of SYS1:.

```
┌──────────────────────────────────────────────────────────────────┐
│                        Current Directory Path                      │
├──────────────────────────────────────────────────────────────────┤
│FS1/SYS1:                                                           │
└──────────────────────────────────────────────────────────────────┘
```

FIGURE 4-8.   Current directory path pointing to volume SYS1:

Press (ENTER), and you are now pointing to your server and a root volume location. Confirm this by checking the current directory as shown in the FILER menu header. If it is not correct, try changing your directory again.

Creating the Directories
APPS and DATA

You are ready to create subdirectories. Move the cursor to the **Subdirectory Information** option and press (ENTER). You will see a Network Directories list. LOGIN, MAIL, PUBLIC, and SYS-TEM are already included in this submenu if you are pointing to a SYS: volume. (In the example in Figure 4-9, the SYS1: volume already contains Open Systems accounting subdirectories.)

Press (INSERT) and you are provided with a box in which to define the name of a new directory. Type **APPS** and press (ENTER). Press (INSERT) again, type **Data**, and press (ENTER). You have created the APPS and DATA directories.

CHANGING CURRENT DIRECTORY TO APPS   Net-W are mappings can be quite long, and syntax and spelling critical. Take this opportunity to practice using the Insert method of defining paths. Press (ESC) to get back to the FILER Available Topics menu. Highlight **Select Current Directory** and press

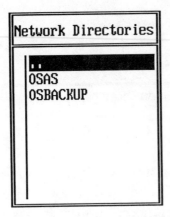

FIGURE 4-9.   FILER Network Directories menu prior to creation of the APPS and DATA directories

(ENTER). Now press (INSERT) to bring up the Current Directory Path box. You should see a screen like that shown in Figure 4-8.

Highlight the directory **DATA** and press (ENTER). DATA is added to the path name in the path box. Of course, it is not DATA but APPS that you want to make the current directory.

At this point you still are in Insert mode. Press (ENTER) again. DATA is taken out of the path definition. This is NetWare's way of letting you quickly correct a mistake while you are in Insert mode.

It is APPS that you want in the path box. Highlight **APPS** and press (ENTER). You should see a screen like that shown in Figure 4-10. To make APPS stay in the path, you must escape out of Insert mode. Just press (ESC) once.

You now are out of Insert mode and back into the FILER Typing mode. The Network Directories submenu disappears, but the Current Directory Path box remains on screen. This tells you that you are in Typing mode. Press (ENTER) and the current directory path changes. Check the FILER menu header to confirm that the current directory is now (servername)/(volume):APPS.

```
┌──────────────────────────────────────────────────────────┐
│                    Current Directory Path                  │
├──────────────────────────────────────────────────────────┤
│FS1/SYS1:APPS                                               │
└──────────────────────────────────────────────────────────┘
```

FIGURE 4-10.   The current directory path pointing to APPS

CREATING READONLY, READWRIT, AND DATABASE SUBDIRECTORIES   Move the cursor down to Subdirectory Information, and use the Insert function to create the READONLY, READWRIT, and DATABASE subdirectories beneath APPS. When you have completed this step, escape back to the FILER Available Topics menu. Highlight Select Current Directory and, using either the Insert or Typing mode, make APPS your current directory.

Current Directory Information

Take a look at the APPS directory configuration. Begin at the FILER Available Topics menu. Highlight **Current Directory Information** and press (ENTER). You will see the menu shown in Figure 4-11.

With **Creation Date** highlighted, press (ENTER) to see the date on which you created the APPS directory (today's date if the server's date is correctly set). Highlight **Current Effective Rights** and press (ENTER). The on-screen information indicates that you have all rights in this directory.

The reason you have all rights is because you are logged in as SUPERVISOR. Users will have no rights (because no trustee assignment has yet been made to APPS or to a directory higher up the APPS directory tree branch).

Since effective rights are a combination of directory mask rights and trustee assignment rights, take a moment to see what the APPS

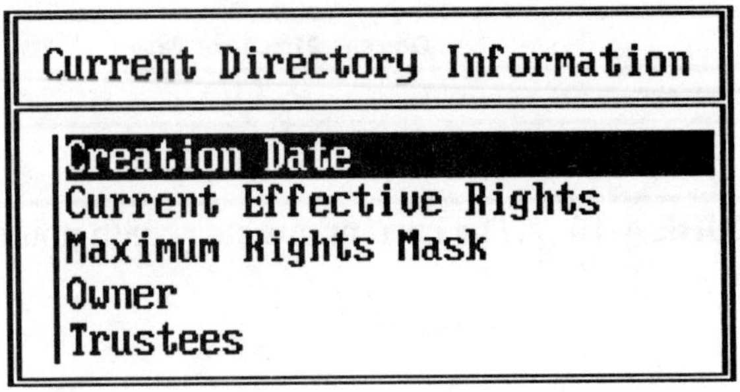

```
┌─────────────────────────────────────────┐
│  Current Directory Information           │
├─────────────────────────────────────────┤
│ ▐Creation Date▌                          │
│ Current Effective Rights                 │
│ Maximum Rights Mask                      │
│ Owner                                    │
│ Trustees                                 │
└─────────────────────────────────────────┘
```

FIGURE 4-11.   The FILER Current Directory Information menu

directory mask looks like. Highlight **Maximum Rights Mask** and press (ENTER). You will see the screen shown in Figure 4-12.

Maximum Rights are those rights contained in the directory rights mask. These are the maximum rights you could have as a user, if appropriate trustee assignments were made. While your Maximum Rights list includes all rights, your effective user rights are still none. Maximum rights are directory mask rights, not effective rights.

Before creating a trustee assignment, take a look at the Owner option within Current Directory Information. Highlight **Owner** and press (ENTER). Assuming you were logged in as SUPERVISOR when you created the directory APPS, SUPERVISOR should be the listed owner.

Making an SOR Trustee Assignment In APPS to EVERYONE

As suggested previously and illustrated in Table 4-3, one trustee assignment of Search, Open, and Read to the directory APPS for the group EVERYONE establishes much of your required APPS directory structure security.

```
┌─────────────────────────────────┐
│        Maximum Rights           │
├─────────────────────────────────┤
│ Create New Files                │
│ Delete Files                    │
│ Modify File Names/Flags         │
│ Open Existing Files             │
│ Parental Rights                 │
│ Read From Files                 │
│ Search For Files                │
│ Write To Files                  │
└─────────────────────────────────┘
```

FIGURE 4-12.   A directory maximum rights mask accessed through FILER

To create an effective right, a trustee assignment must be made. To do this within FILER, highlight **Trustees** and press (ENTER). A blank Trustee Name-Trustee Type-Rights box appears. It is in this box that you will create the list of trustees (users or groups) who will have rights to the APPS directory.

Press (INSERT) to call up the Others submenu (see Figure 4-13). Highlight the group **EVERYONE** and press (ENTER). The group EVERYONE has been added as a trustee to the directory APPS, with the trustee assignment of all rights.

You want EVERYONE to have only Search, Open, and Read rights. With the highlight bar over **EVERYONE** within the Trustee Name-Trustee Type-Rights box, press (ENTER). The Trustee Rights submenu shown in Figure 4-14 appears on the screen.

From this submenu you want to revoke the rights that EVERY-ONE is not to have. Keep the highlight bar over Create New Files and press the (DELETE) key. Confirm that you do, **Yes**, want to **Revoke All Marked Rights** and press (ENTER). The Create right is removed from the Trustee Rights list.

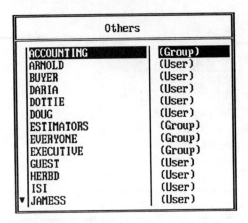

FIGURE 4-13. The Others menu selected for creating trustees

Use the (F5) (Mark) key to mark all other rights you wish to revoke and press (DELETE). Confirm that the marked rights are to be revoked (select **Yes**) and press (ENTER). You should now see

FIGURE 4-14. Trustee rights as initially created in FILER

```
┌─────────────────────────────────┐
│      Trustee Rights             │
├─────────────────────────────────┤
│Open Existing Files              │
│Read From Files                  │
│▐Search For Files               ▌│
│                                 │
│                                 │
│                                 │
│                                 │
└─────────────────────────────────┘
```

FIGURE 4-15.   Trustee rights after revocation (for APPS)

only the Open, Read, and Search rights on the Trustee Rights submenu (see Figure 4-15).

Escape back to the FILER Available Topics menu and press (ESC) or (ALT-F10) to exit the FILER submenu. Leave FILER. In the next section you will use SYSCON to create trustee assignments and a user subdirectory.

MANAGING SECURITY WITHIN THE DATA DIRECTORY STRUCTURE

You have a number of choices about how to manage directory security within the DATA directory and subdirectory structure. For instance, you could make a trustee assignment at the level of the DATA directory to the group EVERYONE and thus create an ability for all users to perform some file-management activities within all of the subdirectories beneath DATA. This is probably not advisable, for reasons to be discussed. But take a moment to consider what such a trustee assignment might look like.

Making an SCW Trustee Assignment
In DATA to EVERYONE

Because trustee rights flow down through a directory structure, a trustee assignment of Search, Create, and Write to the directory DATA would allow users to copy files to any directory under DATA. The name used to identify the file in the directory to which it was copied would have to be a filename not already in use in that directory. This arrangement is analogous to the mail directory security established by NetWare and prevents files from being accidentally overwritten.

The Search right allows users to see what filenames are in use in a subdirectory (and to use the NDIR command with a Sub flag to locate the same filename—which may or may not be the same file—in all lower subdirectories beneath data). See Chapter 8 for instruction on using the NDIR command.

You are not required to make trustee assignments at the DATA level of the directory tree. (And if you do, you will probably decide to add rights back into the subdirectories beneath SHARED and USERS.) The weakness of giving rights at the DATA directory level is that users may mistakenly place files in the SHARED and USERS directories, when they really mean for those files to be in a subdirectory beneath SHARED or USERS.

There are two solutions to this annoying problem:

- Change the SHARED and USERS directory masks to blank, that is, to no rights. No matter what trustee assignments are made to, or fall through to, the SHARED and USERS directories, users will have no effective rights in SHARED or USERS.

- Make no trustee assignments at the DATA, SHARED, or USERS directory levels. Make all your DATA trustee assignments at the lowest level of that portion of the directory tree structure.

The latter approach is used in the trustee assignment examples in the remainder of this chapter, and is illustrated in Table 4-3.

Trustee Assignments
In the SHARED Subdirectories

In the SHARED subdirectories, rights can be varied. In the READONLY subdirectory for the group EVERYONE, rights are set at Search, Open, and Read. Master spreadsheet templates, and master form letters or other word processing documents can be placed in this directory and made available to users without risk of the original file being changed. If a Write and Create trustee assignment is not made at DATA or SHARED to the group EVERYONE, SUPERVISOR or a supervisor-equivalent user will have to place templates, or master form or document files, in the READONLY directory. Alternatively, a specific user or user group can be made responsible for the READONLY directory, and given the additional trustee assignment necessary to manage the directory: Create, Write, and possibly Delete and Modify rights.

To allow users to both read from and write to the READWRIT directory, you can make a Search, Open, Read, and Write trustee assignment to the group EVERYONE (or to another, less inclusive group). You can then assign Modify and Delete rights to a user designated as responsible for monitoring and controlling the contents of READWRIT. As an example, VENESSA will, momentarily, be given these additional rights and responsibilities.

Assumed here is that various types of files may all go into the same directory—Lotus 1-2-3 .WK1 files, word processing files, graphics files, and so forth.

If too many files are stored in a single directory, consider creating subdirectories under one or both of the READONLY and READWRIT directories. In a small organization, READONLY and READWRIT need not become too full of files if

- Users use their home directory, or some other set of work directories, as the place for working copies of files.

- Someone performs routine housekeeping on the READONLY and READWRIT directory files.

Table 4-3 summarizes the trustee assignments you will make to the subdirectories beneath DATA. The next section provides instructions for using SYSCON to create this directory and security arrangement.

CREATING TRUSTEE ASSIGNMENTS AND DIRECTORIES THROUGH SYSCON

Trustee assignments and directories can be created through FILER by any user having Parental (and with that Modify and Create) rights in an appropriate directory. SYSCON can also be used to create trustee assignments and directories, but only by the user SUPERVISOR or a supervisor-equivalent.

Creating Trustee Assignments

As necessary, log in as SUPERVISOR. The following instructions make a trustee assignment to the directory READWRIT.

CREATING A ROSWC TRUSTEE ASSIGNMENT IN READWRIT THROUGH SYSCON   To create a Read, Open, Search, Write, and Create trustee in READWRIT for the group EVERYONE:

1. At the prompt, type **SYSCON** and press (ENTER).

2. At the SYSCON Available Topics menu, select **Group Information** and press (ENTER).

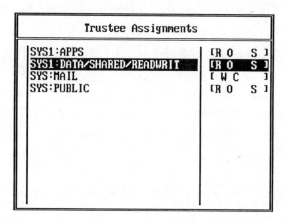

```
┌─────────────────────────────────────────────┐
│            Trustee Assignments                │
│ ┌───────────────────────────────────────────┐ │
│ │SYS1:APPS                    [R O    S ]   │ │
│ │SYS1:DATA/SHARED/READWRIT    [R O    S ]   │ │
│ │SYS:MAIL                     [ W C     ]   │ │
│ │SYS:PUBLIC                   [R O    S ]   │ │
│ │                                           │ │
│ │                                           │ │
│ │                                           │ │
│ │                                           │ │
│ │                                           │ │
│ └───────────────────────────────────────────┘ │
└─────────────────────────────────────────────┘
```

FIGURE 4-16.   Trustee rights as initially created in SYSCON to EVERYONE for the directory Readwrit

3. From the Group Names submenu, highlight **EVERYONE** and press (ENTER).

4. From the Group Information submenu, highlight **Trustee Assignments** and press (ENTER).

5. To create a new trustee assignment to READWRIT, press (INSERT). You will see a current path displayed. Alter that path (using the Typing or the Insert mode) so that it points to (server)/(volume):APPS/READWRIT. Press (ENTER).

You should now see a screen like that shown in Figure 4-16. To add rights to this trustee assignment follow these steps:

1. Highlight the READWRIT trustee assignment and press (ENTER).

2. Press (INSERT).

3. Mark (with (F5)) the rights to be added to READWRIT and press (ENTER).

4. Press (ESC) once and the trustee assignment is complete.

MAKING VENESSA RESPONSIBLE FOR MANAGING READWRIT To periodically clean up the READWRIT subdirectory, a user needs Delete rights. To round out plans for managing this directory, provide the user VENESSA Search, Open, Read, Write, Create, and Delete trustee assignment in READWRIT.

1. From the SYSCON Available Topics menu, select **User Information**.

2. Highlight **Venessa** and press (ENTER) to call up the User Information screen.

3. Select **Trustee Assignments** and press (ENTER) to view the Directory in Which Trustee Should Be Added box.

4. Press (INSERT) to define the path to which the trustee assignment is to flow: (server)/(volume):APPS/READWRIT. Be sure to press (ESC) to go from Insert back to Typing mode before pressing (ENTER).

5. To alter VENESSA's trustee rights in READWRIT, highlight the current trustee assignment and press (ENTER). This displays the Trustee Rights Granted screen. Press (INSERT) to call up and add in the additional rights to be granted. (Use (DELETE) to remove any rights not desired.)

When you are finished you should see a list like that shown in Figure 4-17.

TRUSTEE ASSIGNMENTS IN USER HOME SUBDIRECTORIES Following the principle of making trustee assignments under DATA at the lowest levels of the directory structure, you will give each user a trustee assignment to only his

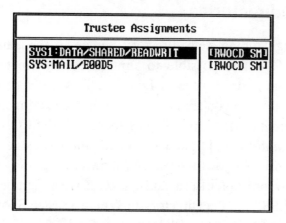

```
                    Trustee Assignments

 SYS1:DATA/SHARED/READWRIT         [RWOCD SM]
 SYS:MAIL/E00D5                    [RWOCD SM]
```

FIGURE 4-17.   Trustee assignment to VENESSA in Readwrit

or her own user subdirectory. These individual user trustee assignments can be for all rights, or for all rights except Parental. In either case, each user has access to his or her home directory, but no one else has any access (unless they log in as SUPERVISOR or as a supervisor-equivalent user).

The Parental right allows both for creation of subdirectories and for a user making trustee assignments, from that point in the directory structure downward. Some LAN managers choose to give a user all rights except Parental in the home directory. But heavy users of home directories may find a need for subdirectories. The Parental right allows a user to determine which other users or groups may have access to his or her user directory or subdirectories (on a basis the user controls).

One other note about user subdirectories: Always name the user's subdirectory with the user's login name. This allows use of a %LOGIN_NAME parameter in a directory mapping in the system login script (see Chapter 7 for details).

User Home Subdirectories

Through typing new directory names in the path box within SYSCON it is possible to simultaneously create both a new directory and a trustee assignment. This is a particularly useful shortcut when you are creating user home subdirectories.

From the Available Topics menu of SYSCON, select **User Information**, highlight **Venessa** and then **Trustee Assignments**. This will take you to the screen shown in Figure 4-17.

Now, press (INSERT) to add a new trustee assignment for the user VENESSA. In the Directory in Which Trustee Should Be Added box, type or insert a path leading to DATA/USERS. For instance

FS1/SYS:DATA/USERS

Be sure you are in Typing mode, and then complete the path with addition of a VENESSA subdirectory: /VENESSA. Press (ENTER) and select **Yes** in the Verify Creation of New Directory submenu. Press (ENTER) to complete the creation of the trustee assignment.

As shown in Figure 4-18, you have three trustee assignments made directly to VENESSA. In all probability, the trustee assignment to VENESSA in her VENESSA home directory is only for Search, Open, and Read rights. Highlight the trustee assignment, press (ENTER) and then (INSERT), and from the Rights Not Granted menu select those additional rights to grant. In this case, add all rights except Parental. (Using the (F5) Mark key to select these additional rights for the trustee assignment is the quick approach.) The final result is shown in Figure 4-19. Press (ESC) once to complete the trustee assignment modification.

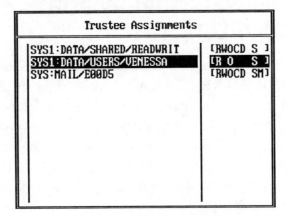

```
            Trustee Assignments
|SYS1:DATA/SHARED/READWRIT    [RWOCD S ]
|SYS1:DATA/USERS/VENESSA      [R O   S ]
|SYS:MAIL/E00D5               [RWOCD SM]
```

FIGURE 4-18.   Read, Open, and Search rights in
Data/Users/Venessa

```
            Trustee Assignments
|SYS1:DATA/SHARED/READWRIT    [RWOCD S ]
|SYS1:DATA/USERS/VENESSA      [RWOCD SM]
|SYS:MAIL/E00D5               [RWOCD SM]
```

FIGURE 4-19.   Amended Data/Users/Venessa trustee
assignment for the user VENESSA

DELETING VENESSA'S SUPERVISOR SECURITY EQUIVALENCY

In Chapter 3 you made VENESSA a supervisor-equivalent user. This means that VENESSA will have all rights in all directories, regardless of how limited her actual trustee assignments happen to be. For exercises you complete in later chapters you may log in as VENESSA, and you will want to be working with restricted effective rights. Therefore, take a moment at this point to delete VENESSA's supervisor equivalency. You must do this while logged in as SUPERVISOR.

From the SYSCON Available Topics menu select **User Information** and press (ENTER). Move the cursor to Venessa and press (ENTER). Select **Security Equivalencies** and press (ENTER). Highlight the SUPERVISOR security equivalency and press (DEL). Confirm that, **Yes**, you wish to delete the SUPERVISOR security equivalency, and press (ENTER). VENESSA should now no longer be equivalent to the user SUPERVISOR.

FILE FLAGS

Thus far, discussion has focused on NetWare security at the directory or subdirectory level. The security arrangements summarized in Tables 4-2 and 4-3 apply equally to all files in a particular directory. In some instances, you may wish to place a file in a directory in which all security rights are effective, but *flag* the file for special use.

The file flags available in NetWare are

- Normal

- Shareable or Non-shareable

- Read-Write or ReadOnly

- TTS

- Hidden

Flags are not mutually exclusive: a file can be flagged Shareable/ReadOnly or Non-shareable/ReadOnly. The Normal flag configuration, which is the default for newly created files, is Non-shareable/Read-Write. Non-shareable/Read-Write files can be opened for use by only one user at a time and can be overwritten.

Flagging Files ReadOnly

If you place a file in a directory where users have all rights, but you want to ensure that users do not inadvertently delete that particular file, flag the file as ReadOnly, either Shareable or Non-shareable.

Flagging SYSTEM directory files ReadOnly can prevent their being overwritten, and helps avoid (but does not prevent) their deletion by SUPERVISOR or a supervisor-equivalent. If you upgrade to a higher version of NetWare (from 2.12 to 2.15, for instance) you will need to change ReadOnly file flags back to Read-Write before copying the updated NetWare System files to the server. And some SYSTEM files must be written back by NetWare. Thus, you should change flags with caution.

Flagging Files Shareable

A file is normally flagged as Shareable only if the application package in which the file is used has the ability to keep track of multiple, simultaneous use. In those instances, reflagging the file may not be necessary. Application programs written to run on a NetWare server seem to have the ability to handle this transparently, in the background. But on occasion, application software documentation will ask you to flag certain files as Shareable or Shareable/ReadOnly at the time of installation.

Hidden Files

A file flagged Hidden does not appear in directory listings of users, even though the file is located on the server hard disk. This is another way to keep users from inadvertently deleting a file. On the other hand, if they try to save a file in a directory using a name already in use by a hidden file, they may not understand why NetWare disallows their use of that filename.

Transaction Tracking Services (TTS)

The TTS flag is a database system fault tolerance feature. You must be running SFT NetWare 286 and have TTS installed to use this flag. A database file flagged TTS has NetWare's transaction tracking database integrity checks applied to it.

Summary

From this chapter you have gained an understanding of how directory mask rights combine with group and individual trustee rights to yield effective rights in NetWare server directories and subdirectories. Directory mask rights apply to all users and are specific to a directory or subdirectory. Trustee assignments made to a user or to a group (and its members) fall downward through the directory structure.

While this may seem a complex security mechanism, careful planning and use of groups as the object to which many trustee assignments are made make NetWare directory security an elegant mechanism for establishing directory security arrangements.

- One trustee assignment is made in the directory PUBLIC to the group EVERYONE: Search, Open, and Read.

- One trustee assignment is made in MAIL to the group EVERYONE: Create and Write.

- One trustee assignment is made for each user in his or her own home subdirectory under MAIL: all rights except Parental.

In Chapter 6 you are challenged to design an equally elegant security arrangement for your planned directory structure.

You also learned that through use of file flags, directory security can be supplemented with file level security.

Finally, you were provided with an opportunity to use both FILER and SYSCON to create both directories and trustee assignments.

chapter **5**

RUNNING APPLICATIONS ON A LAN

Application software is the life blood of PCs. Spreadsheet, word processing, database, and other applications make the PC a useful tool. In giving up PC independence for life on a LAN, you naturally expect application packages in the LAN environment to provide bigger and better rewards than obtained in your standalone PC environment.

In that expectation you may be rewarded, or greatly disappointed. The difference in experience has a lot to do with how well you know an application. It also depends on how well and how creatively the application is installed on the server.

This chapter introduces you to what you can expect from application packages on a LAN and of questions to ask when you are selecting application software. Attention is directed to these important issues:

• multiuser characteristics of application packages

• whether these packages may be used in a multioperating environment

• whether these packages take advantage of distributed processing

To benefit from the discussion contained in this and the next chapter you do not need to be using on your LAN the application software packages discussed here. But learning how these application packages are installed on and perform on a NetWare server is most instructive, and well worth reading about.

Special attention is given to Lotus 1-2-3 Release 2.01, WordPerfect version 5.0, and Paradox Release 3.0. While these packages are selected for convenience—the author's familiarity with them—they illustrate quite well the questions and situations you will encounter in installing applications on a LAN. Take time to read this chapter, even if you do not currently support or plan to use these particular application packages on your LAN.

The following discussion is intended neither to promote, nor detract from, these or other application packages. It is intended to help you make informed software purchase, installation, and usage decisions. LAN applications are fundamentally different from standalone PC applications, so you should take the time to read this chapter thoroughly.

SINGLE-USER APPLICATIONS ON THE LAN: LOTUS 1-2-3 RELEASE 2.01

Is it possible to install a single-user standalone version of an application package on a file server? Will you be disappointed in how the application package performs? With investments already made in single-user, standalone software applications, these are important questions.

Unfortunately, using single-user software in an environment where several users are simultaneously trying to access the application can yield unexpected or erratic events. The best way to avoid disappointment is to purchase, install, and learn to use application packages that are LAN-ready (and Novell NetWare-ready) packages. (And before investing money in a package, check with other users, preferably people using the application on a NetWare server.)

Lotus Development Corporation now offers a LAN pack version of 1-2-3 that allows for simultaneous use by several users, at a lower overall purchase cost than if the same number of standalone copies of 1-2-3 had been purchased. However, the 1-2-3 discussion in this chapter is intended to illustrate how a standalone application package may perform in a LAN environment. Thus, all references to Lotus 1-2-3 assume you are using one or another of Lotus Development Corporation's non-LAN versions of Lotus 1-2-3, for example, Release 2.01.

That said, the question remains: Can you install single-user application software on a server and have it ever perform reliably? In fact, the answer is yes. But *reliably* does not mean 1-2-3 will behave exactly as you are used to seeing the package perform on a standalone machine.

How NetWare Handles Lotus 1-2-3 Release 2.01

You can copy Lotus 1-2-3 Release 2.01 to the server and allow several users to access one copy of the package from the server. This works because of how the 1-2-3 program files are handled at the server.

When copied to the server, the program files are flagged as Normal: as Non-shareable, Read-Write files. When at a prompt you type **123** and press (ENTER), NetWare does as follows:

1. goes to the server hard disk for a copy of the required 123 executable and command files

2. copies the files into the RAM of the server (at which point the hard disk files are closed)

3. transmits the files across the LAN to the workstation from which the request originated

4. closes the 123 files in the server RAM

Since the files are closed, they can be opened by any other user on the network who has Search, Open, and Read rights in the directory in which the 1-2-3 program files are located.

If VENESSA now types **123** and presses (ENTER), the same steps occur as just described, except that the files are forwarded to the requesting workstation directly from the RAM of the server, if they are still in the server's RAM cache.

In essence, each workstation receives and runs 1-2-3 as a single-user, standalone application. It just happens to be the same copy of the program files (a violation of licensing agreements). NetWare handles the opening and closing of files reliably. At worst, you experience a slight delay in accessing 1-2-3. You and VENESSA are happy campers, for the moment. However, disappointment lurks close by.

Lotus 1-2-3 Release 2.01 Is Not Multiuser

One great disappointment comes when you and VENESSA simultaneously use the same Lotus spreadsheet file from the same directory. You make changes and save the spreadsheet back to the same directory under the same filename. VENESSA now saves her changes to the same directory, using the same filename. When you next access the file, only the changes made by VENESSA are present. If there exists a happy camper, it is VENESSA, not you.

In the standalone PC world, VENESSA could not change the file while you are using it. Only one of you can work on the PC at a time. But the LAN world is a multiuser, simultaneous-use world. Beginning with Release 2.2 of 1-2-3, a *file reservation* system is implemented that prevents users from inadvertently overwriting each other's changes to a spreadsheet. Unfortunately, earlier standard editions of Lotus 1-2-3 are not multiuser application packages.

Lotus 1-2-3 Release 2.01 is not aware of users simultaneously using a 1-2-3 file. No one is keeping track of this fact, and there lies the problem. While the 1-2-3 program and spreadsheet files are flagged in NetWare as Non-shareable, this means only that the file may not be held open for multiple access. Multiple copies can be made available one at a time.

Applications adapted to a LAN environment use techniques to avoid users writing over each others file changes. Lotus 1-2-3 Release 2.01 is a single-user application running in a multiuser work environment.

What Are the Defaults?

A second complication is how a single-user application handles default settings, and who is allowed to change those settings.

THE DEFAULT DRIVE POINTER   Lotus 1-2-3 can be configured with a default drive to which it points when loaded at your workstation. If you have a hard drive on your workstation, you may choose to have Lotus 1-2-3 point to drive C:\ when it is loaded. However, the default of C:\ in 1-2-3 means that the application locks up when requested from a workstation with only two floppy drives. Making the default A:\ does not help at all if you have diskless workstations.

As it happens, this particular problem can be avoided. The trick is to set the default drive for 1-2-3 to a blank drive. Go to the 1-2-3 default menu, select default drive, backspace over the existing default until the default field is blank, and then immediately save the defaults back to the Lotus 1-2-3 program directory.

With the default drive blank, 1-2-3 adopts whatever drive a user is pointing to at the time 1-2-3 is requested. This is a nifty feature. It means that if you point to the directory in which you wish to work before entering 1-2-3, 1-2-3 will always point to your working directory. (You must, however, have the 1-2-3 program directory defined as a NetWare search drive.)

This particular way around the default drive setting is not mentioned to encourage you to use 1-2-3 from the server. Rather, it is to illustrate a technique that works with some other LAN multiuser packages (including Paradox) and with some single-user packages.

The current drive becoming the default drive if the default is left blank does not work with all applications, in single-user or LAN version. For instance, WordPerfect 5.0 requires that certain drive pointers and paths be explicitly defined in its setup procedures.

THE DEFAULT PRINTER   What about printer defaults or other default files? Fortunately, Lotus 1-2-3 can be set up to remember and have available more than a single print driver default. With two print drivers installed as defaults in 1-2-3, you pick which to use at the time of printing. But who gets to change the defaults?

When you go to print a 1-2-3 spreadsheet to your printer tomorrow, you will want the 1-2-3 defaults set the same as today. This may not happen if just anyone can change the 1-2-3 system defaults.

The file in which 1-2-3 default settings are stored is copied to the server hard disk as a Non-shareable, Read-Write file. In theory, any user can change the 1-2-3 system defaults at any time. In practice, you may (as recommended in Chapter 4) place the Lotus program files (including the system defaults file) in a directory that has only Search, Open, and Read rights. Now a user can access 1-2-3 with whatever defaults have been set (including a blank default directory), but will be unsuccessful in writing changes to the defaults back to the server. The trade off is that no one else can change the defaults (unless they are a user given Lotus 1-2-3 LAN management responsibilities, or they are the user SUPERVISOR or a supervisor-equivalent).

Even with multiuser LAN applications, it is beneficial to place system default files in a directory restricted to Search, Open, and Read rights. If these defaults require permanent individual customizing, the application package must make allowance for this. 1-2-3 does not, in part because it cannot use multiple drive pointers to point to multiple directories. (An example of how this does occur within WordPerfect is discussed later in this chapter.)

To return to the original question: Can you support Lotus 1-2-3 on the server? Yes. Should you support Lotus 1-2-3 from the server? You had better not.

The Problem of License Agreements

Most application packages developed for standalone PCs expressly allow use of the package on only one personal computer. Using Lotus 1-2-3 at the workstation, while it resides at the server, may in itself constitute a violation of the license agreement, even if only one person at a time uses the package at a workstation. If several users simultaneously use the one licensed copy of the application, this is a clear violation of the license agreement.

 Lotus Development Corporation could take your business away from you for this violation of their license agreement.

What If You Have Multiple Standalone Licenses Now?

To be legal, many companies purchased multiple copies of standalone application packages, such as Lotus 1-2-3. Do they now have to purchase LAN packs of these applications to be legal?

Software exists that can be installed on the server to track how many users are simultaneously using a particular (standalone) application package. If you have ten licenses for Lotus 1-2-3, you can

- place Lotus 1-2-3 on the server

- install a separate software package to keep track of how many copies of Lotus 1-2-3 are running simultaneously

- have the specialized tracking software automatically lock the Lotus 1-2-3 files from further access when the simultaneous user count reaches ten

You are now living within the spirit of the original license agreements. But are you violating the letter of the license agreement? The answer depends on the company that developed and licensed the application. The real issue is: would Lotus Development Corporation be sympathetic to the approach just outlined. You will have to call Lotus to find out.

MULTIUSER APPLICATIONS IN A SINGLE OPERATING ENVIRONMENT: WORDPERFECT 5.0 LAN VERSION

WordPerfect 5.0 can be purchased in a LAN-ready version, supporting multiple users, and it is this version to which reference is made in this book.

In both its LAN and standard versions, WordPerfect 5.0 expands the world of word processing in several important respects. For instance, it incorporates graphics features formerly found only in desktop publishing packages. However, the package is discussed here for its LAN features. These include the following:

- A system for file locking to ensure that network users do not overwrite each other's work.

- A system for managing temporary, user-specific files.

- Allowance for user-specific default printer configurations, stored in a directory location that WordPerfect remembers.

- Ability to reference server-installed printers from within WordPerfect.

- Allowance for user-specific dictionaries, also stored in a directory separate from other files, a directory with its own NetWare effective rights.

The strengths and limitations of these multiuser features are briefly reviewed here.

File Locks

WordPerfect's file-locking scheme is well thought out and reliable. It applies when you and another user simultaneously use the same named file from within the same directory. (Files with the same name but in different directories are treated by WordPerfect as different files.)

When you first access a file, WordPerfect checks to see if another user is already using that same file (meaning that a user has accessed the file). WordPerfect does not know whether that first user is merely viewing the file or is changing the file.

If the file is in use, a copy is made available to you. However, you are not allowed to save the file back to the server, in the same directory, using the same filename. You are *not* prohibited from editing the file at your workstation nor are you prevented from saving the file under another name to the same or a different directory, within the limits set by NetWare directory security rights. (You need Create and Write rights in a directory to save a new file to that directory.)

Essentially, you and the other users are working on a copy of the same file, each independently at your own workstations. Because the other user was first to access the file, you *must* save your copy of the file under a new name, if you save it to the directory from which it originated. This is true even if the other user is no longer using the document and has, perhaps, even logged out of the server. If you try to save a file in use when you requested the file, you will receive an "error: File Locked" message.

The system for locking a file is not sophisticated, but it certainly goes a long way toward ensuring that users do not walk over each other in the process of doing their own work. Two limitations are

- a user is not really informed that the file is in use when he or she calls it up

- the "error: File Locked" message is cryptic at best

Network users must be educated on how WordPerfect works in a network environment and why they receive the error messages they do.

WordPerfect's file locking does not allow users to interactively work on the same document at the same time: VENESSA cannot edit Section I of a report while you edit Section II, for instance. But this may be too much to expect, not just from WordPerfect (which is rich in features), but from users who are used to working independently, unencumbered by the constraint of what other users are doing.

Temporary Files

Like many LAN packages, WordPerfect creates a number of temporary files to manage the multiuser word processing environment. WordPerfect's approach allows multiple users to work freely within the same directory, within the limits of file saving just mentioned.

When you enter the WordPerfect application, you are asked to provide a user identification of up to three characters in length. For instance, the user VENESSA might enter the user ID **VEN**. The three letters provided are embedded in the names of a number of permanent and temporary files that WordPerfect creates. If VENESSA exited to the DOS shell while in WordPerfect and listed the directory she was in when entering WordPerfect, she might find that these files had been created:

```
WPVEN{.CHK
WPVEN{.TV1
WPVEN{.BV1
WPVEN{.SPC
```

These temporary files are deleted when users exit WordPerfect. Automatic creation and deletion of temporary files by WordPerfect raises two important points in regard to design of NetWare directory security:

- If you are to use WordPerfect, you must enter WordPerfect while pointing to a directory in which you have effective NetWare Create and Write rights, those minimal rights necessary to create new files. If WordPerfect cannot create its required temporary files, it denies you access.

- If temporary files are to be automatically deleted by WordPerfect upon your leaving the application, you must have an effective NetWare Delete right within this directory.

Not being able to delete temporary files is more of a nuisance than a real problem. If you do not have delete rights, you will successfully exit WordPerfect, but the temporary files will remain, until and if another user (perhaps SUPERVISOR) comes along and deletes these files. You may not want to litter your server directories with permanent temporary files, but if space is not a consideration, no harm is done. You may, however, encounter one annoyance.

If you again enter WordPerfect in a directory with a user ID for which temporary files already exist, you are prompted to answer whether there are other users using WordPerfect on the network. While you can answer no and enter the package, this is at best counter-intuitive and confusing to the average user.

Thus, you generally will want to have Search, Create, Write, Read, and Delete effective rights in those directories in which you expect to enter and use WordPerfect. This does not mean that you have to have these rights in all directories containing files you want to use.

A Use for Your Home User Directory

If you enter and exit WordPerfect while pointing to your home user directory, in which you have all effective rights except Parental (see Chapter 4), you will enter and leave WordPerfect as designed, with temporary files automatically created and deleted. Once within WordPerfect, and while still having WordPerfect point to your home directory as the default directory, you can call up a file from any other directory simply by providing a path and filename. For instance, you could point to

FS1/SYS1:DATA/SHARED/READONLY/CONFIRM.LTR

and call the file CONFIRM.LTR into WordPerfect from a directory where you have only Read, Open, and Search rights. Similarly, you can write a file to a directory that is not your default directory. For instance:

FS1/SYS1:DATA/SHARED/READWRIT/CONF1028.PYA

Working in one directory while accessing other directories is a common practice on a LAN. Fortunately, the process is simplified ·
through use of the multiple drive pointers available through Net-

Ware. Also typical is automatic creation and deletion of files by the LAN application, the creation and deletion occurring in a directory separate from where the main application program files are located.

User-Specific Printer Defaults

As with nearly all PC applications, WordPerfect allows for permanent printer defaults and temporary printer defaults. Temporary defaults can be set at any time and are saved along with a word processed document when that document is saved to disk. Document-specific defaults are automatically, temporarily invoked when the document is later called to a workstation (if the default print driver can be located).

When you first enter WordPerfect, default settings are always made available: either a general set of print defaults can be defined, available to any or all users on the network, or user-specific default printer settings can be defined.

The term *user* has a somewhat different meaning in WordPerfect than it does in NetWare. WordPerfect does not associate user printer default settings with NetWare user names but uses the three-character user ID just mentioned. This ID is embedded in the filename that contains WordPerfect user-specific printer defaults.

If there are no user-specific default filenames that include (embedded at the appropriate spot in the filename) the three-letter code you used to identify yourself as a WordPerfect user, Word-Perfect loads at your workstation the main system printer defaults. You will also receive the system default if—because of the NetWare and/or WordPerfect installation—WordPerfect cannot find the directory in which user-specific printer defaults are located.

User-specific print defaults will be loaded under the following circumstances:

- the directory in which user printer default files are located has been made known to WordPerfect through installation

- a user printer default file with the given three-character user ID embedded exists

These user-specific printer files may be stored in a directory separate from the main system printer defaults. Again, this means you can limit effective rights to the system defaults to only Search, Open, and Read but choose to allow users Create and Write rights in the directory containing their user-specific printer settings. Any user can access a particular printer setup default file just by providing the appropriate WordPerfect three-letter code.

However, no two users can use the same three-character user ID while working in the same directory, because temporary file conflicts would occur. For instance, if NetWare user VENESSA routinely used a set of WordPerfect printer defaults known to WordPerfect through the ID VEN, you could enter WordPerfect with the VEN letters and receive those printer defaults for your work, as long as another user was not already in use in the same directory with the VEN user ID.

There lies the limitation on how WordPerfect handles user-specific printer defaults. The file is actually copied to the directory in which a user is working at the time they enter WordPerfect, and only one user at a time may work in that directory with the same user ID, though multiple users may work in the same directory under different WordPerfect user ID names.

A point about all of this: Always ask whether and how an application handles multiple default settings (including printer settings). This may not be the most important question to ask, but knowing about this may tell you a lot about how multiuser the application really is, and what limitations apply.

Transparent Access to Server Printers

WordPerfect, through its install routine, can be told of the existence of network printers (printers attached to a file server). Users can then access a network printer from within WordPerfect without having to worry about issuing an appropriate NetWare CAPTURE command. (See Chapter 9 for information on CAPTURE.) This, too, is a feature you would like to see in a truly multiuser operating environment.

 WordPerfect manages sending print jobs to a printer or to the server through its own internal print buffer. While there is usually no conflict between how WordPerfect handles print jobs and how NetWare at the server handles those jobs, some complications can arise, particularly if you are printing a long WordPerfect document from disk that contains complicated formatting or font changes. (See the discussion in Chapter 9 of the Timeout parameter used in conjunction with the NetWare CAPTURE command.)

User Dictionaries

WordPerfect allows for user-defined dictionaries in addition to the main dictionary used in spell checking. In this way, special or technical terms can be spell checked without those terms having to be made part of the main, general dictionary. For instance, you can place *Novell* in a supplemental user dictionary and spell check this page using that dictionary, along with the main dictionary. WordPerfect will know that *Novell* is an acceptably spelled word. Later, you can spell check a document using only the main dictionary, and WordPerfect will highlight *Novell* as a misspelled word, and offer *novel* as one alternative for a correct spelling.

Unlike printer default setting files, supplemental dictionaries can be named by the user rather than by WordPerfect. Supplemental dictionaries may be maintained in a separate directory from where you are doing your WordPerfect document development.

You need to decide in exactly which directory to place the supplemental files, and to determine what NetWare directory level effective rights are appropriate. In particular, do you want to include an effective Write right, thereby allowing any user to add words to the supplemental dictionary file? This is one example of the many options presented with LAN applications, options that required knowledgeable decisions by you.

In Chapter 6 an elaboration of the directory structure and security discussed in Chapter 4 is provided with specific reference to WordPerfect 5.0 considerations. For now, just note that Net-Ware directory security features are used to supplement WordPerfect's own application design. It is NetWare that allows the main dictionary to be protected from modification, not Word-Perfect. This creative merging of NetWare and application software features is an exciting, if sometimes demanding, aspect of using application software in a LAN environment.

The WordPerfect License Agreement

WordPerfect has a unique license agreement. When you purchase WordPerfect in its LAN version, you specify how many user modules you wish to purchase: four, six, eight, or any number. No matter how many user modules you purchase, you receive only one copy of the software. You do receive extra copies of the same documentation.

Once you install WordPerfect on the server, there is no apparent limit on the number of users who may simultaneously use it. If you purchased six user modules, for instance, seven, eight, or more users can simultaneously use WordPerfect.

What does this imply about the license agreement and your adherence to it? One interpretation is that WordPerfect Corporation is licensing your server. But the company expects you to purchase one user module up to the number of users you expect to simultaneously use WordPerfect. You may wish to contact Word-Perfect Corporation for clarification, or to ask for a discount rate for a large number of users.

One other feature of WordPerfect is also discussed in this book: user-defined macros. That topic is reserved for Chapter 7 and the discussion of NetWare search drives.

TOWARD DISTRIBUTED PROCESSING: PARADOX3

A rather spiffy multiuser package is Paradox Release 3.0. If you want to know what your LAN database application should do for you, take time to read the parts of this chapter (and Chapter 6) that discuss Paradox. Because of what it illustrates about truly multiuser application packages, Paradox is a particularly useful package to review and learn about, even if you do not plan to use this package on your LAN.

Paradox was one of the first well-behaved, well-designed LAN application packages. Release 2.0 of Paradox was multiuser and LAN-ready. Paradox Release 3.0 is also LAN-ready, regardless of whether it is purchased in its LAN pack (six-user) version or as a single-user package. The only difference between the single-user and LAN pack version is the number of serial numbers that come with the package (on which more is said later).

Most of the discussion that follows applies equally to Paradox Releases 2.0 and 3.0. The Paradox database development package, marketed by Borland International, is particularly interesting in these respects:

- It allows you to develop database applications that are network-ready, without having to do any programming.

- It employs a sophisticated file- and record-locking scheme.

- It allows users to see changes being made to records by other users, automatically.

- It includes security features that go beyond and supplement NetWare security.

- It uses a system for creating and deleting temporary files that fits with NetWare's basic directory design.

Paradox also steps close to distributed processing.

Viewing Records

Any number of users may view a Paradox database record simultaneously. This is possible because of a system of least-restrictive locks that Paradox automatically places on files and records.

When you open a file and call a particular record to a screen in View mode, by definition you will not be making any changes to this record. Thus, it is alright for another user to actually change the record, in one of two editing modes: Edit or Coedit. You can view a record while another user changes that same record. And when that other user has completed his or her changes (when he or she leaves the table, if in Edit mode, or when that user switches to another record, if in Coedit mode) a copy of the change is directed to your workstation, automatically.

Edit Versus Coedit Mode

In Edit mode, only one user may be changing a record in a table, or related tables, at a time. If you call up a record from table CLIENT in Edit mode, a lock is placed on the entire table, disallowing anyone else editing a record in that table, until you complete your work and release the CLIENT table edit lock. (Other users can view that same table, and record while you edit the table records.)

In Coedit mode, Paradox allows multiple users to all enter the same table for record editing purposes, though no one else may edit a record you have already begun to edit.

Use of NetWare Bindery File Information

If you are in Coedit mode along with JANE (who is on another workstation in another part of the building) and you try to edit a record that JANE is already editing, you will be sent a message that says the record is locked by JANE. That's right: Paradox knows what NetWare user name is logged in at a workstation and sends messages using the NetWare user name.

Automatically updating screens on a workstation based on activities at other workstations, and sending information about who is working at other workstations, is the beginning of what *distributed processing* is all about. It also means that Paradox is tapping into information contained in NetWare's bindery file, the file where user and group names and security information resides.

Paradox3 Added Security

You cannot view Paradox database tables unless you have Net-Ware Search, Open, and Read effective rights in the directory in which those tables reside. Nor can you change records, which must be written back to a file, if you lack a NetWare Write effective right. NetWare security is not overridden by Paradox. You use NetWare security to protect your Paradox database from user abuse.

Paradox does, however, allow you to take security one step further. As often is the case, a database record has fields that it may be inappropriate for some users to view. NetWare is of no assistance here. Either you can view a file, and all fields of all records, or you cannot. But from within Paradox you can set passwords that must be provided when entering a Paradox application. These passwords attach to defined rights, which determine what database tables (files) a user is allowed to view and, within records of a table, what fields the user is allowed to view. These passwords are unrelated to NetWare's user login password. The passwords are set by you, as are the associated rights of a user providing a particular password.

Paradox security works in addition to whatever NetWare directory and file security you have already established. Because users become confused the more levels of security they encounter, it is suggested you use the Paradox security features only when NetWare is not sufficiently restrictive.

Temporary Tables and Files

In the course of doing its magic, Paradox automatically creates a number of temporary tables or files. If you demand of a database table "Show me all customers who have placed an order of $500.00 or more in the last month," Paradox places the answer in a temporary table named Answer.db. Answer.db stays temporarily in existence until you leave the Paradox program or clear the Paradox active workspace on your workstation. But what if another user asks a question through Paradox before you are finished using the information in Answer.db?

The answer is that Paradox goes about its business of creating Answer.db without regard to the number of users simultaneously using Paradox. If both users are having their Answer.db table stored in the same directory, the second replaces the first.

Paradox can manage multiple Answer.db tables. Here is how: Paradox creates its temporary tables and files in a specified default directory. A drive pointer is used to designate the default drive. The pointer can be a network drive pointer, but a specific path does not have to be defined within Paradox.

For instance, you could use the drive letter T:\. If all users are pointing to (are mapped to) the same default directory location with T:\, they will overwrite each others temporary files, and confusion reigns. But NetWare allows you to map users to different locations using the same drive pointer. You will need to give all Paradox users a mapping using the drive pointer T:\, but with T:\

pointing to different locations for each user. The user directories you set up in Chapter 4 are the logical place for T:\ to point to. (If you use G:\ to point users to their home directories, you will not also need a T:\ mapping if you set the Paradox temporary file default to G:\ .) In Chapter 7 you will see how to use NetWare login script parameters to easily accomplish this G:\ mapping task.

Mapping each user, using the G:\ pointer, to his or her home user directory, Paradox places temporary files in a different directory for each user. A file named Answer.db located in the subdirectory FS1/SYS1:DATA/USERS/VENESSA is never overwritten when a second Answer.db is placed in FS1/SYS1:DATA/USERS/SAM.

 The default pointer for temporary files must be the same for all Paradox users. You cannot set the default location as C:\ for yourself and T:\ for other users. However, you or any other user can temporarily change the default location to which Paradox stores temporary files once you are in a session of Paradox work.

Storing Temporary Files On the Server or Workstation

A frequently encountered LAN application question is whether to store temporary files at the server or the workstation. The Paradox documentation suggests storing them at the workstation hard disk. This is intended to reduce LAN traffic and speed Paradox processing. However, the recommendation is not an absolute, for two reasons.

First, on a LAN with few users and not much LAN traffic, and where the server has considerable RAM available for file caching, there may be no speed gain from storing files on a local workstation hard disk. In fact, processing may be slower than if the temporary files are stored on the server.

Second, Paradox needs to initially find the default pointer where it is to place temporary files. This is known as your Private directory, and within Paradox can be temporarily changed at any time (through the TOOLS, NET, SETPRIVATE function). However, if you say that the standard default location is C:\ and your workstation does not have a hard disk, you could experience difficulties.

A solution might seem to be to leave the default for the temporary file directory pointer blank. The difficulty is that in Paradox a blank Private directory default is just that, blank. Because it is a common practice to point to the directory in which your data files are located before calling up and entering Paradox, you would end up placing your temporary files in the data directory (assuming you had sufficient NetWare effective rights to do so), if the private directory default is blank. But other users, following the same procedure, would also point to and place their temporary files in the data directory in which you are working. You are then back to the problem of users overwriting each others temporary files.

You could always change your Private directory through Paradox after entering that program, and train all your users to do the same. But this is extra work and not an elegant solution. The alternative is to store temporary files in user home directories on the server. If you are consistent in which drive pointer you use to point users to their server home directory (always using G:\, for instance) you can then change the permanent Private directory default within Paradox to G:\. As long as each user on the server who is using Paradox has a NetWare G:\ mapping, which points to his or her own , unique directory, temporary file creation and deletion will be managed by Paradox with no conflicts among users.

The PARADOX.NET File

Paradox keeps track of locks placed on files independent of NetWare. This information is stored in a file named PARA-

DOX.NET. When you install Paradox, you tell it where this
PARADOX.NET file is located. You must place the PARA-
DOX.NET file in a directory where all users have Search, Open,
Read and Write rights. The directory in which PARADOX.NET
is located may be the directory in which you have located your
Paradox database objects: tables, report and form formats, and so
forth. You probably would *not* want to locate PARADOX.NET in
the same directory with the Paradox application executable and
command files.

This is one more example of how LAN applications require
some thoughtful planning of directory structure, on which more
will be said in the next chapter.

The Paradox Licensing Agreement
And Multiple Serial Numbers

Paradox, like WordPerfect, is not copy-protected. But unlike
WordPerfect, Paradox does limit the number of users who can
simultaneously use Paradox. It does this through a table of Paradox
authorized serial numbers.

There is no difference between the Paradox single-user package
and the Paradox LAN package, except that the LAN pack comes
with six authorized serial numbers. While you only need one copy
of Paradox running at the server to support any number of users,
you do need multiple serial numbers.

Serial numbers can be added to any existing serial numbers. If
you have purchased the single-user version of Paradox (which is
really multiuser, except for the lack of serial numbers), and then
purchase the LAN pack (an additional six serial numbers), you will
not need to reinstall Paradox. You will want to install the additional
six serial numbers. Then any user, up to a total of seven users, can
simultaneously use Paradox.

FUTURE APPLICATIONS
IN A DISTRIBUTED,
MULTI-OPERATING ENVIRONMENT

For all their advances, current application software has certain inherent limitations. In particular, current software is not highly distributed in its implementation, nor does it allow for transparent sharing of files between workstations running different operating systems.

Interoperability Between Workstations

While NetWare interacts with DOS to establish a multiple operating system environment, most application packages do not know how to talk across different workstation operating systems: for example, DOS, UNIX, and Macintosh. Current LAN application software is basically single workstation operating system software.

Application software such as WordPerfect is available in versions that run on other than DOS workstations—on the Macintosh, for instance. And NetWare 2.15 allows an AppleTalk network topology to be linked to DOS workstations (on any of a variety of topologies) through the NetWare server.

Unfortunately, the file formats used by these different operating systems are not entirely compatible. While NetWare allows you to import into a DOS version of WordPerfect a document file developed under WordPerfect running on a Macintosh, parts of the file may be lost in the conversion process. This situation will change dramatically in the next few years, with application software combining with server software advances to allow for transparent interoperability across diverse workstation operating systems.

There certainly is no question that operating system inter-operability is possible. After all, you are already operating in a LAN environment that links one workstation operating system (DOS in this instance) with the server environment (NetWare).

Toward Highly Distributed Processing Applications

In its manner of placing locks on tables and of informing users about who is using a database file or record, Paradox takes advantage of the distributed processing concept much more than does WordPerfect. But even Paradox only hints at truly distributed processing.

For instance, Paradox does not allow users across the LAN to share workstation hard disk space or RAM resources. Nor is Paradox highly distributed in terms of the server-workstation relationship. Like WordPerfect, Paradox does most of its work at the PC workstation. When you ask Paradox a question of a data table (when you query it), every record is passed to the workstation for checking against the query criteria. In a table with 10,000 records, all 10,000 must pass across the LAN wires to the workstation, which then checks each record against the query criteria.

Moreover, all qualified records must reside at the workstation to be further manipulated or acted upon. If the workstation has limited RAM, this may mean more LAN or workstation activity, as overflow must be stored temporarily to some location.

In a truly distributed LAN database package, some activities would be performed at the server: either the NetWare server or a specialized, separate database server. When a table or file of 10,000 records was queried, the sorting and selection of records would occur at the server, and only the results (the qualifying records) passed to the workstation. Or, if you wanted a sum total of all purchases for the last six months, both the selecting and summing processes could be done at the server, and only the value of Total Last Six Month Purchases transmitted across the LAN to the workstation.

In defense of Paradox, Borland International is working on means to use Paradox as a front end to a truly distributed database that uses structured query language (SQL) technology. So, if you are using Paradox, there is some chance what you learn will help carry you into the future.

In the case of WordPerfect, Paradox, and almost all other current LAN application packages, you have a great package today, an application package that allows you to take advantage of the multiuser LAN operating environment to do things you could not possibly do on a standalone PC. You also have application packages unlike those that will be available in ten, five, or even two years. But you have to do work today. How do you decide to select a particular package?

WHAT TO LOOK FOR
IN LAN APPLICATION SOFTWARE

Ultimately, you must decide which is best for you. Among the questions to ask are these:

- Is the package a multiuser package, not just a single-user package that can be used on a LAN?

- How does the application handle default settings? Is it flexible?

- What does the license agreement allow? (If need be, call the licensing company.)

- Can you access network printers from within the application?

In addition to these questions, you will want to consider ease of use, overall cost, and level of user support. WordPerfect Corporation is known for its excellent user support. And Paradox is notable for its Lotus-like menu and relative ease of use, as well as for its innovations. But ultimately you must decide. It is hoped the discussions presented in this chapter will help you make a more informed decision.

A FINAL WORD ABOUT MULTIPLE DRIVE POINTERS AND MAPPINGS

Beyond file locking, the most notable feature of LAN application packages is their ability to know of and use multiple drive pointers and drive mappings. This ability carries implications for how you establish and use your NetWare drive pointers.

First, it is very important to be consistent across users in what drive pointers are used to point to a particular path. And it is advisable to discourage users from redefining their NetWare drive mappings.

Also, get out of the habit of using the DOS change directory (CD\) command. You may accidentally unmap yourself from a location that your application needs to have defined to perform its functions. Or you may map yourself to a directory in which you have insufficient effective rights for the application to perform its functions.

The main keys to successful application use are a well-planned NetWare directory and security structure, and appropriate user drive mappings that allow your application software to take advantage of the planned directory and security structure.

Summary

In this chapter you were briefly introduced to how single-user and multiuser packages operate on a LAN. Using single-user packages such as Lotus 1-2-3 has inherent limitations, and likely violates your licensing agreement with Lotus Development Corporation.

WordPerfect Version 5.0 is multiuser and LAN-ready. It performs file locking reliably and allows for multiple default printer settings. It also allows you to use NetWare directory security to protect program and special utility files, such as the main dictionary file, from corruption. On the other hand, WordPerfect does not allow users to interact with each other in writing or editing a document. Two users cannot simultaneously edit different parts of a document and have their changes saved back to the same file.

Paradox is a powerful, relatively easy-to-master database development tool. It is inherently multiuser, even allowing for multiple user editing of different records in the same database file (or in a group of related files). And it offers some flexibility in how you configure Paradox on your LAN, as with the choice of placing temporary files at the workstation or on the server. If it is not a fully distributed database development tool, it is among the most advanced packages available to date, and Borland International is forward looking in its software updates.

PLANNING YOUR USER, GROUP, DIRECTORY, AND SECURITY STRUCTURE

Group to Individual Crosswalk
Directory Structure and the Rights Planning Forms
Multiserver Considerations
Summary

This chapter presents a structured procedure for planning a NetWare server installation. The foundation of a successful installation is considered thought on what your directory structure may look like, what groups will be established to help manage security, and what trustee assignments to make to groups and users.

The forms and procedures offered here will help you achieve a well-planned, thoughtful server installation. The forms and procedures are equally applicable to planning a multiserver installation.

The objective is to get it right the first time. Blank copies of forms are provided in Appendix A.

GROUP TO INDIVIDUAL CROSSWALK

In designing a server installation, your first decision is what groups and users to set up on your server. As a beginning, take a blank piece of paper and brainstorm a list of group names you might wish to create. In all likelihood, you will later decide some of the groups are unnecessary but, for now, be generous in your listing. For instance, is there to be a WORD_PROCESSING group? What about one or more database groups: one for each unique database you are supporting on your server?

Here is a list of possible groups to stimulate your thinking:

```
EVERYONE
EXECUTIVE
ESTIMATORS
OPERATIONS
PROJECTS
SECRETARY
ACCOUNTING
INVENTORY
PAYABLE_CLERKS
RECEIVABLE_CLERKS
WP50_MGR
WP50_USERS
LOTUS_MGR
MODEM_USERS
GATEWAY_USERS
```

The NetWare designations Console Operator and Print Queue Operator do not need to be listed. These special user responsibilities can be directly assigned later.

Next, on a piece of paper, list user names for all (or a good sampling) of the persons who will use the server. Be prospective.

Think about what groups you may need, and what users may be accessing the server 12 or 18 months from now. Avoid developing a "just to get started" server installation plan. Develop a comprehensive plan, even if you choose to install only portions of that plan right now. Adding parts of the comprehensive plan later is much easier than undoing a great short-term plan that does not meet your long-term needs. Include among your group and user lists functions, departments, and individuals who will benefit from the LAN environment when it has proven its utility, even if they are not part of your current plans.

The Group EVERYONE
Versus Application User Groups

As you will see momentarily, the approach used in this chapter is to have the group EVERYONE establish security in most of the software application program directories. If you take this approach, separate application user groups (WP50_USERS, for example) may not be essential to planning the application program directory security.

However, there are two instances in which application user groups may be useful. First, you may have some applications to which you do not want all users to have access. Particularly on an internetwork—where users unknown to you may attach to your server and where software licensing agreements could be violated if attached users access a software package—you may choose to establish an application user group to keep under your control access to a particular software package.

Second, you may have application-specific data directories to which you do not want all users to have access. For instance, you might find a WP50_USERS group or a PARADOX_USERS group useful, even if you choose to allow EVERYONE access to these application program directories.

Setting up application user groups requires some extra on-going work. As you add users to the server, you will have to add the user to each of his or her appropriate application user groups. In contrast, by establishing application security through EVERY-ONE, effective rights necessary to use applications is automatic, because new users are automatically added by NetWare to the group EVERYONE.

If you are going to assign responsibility to a user other than yourself for managing application directories, you may find it convenient to establish application manager groups (WP50_MGR, for instance). While you can make trustee assignments directly to the user designated as manager for all or some portion of an application, the group definition makes it easy to change who is in charge, as people come into and leave you organization or assume different jobs within the organization.

The Server Crosswalk Form

The next step is to decide which users are members of which groups. This is not a permanent decision, but one you should try

	EVERYONE	BACKUP_MGR	WP50_MGR	CUSTOMER_DB	EQUIPMENT_DB	WP50_USERS	EXECUTIVE
GUEST	X						
SAM	X				X		X
VENESSA	X		X				
VIKI	X	X			X		
MARK	X			X			X
DOUG	X						
BARBARA	X			X			X
	X						

TABLE 6-1. Group-to-User-Crosswalk Form

to make now. It will help you later when you plan your directory security structure.

As an aid, use the Server Crosswalk form in Appendix A. List the groups you are considering establishing across the top of the form and users down the left column. EVERYONE and the user GUEST are already listed for you, but need not appear on every page of the form if your listing runs to multiple pages. An example of a completed crosswalk form is shown in Table 6-1.

If you have multiple servers on your network, you should complete a separate group-to-user crosswalk form for each server, keeping in mind you have the option of doing either of the following:

- Setting the same user up on separate servers, including keeping the user GUEST on each server.

- Setting users up on only one server, but allowing attachments from other servers as GUEST, or as another user you set up on your server.

DIRECTORY STRUCTURE AND THE RIGHTS PLANNING FORMS

The next forms to complete are for planning effective security. These planning forms were introduced in Chapter 4 in a combined format (Table 4-2). You will find it convenient to have separate forms for group and individual user security planning. Blank copies of these forms are provided in Appendix A. Make several copies of the forms before beginning your planning.

Developing a Directory Tree Diagram

Before completing the security planning forms, you will find it helpful to develop a tree diagram of your proposed directory

structure, taking into account recommendations in your application software documentation. Read your application software installation instructions, sketch out a tree diagram, and only then
complete the security planning forms. If you jump into the security
planning forms first, you will likely leave out subdirectories and
end up rewriting them.

An example tree directory, which goes beyond that found in
Chapter 4, is shown in Figure 6-1.

Lotus 1-2-3 Release 2.1, WordPerfect Version 5.0, and Paradox
Release 3.0 are used as example applications in this directory
structure design. Your directory structure may be more or less
elaborate. For instance, you might choose to place WordPerfect
keyboard layouts in a directory separate from macros. Or, you
could choose to place both these special-purpose items inside the
main WP50 directory. The question is: Whom do you want to
manage the setting up of keyboard layouts and general purpose
macros? (Note that users can override the WordPerfect default
locations for keyboard and macro files during any session in
WordPerfect.)

In the example in this chapter, all application system defaults
will be contained in the main program directories. User-specific
defaults and auxiliary files (dictionaries, style sheets) are placed
in separate directories. Users can temporarily change these defaults
during a session on the network, but will always receive the system
defaults when they log in.

Group-to-Directory-Rights
Planning Form

Beginning with a blank Group-to-Directory-Rights planning form,
list the groups you expect to establish on your server down the left

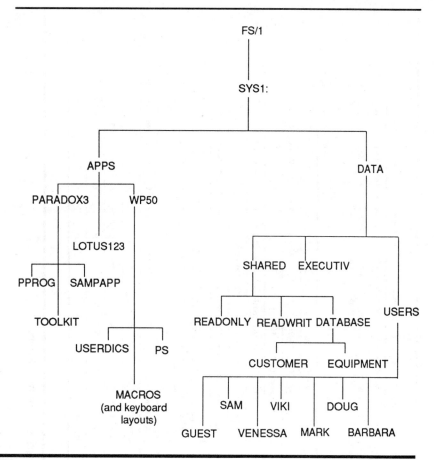

FIGURE 6-1.   APPS and DATA subdirectory structure

column. To avoid having to rewrite this information, make several copies of the partially completed form. You may find it advisable to work in pencil with an eraser handy. Some backtracking now, on paper, is a lot easier than trying later to fix a poorly documented server security structure.

Row	Column 1	Column 2	Column 3	Column 4	Column 5	Column 6	Column 7	Column 8
	Dir. Rights < >	TAPEBACK	APPS/	APPS/ LOTUS123	APPS/ WPS0/	APPS/ WPS0/ USERDICS	APPS/ WPS0/ MACROS	APPS/ WPS0/ PS
1	< CDMOPRSW >	< CDMOPRSW >	< CDMOPRSW >	< CDMOPRSW >	< CDMOPRSW >	< CDMOPRSW >	< CDMOPRSW >	< CDMOPRSW >
2	Trustee Assignment ( ) Effective Rights [ ]							
3	EVERYONE (TA)	(_ O_RS_)	(_ O_RS_)	~	~	(C_ O_RSW)	~	(C_ O_RS)
4	[ER]	[_ O_RS_]	[_ O_RS_]	[_ O_RS_]	[_ O_RS_]	[C_ O_RSW]	[_ O_RS_]	[C_ O_RSW]
5	BACKUP_MGR (TA)	(C_ O_RSW)	~	~	~	~	~	~
6	[ER]	[C_ O_RSW]	[none]	[none]	[none]	[none]	[none]	[none]
7	WPS0_MGR (TA)	~	~	~	(CDMOPRSW)	~	~	~
8	[ER]	[none]	[none]	[none]	[CDMOPRSW]	[CDMOPRSW]	[CDMOPRSW]	[CDMOPRSW]
9	EXECUTIVE (TA)	~	~	~	~	~	~	~
10	[ER]	[none]	[none]	[none]	[none]	[none]	[none]	[none]
11	CUSTOMER_DB (TA)	~	~	~	~	~	~	~
12	[ER]	[none]	[none]	[none]	[none]	[none]	[none]	[none]
13	EQUIPMENT_DB (TA)	~	~	~	~	~	~	~
14	[ER]	[none]	[none]	[none]	[none]	[none]	[none]	[none]
15	WPS0_USER (TA)	~	~	~	~	~	~	~
16	[ER]	[ ]	[ ]	[ ]	[ ]	[ ]	[ ]	[ ]

TABLE 6-2. Group Security Planning Form

Row	Column 1	Column 9 <CDMOPRSW>	Column 10 <CDMOPRSW>	Column 11 <CDMOPRSW> APPS/PARADOX3/	Column 12 <CDMOPRSW> APPS/PARADOX3/ PPROG	Column 13 <CDMOPRSW> APPS/PARADOX3/ TOOLKIT	Column 14 <CDMOPRSW> APPS/PARADOX3/ SAMPAPP	Column 15 <CDMOPRSW> DATA/
1	Dir. Rights < >							
2	Trustee Assignment ( ) / Effective Rights [ ]							
3	EVERYONE (TA)	< >	< >	< >	< >	> (CD_O_RSW)	(CD_O_RSW) <	< >
4	[ER]	[ ]	[ ]	[_O_RS_]	[_O_RS_]	[_O_RS_]	[CD_O_RSW]	[none]
5	BACKUP_MGR (TA)	< >	< >	< >	< >	< >	> (CDMOPRSW)	< >
6	[ER]	[ ]	[none]	[none]	[none]	[none]	[CDMOPRSW]	[none]
7	WP50_MGR (TA)	< >	< >	< >	< >	< >	< >	< >
8	[ER]	[ ]	[none]	[none]	[none]	[none]	[none]	[none]
9	EXECUTIVE (TA)	< >	< >	< >	< >	< >	< >	< >
10	[ER]	[ ]	[none]	[none]	[none]	[none]	[none]	[none]
11	CUSTOMER_DB (TA)	< >	< >	< >	< >	< >	< >	< >
12	[ER]	[ ]	[none]	[none]	[none]	[none]	[none]	[none]
13	EQUIPMENT_DB (TA)	< >	< >	< >	< >	< >	< >	< >
14	[ER]	[ ]	[none]	[none]	[none]	[none]	[none]	[none]
15	WP50_USER (TA)	< >	< >	< >	< >	< >	< >	< >
16	[ER]	[ ]	[none]	[none]	[none]	[none]	[none]	[none]

TABLE 6-2. Group Security Planning Form (continued)

Row	Column 1	Column 16	Column 17	Column 18	Column 19	Column 20	Column 21	Column 22
1	Dir. Rights < >	<CDMOPRSW>	<CDMOPRSW>	<CDMOPRSW>	<CDMOPRSW>	<CDMOPRSW>	<CDMOPRSW>	<CDMOPRSW>
2	Trustee Assignment ( )	DATA/ EXECUTIV	DATA/ SHARED/	DATA/ SHARED/ READONLY	DATA/ SHARED/ READWRIT	DATA/ SHARED/ DATABASE/	DATA/ SHARED/ DATABASE/ CUSTOMER	DATA/ SHARED/ DATABASE/ EQUIPMNT
	Effective Rights [ ]							
3	EVERYONE (TA)	( )	( )	(__O_RS_)	(CD_O_RSW)	( )	( )	( )
4	[ER]	[none]	[none]	[_O_RS_]	[CD_O_RSW]	[none]	[none]	[none]
5	BACKUP_MGR (TA)	( )	( )	( )	( )	( )	( )	( )
6	[ER]	[none]	[none]	[none]	[none]	[none]	[none]	[none]
7	WP50_MGR (TA)	( )	( )	( )	( )	( )	( )	( )
8	[ER]	[none]	[none]	[none]	[none]	[none]	[none]	[none]
9	EXECUTIVE (TA)	(CDMOPRSW)	( )	( )	( )	( )	( )	( )
10	[ER]	[CDMOPRSW]	[none]	[none]	[none]	[none]	[none]	[none]
11	CUSTOMER_DB (TA)	( )	( )	( )	( )	( )	(C_O_RSW)	( )
12	[ER]	[none]	[none]	[none]	[none]	[none]	[CC_O_RSW]	[none]
13	EQUIPMENT_DB (TA)	( )	( )	( )	( )	( )	( )	(C_O_RSW)
14	[ER]	[ ]	[ ]	[ ]	[ ]	[ ]	[ ]	[CC_O_RSW]
15	WP50_USER (TA)	( )	( )	( )	( )	( )	( )	( )
16	[ER]	[none]	[none]	[none]	[none]	[none]	[none]	[none]

TABLE 6-2. Group Security Planning Form (*continued*)

Next, list your directory structure across the top of the Group-to-Directory-Rights planning form. Follow these two suggestions to avoid having to backtrack later:

- List *every* directory and *every* subdirectory across the top of the planning form. This will help ensure that you accurately place trustee assignments at a correct level of your directory structure.

- When shifting between branches or subbranches of your directory structure, leave a couple of blank columns. You may decide later to elaborate your directory tree structure, and leaving blanks gives you a place to insert additional subdirectories.

Table 6-2 shows a completed Group-to-Directory-Rights planning form.

DIRECTORY MASKS   Directory mask rights apply to all users on the network, but are specific to directories. With effective use of trustee assignments, you can leave the planned directory masks with all rights included, which is the default configuration when you create a directory. This is illustrated in row 1 of Tables 6-2 and 6-3 where every directory mask has been left with all rights included.

MINIMUM TRUSTEE ASSIGNMENTS IN THE HIGHER DIRECTORIES   Before making any additional trustee assignments, try to figure out what effective rights already exist for your users. Remember, existing trustee assignments filter downward through the directory structure. For instance, NetWare created a trustee assignment of Read, Open, and Search rights to the group EVERYONE in the directory PUBLIC. This trustee assignment falls through to each of the DOS directories under PUBLIC, without any additional trustee assignments having to be made. (For

Row	Column 1	Column 2	Column 3	Column 4	Column 5	Column 6	Column 7	Column 8
1	Dir. Rights < >	<CDMOPRSW>	<CDMOPRSW>	<CDMOPRSW>	<CDMOPRSW>	<CDMOPRSW>	<CDMOPRSW>	<CDMOPRSW>
2	Trustee Assignment ( )	TAPEBACK	APPS/	APPS/ LOTUS123	APPS/ WP50/	APPS/ WP50/ USERDICS	APPS/ WP50/ MACROS	APPS/ WP50/ PS
	Effective Rights [ ]							
3	GUEST (TA)	< >	< >	< >	< >	< >	< >	< >
4	[ER]	[C_O_RSW]	[_O_RS_]	[_O_RS_]	[_O_RS_]	[C__ORSW]	[_O_RS_]	[C__ORSW]
5	SAM (TA)	< >	< >	< >	< >	< >	< >	< >
6	[ER]	[none]	[_O_RS_]	[_O_RS_]	[_O_RS_]	[C__ORSW]	[_O_RS_]	[C__ORSW]
7	VENESSA (TA)	< >	< >	< >	< >	< >	< >	< >
8	[ER]	[none]	[_O_RS_]	[_O_RS_]	[CDMOPRSW]	[CDMOPRSW]	[CDMOPRSW]	[CDMOPRSW]
9	VIKI (TA)	< >	< >	< >	< >	< >	< >	< >
10	[ER]	[C_O_RSW]	[_O_RS_]	[_O_RS_]	[_O_RS_]	[C__ORSW]	[_O_RS_]	[C__ORSW]
11	MARK (TA)	< >	< >	< >	< >	< >	< >	< >
12	[ER]	[none]	[_O_RS_]	[_O_RS_]	[_O_RS_]	[C__ORSW]	[_O_RS_]	[C__ORSW]
13	DOUG (TA)	< >	< >	< >	< >	< >	< >	< >
14	[ER]	[none]	[_O_RS_]	[_O_RS_]	[_O_RS_]	[C__ORSW]	[_O_RS_]	[C__ORSW]
15	BARBARA (TA)	< >	< >	< >	< >	< >	< >	< >
16	[ER]	[none]	[_O_RS_]	[_O_RS_]	[_O_RS_]	[C__ORSW]	[_O_RS_]	[C__ORSW]

TABLE 6-3.   User Security Planning Form

Row	Column 1	Column 9 <CDMOPRSW>	Column 10 <CDMOPRSW>	Column 11 <CDMOPRSW> APPS/ PARADOX3/	Column 12 <CDMOPRSW> APPS/ PARADOX3/ PPROG	Column 13 <CDMOPRSW> APPS/ PARADOX3/ TOOLKIT	Column 14 <CDMOPRSW> APPS/ PARADOX3/ SAMPAPP	Column 15 <CDMOPRSW> DATA/
1	Dir. Rights < >							
2	Trustee Assignment ( ) Effective Rights [ ]							
3	GUEST (TA)	( )						
4	[ER]	[ ]	]	[_O_RS_]	[_O_RS_]	[_O_RS_]	[CD_O_RSW]	[none]
5	SAM (TA)	( )						
6	[ER]	[ ]	]	[_O_RS_]	[_O_RS_]	[_O_RS_]	[CD_O_RSW]	[none]
7	VENESSA (TA)	( )						
8	[ER]	[ ]	]	[_O_RS_]	[_O_RS_]	[_O_RS_]	[CD_O_RSW]	[none]
9	VIKI (TA)	( )						
10	[ER]	[ ]	]	[_O_RS_]	[_O_RS_]	[_O_RS_]	[CD_O_RSW]	[CDMOPRSW]
11	MARK (TA)	( )						
12	[ER]	[ ]	]	[_O_RS_]	[_O_RS_]	[_O_RS_]	[CD_O_RSW]	[none]
13	DOUG (TA)	( )						
14	[ER]	[ ]	]	[_O_RS_]	[_O_RS_]	[_O_RS_]	[CD_O_RSW]	[none]
15	BARBARA (TA)	( )						
16	[ER]	[ ]	]	[_O_RS_]	[_O_RS_]	[_O_RS_]	[CD_O_RSW]	[none]

TABLE 6-3.   User Security Planning Form (*continued*)

Row	Column 1	Column 16	Column 17	Column 18	Column 19	Column 20	Column 21	Column 22
1	Dir. Rights < >	<CDMOPRSW>	<CDMOPRSW>	<CDMOPRSW>	<CDMOPRSW>	<CDMOPRSW>	<CDMOPRSW>	<CDMOPRSW>
2	Trustee Assignment ( ) Effective Rights [ ]	DATA/ EXECUTIV/	DATA/ SHARED/	DATA/ SHARED/ READONLY	DATA/ SHARED/ READWRIT	DATA/ SHARED/ DATABASE/	DATA/ SHARED/ DATABASE/ CUSTOMER	DATA/ SHARED/ DATABASE/ EQUIPMNT
3	GUEST (TA)	~	~	~	~	~	~	~
4	[ER]	[none]	[none]	[_O_RS_]	[C__ORSW]	[none]	[none]	[none]
5	SAM (TA)	~	~	~	~	~	~	~
6	[ER]	[CDMOPRSW]	[none]	[_O_RS_]	[C__ORSW]	[none]	[CC__ORSW]	[C__ORSW]
7	VENESSA (TA)	~	~	~	~	~	~	~
8	[ER]	[none]	[none]	[_O_RS_]	[C__ORSW]	[none]	[CC__ORSW]	[none]
9	VIKI (TA)	~	~	~	~	~	~	~
10	[ER]	[CDMOPRSW]	[CDMOPRSW]	[CDMOPRSW]	[CDMOPRSW]	[CDMOPRSW]	[CDMOPRSW]	[CDMOPRSW]
11	MARK (TA)	~	~	~	~	~	~	~
12	[ER]	[CDMOPRSW]	[CDMOPRSW]	[_O_RS_]	[C__ORSW]	[none]	[CC__ORSW]	[none]
13	DOUG (TA)	~	~	~	~	~	~	~
14	[ER]	[none]	[none]	[_O_RS_]	[C__ORSW]	[none]	[none]	[none]
15	BARBARA (TA)	~	~	~	~	~	~	~
16	[ER]	[none]	[none]	[_O_RS_]	[C__ORSW]	[none]	[CC__ORSW]	[none]

TABLE 6-3.   User Security Planning Form (*continued*)

Row	Column 1	Column 23	Column 24	Column 25	Column 26	Column 27	Column 28	Column 29	Column 30
1	Directory Rights < >	<CDMOPRSW>	<CDMOPRSW>	<CDMOPRSW>	<CDMOPRSW>	<CDMOPRSW>	<CDMOPRSW>	<CDMOPRSW>	<CDMOPRSW>
2	DIRECTORY\ SUBDIRECTORY	DATA/ USERS	DATA/ USERS/ GUEST	DATA/ USERS/ SAM	DATA/ USERS/ VENESSA	DATA/ USERS/ VIKI	DATA USERS/ MARK	DATA/ USERS/ DOUG	DATA/ USERS/ BARBARA
	GROUPS and USERS Trustee Assignment ( ) Effective Rights [ ]								
3	GUEST (TA)	( )	(CDMO_RSW)	( )	( )	( )	( )	( )	( )
4	[ER]	[ ]	[CDMO_RSW]	[ ]	[ ]	[ ]	[ ]	[ ]	[ ]
5	SAM (TA)	( )	( )	(CDMO_RSW)	( )	( )	( )	( )	( )
6	[ER]	[ ]	[ ]	[CDMO_RSW]	[ ]	[ ]	[ ]	[ ]	[ ]
7	VENESSA (TA)	( )	( )	( )	(CDMO_RSW)	( )	( )	( )	( )
8	[ER]	[ ]	[ ]	[ ]	[CDMO_RSW]	[ ]	[ ]	[ ]	[ ]
9	VIKI (TA)	( )	( )	( )	( )	(CDMO_RSW)	( )	( )	( )
10	[ER]	[CDMOPRSW]	[CDMOPRSW]	[CDMOPRSW]	[CDMOPRSW]	[CDMOPRSW]	[CDMOPRSW]	[CDMOPRSW]	[CDMOPRSW]
11	MARK (TA)	( )	( )	( )	( )	( )	(CDMO_RSW)	( )	( )
12	[ER]	[ ]	[ ]	[ ]	[ ]	[ ]	[CDMO_RSW]	[ ]	[ ]
13	DOUG (TA)	( )	( )	( )	( )	( )	( )	(CDMO_RSW)	( )
14	[ER]	[ ]	[ ]	[ ]	[ ]	[ ]	[ ]	[CDMO_RSW]	[ ]
15	BARBARA (TA)	( )	( )	( )	( )	( )	( )	( )	(CDMO_RSW)
16	[ER]	[ ]	[ ]	[ ]	[ ]	[ ]	[ ]	[ ]	[CDMO_RSW]

TABLE 6-3. User Security Planning Form (*continued*)

further explanation, refer back to Chapter 4 and Table 4-2, columns 4 through 8.)

Following the NetWare PUBLIC security example, you can make one trustee assignment to the directory APPS and create most of the effective rights users require in the APPS subdirectories. Specifically, make a Search, Open, and Read trustee assignment to the group EVERYONE at the APPS directory level (as illustrated in Table 6-2, row 3, column 3). Be sure to make this trustee assignment to the APPS main directory, not to the APPS subdirectories. As a rule, make minimal trustee assignments at the higher level of the APPS directory structure, and then add back in additional rights at lower levels.

ADDING TRUSTEE RIGHTS BACK INTO THE APPS SUB-DIRECTORIES   Users can be allowed additional rights in the WordPerfect 5.0 application subdirectories through group trustee assignments. The following additional trustee assignments are made to the group EVERYONE in selected subdirectories:

- C, O, R, S, and W to APPS/WP50/USERDICS (see Table 6- 2, row 3, column 6)

- C, O, R, S, and W to APPS/WP50/PS (see Table 6-2, row 3, column 8)

All users can now manage WordPerfect user printer settings. They can also create supplemental dictionaries, using a new filename, and add words to those dictionaries. (See Chapter 5 for an explanation of what constitutes a WordPerfect user.) Table 6-2 shows the resulting effective rights that flow from these trustee assignments (row 3, columns 6 and 8).

Note that the group EVERYONE was not used to add rights back into the MACROS subdirectory (Table 6-2, column 7).

Management of this subdirectory is reserved to the user or users who are made a member of the WP50_MGR group, to which an additional trustee assignment of all rights is made in the APPS/WP50 directory. This trustee assignment is shown in Table 6-2, row 7, column 5. The consequent effective rights for the WP50_MGR group are shown in row 8, columns 5 through 8 of Table 6-2.

If you followed through with your group and user installation plan detailed in Table 6-1, VENESSA will be made a member of the group WP50_MGR and will inherit these effective rights (as illustrated in Table 6-3, row 8, columns 5 through 8).

THE DATA SUBDIRECTORIES   Some of the trustee assignments for the data directories were developed in Chapter 4; specifically, the trustee assignments to the subdirectories DA-TA/SHARED/READONLY and DATA/SHARED/READ-WRIT. In this chapter it is the additional directories for database and executive use to which your attention is directed.

In both instances, the decision has been made to restrict access to these directories to subgroups of users. The following group trustee assignments support that decision:

- to EXECUTIVE, all rights (CDMOPRSW) in DATA/EXE-CUTIV (Table 6-2, row 9, column 16)

- to CUSTOMER_DB, C, O, R, S, and W, in DATA/DATA-BASE/CUSTOMER (Table 6-2, row 11, column 21)

- to EQUIPMENT_DB, C, O, R, S, and W, in DATA/DATA-BASE/EQUIPMNT (Table 6-2, row 13, column 22)

The EXECUTIV directory is a shared type directory for top company officials. Members of the EXECUTIVE group have

Parental rights, are allowed to create subdirectories under the EXECUTIV directory, and can manage trustee assignments and effective rights in those subdirectories.

The trustee assignments, and resulting effective rights, for the CUSTOMER_DB and EQUIPMENT_DB groups should by now be self-explanatory. You will allow only controlled access to database files in the CUSTOMER and EQUIPMENT subdirectories beneath DATA/SHARED/CUSTOMER (columns 21 and 22 of Table 6-2) by including as group members of CUSTOMER_DB and EQUIPMENT_DB those users who have a valid, legitimate need to use data in these files.

As discussed in Chapter 5, you can further restrict which fields of a database table a particular user can access, if you are using Paradox as your database manager. Paradox provides data security that adds to and goes beyond NetWare's security features. (This added security is not shown in the Table 6-2 or 6-3 planning forms, as it is security specific to Paradox.)

Be sure you have not made redundant trustee assignments at lower levels of the directory structure. As shown in Table 6-2, only a few trustee assignments need to be made. Most of the table cells show only effective rights, based on trustee assignments that flow downward from higher level directories.

Individual-to-Directory-Rights Planning Form

Proceed with completion of the Individual-to-Directory-Rights planning form only when you are satisfied with your established group security arrangements. As you will see shortly, most of your work is complete.

You will find it useful to have available your completed Server Crosswalk form while completing the Individual-to-Directory-Rights form. You may want to work in pencil and have an eraser handy.

First, list users (or a sample of them), down the left side of the form. Then make copies of this form before entering the directories and subdirectories across the top of the form. Show all of the directories and subdirectories listed on the Group-to-Directory-Rights planning form across the top of the Individual-to-Directory-Rights planning form (Table 6-3).

User by user, and directory by subdirectory, determine what each user's effective rights are, based on membership in the group EVERYONE and any other groups of which a user is a member. Recall that the user GUEST is also a member of the group EVERYONE. No users, GUEST or otherwise, are members of any other group, unless you decide to make them a member. With the exception of a trustee assignment to each user in his or her own home directory (Table 6-3, rows 3, 5, 7, 9, 11, 13, and 15; columns 24 through 30, respectively), your work is complete.

 Don't make any unnecessary trustee assignments.

SPECIAL EFFECTIVE RIGHTS FOR SELECTED USERS

You will notice in Table 6-3 that some users appear to have more rights in some directories than do others, even though no additional trustee assignment has been made to those users. This is due to these users' membership in a special-purpose group (as documented in Table 6-1).

VENESSA has special rights in the APPS/WP50 directory and subdirectories (Table 6-3, row 8, columns 5 through 8) because of her being made a member of the group WP50_MGR. No additional trustee assignment was required to accomplish this. If you are comfortable with this arrangement, and VENESSA is aware of her special rights and responsibilities, leave unchanged the trustee assignments that led to these effective rights.

VIKI acquires Create, Open, Read, Search, and Write effective rights in the TAPEBACK directory (row 10, column 2 of Table 6-3) by virtue of her membership in the BACKUP_MGR group.

This is appropriate and necessary to performing a tape archiving session. Unfortunately for data security, VIKI also has acquired all rights in every DATA subdirectory, including all user sub-directories (Table 6-3, row 10, columns 15 through 30).

In practice, only Open, Read, and Search rights are necessary to perform a tape backup of DATA directory and subdirectory files. Whether you want VIKI to have even these rights in every DATA directory (on a day-to-day basis) is debateable. You may wish to consider:

- Limiting the trustee assignment for the BACKUP_MGR group to the DATA directory to Open, Read, and Search rights. (Alter column 15, row 5 of Table 6-2 to be O, R, and S).

- Creating a user name separate from VIKI (perhaps named BACKUP), which you will make a member of the group BACKUP_MGR in place of VIKI (and for which a password must be provided when logging into the server).

Now any member of the BACKUP_MGR group, including VIKI, must log in as BACKUP (in the process providing the appropriate password) in order to perform file backups or archiving of the DATA directories. VIKI will not routinely have Read, Open, and Search rights to other users' home data directories, nor to other directories to which she would normally be excluded while performing her usual daily functions within the organization.

THE USER GUEST   Before making any further trustee assignments, take a moment to consider the user GUEST. In a multiserver environment, users on servers other than the one you are planning will be able to access any directory the user GUEST can access simply by attaching to this server as GUEST and mapping themselves to those server directories. In essence, during their time of attachment, they are equivalent to the user GUEST.

Does GUEST have any effective rights in directories in which you would not want outsiders to have access? In the APPS directory and subdirectories, probably not. However, if the answer is yes, do not panic. You have two choices:

- Delete the user GUEST from the group EVERYONE, and create whatever effective rights you do want GUEST to have through individual trustee assignments to GUEST.

- Go back and rethink your directory structure (are rights flowing down to directories in which you do not want EVERYONE, and GUEST, to have effective rights?) or your earlier trustee assignments to EVERYONE (should any of these be made to another group, in which GUEST is not a member?).

If you need to use application user groups to adequately manage your server security, get going with your eraser and make appropriate changes now on your planning forms.

MORE ON ADDING BACK EFFECTIVE RIGHTS   In several instances, you have made limited trustee assignments at higher levels of a directory structure and allowed trustee assignments to effectively fall through a subdirectory structure. This has not precluded making a trustee assignment that adds rights back into a particular subdirectory. An example of this is illustrated in the trustee assignment for the group EVERYONE to the directory APPS/PARADOX3/SAMPAPP (column 14, row 3 of Table 6-2).

The purpose of this trustee assignment (and associated effective rights as shown in row 4, column 14) is to allow any user on the network to run or view a stock market simulation that comes with Paradox. To run or use this simulation, which illustrates multiuser and graphics features built into Paradox, a user must have rights that go beyond Open, Read, and Search.

By adding rights back into a subdirectory through a trustee assignment to the group EVERYONE, you create a situation where at any time for any users you can run the Paradox demonstration application. You will have to provide the required mappings to APPS/PARADOX3 and to APPS/PARADOX3/SAMPAPP, but the necessary effective rights are in place. And by making the more inclusive rights trustee assignment at the lower level of the directory structure, you avoid any risk of files in the APPS/PARADOX3 subdirectories (PPROG and TOOLKIT) being abused.

MULTISERVER CONSIDERATIONS

If you are planning a network of connected servers or are installing a new server on an internetwork, take the time to complete the planning forms for each server. Not only will this be good documentation later, it will help you make good internetwork decisions now.

There are, of course, additional considerations in an internetwork, multiserver environment. Alluded to already are these:

- Whether to set up an individual as an actual user on multiple servers or to restrict their setup to one server and allow access to other servers through the ATTACH command.

- What trustee assignments (and resultant effective rights) to grant to the group EVERYONE and, as a consequence, to the server's user GUEST (or whether, for a particular server, to remove GUEST from membership in EVERYONE).

As a rule, it is best to leave GUEST as a member of EVERYONE on every server and to make trustee assignment changes to groups other than EVERYONE, if server security is an issue. It is not particularly necessary to create an individual as a user on multiple servers. The NetWare ATTACH command's purpose is to make multiple setups unnecessary.

SERVER NAME

USER LIST	SERVER	SERVER	SERVER	SERVER	SERVER	SERVER	SERVER
GUEST							

TABLE 6-4.   Server-to-User-Crosswalk Form

What you will need to know is to which servers a user is attached. The Server-to-User-Crosswalk form, shown in Table 6-4, can be used to document either attachment or multiserver setup plans.

Multiserver Directory Structures

Ultimately, multiserver planning starts with this question: What applications and shared or restricted data directories do I want to have on a particular server? Except for application licensing agreement restrictions, there is no real reason to have an application program installed on multiple servers. Placing PARADOX on only one server and allowing access to users on other servers through the ATTACH command are economical in terms of setup time, disk space usage, and, one hopes, licensing fees (though you do need to read licensing agreements carefully).

Similarly, nothing dictates that the server on which an application is installed should be the server on which the data or document files reside. It is quite feasible to have NetWare point you to a directory on one server to call up WordPerfect 5.0 program functions while retrieving and saving document files to directories on another server.

The 21 network drive pointers available to a user at a workstation can point to any location on an internetwork, after the user has first attached to each of the servers to whose directories he or she wishes to point.

As with planning security on a single server, multiserver planning begins with a good directory structure. If you are planning server installation on an internetwork, always start with a picture of the existing and planned directory tree for each server and each volume on a server. It may take a little extra time, but developing directory tree diagrams is excellent documentation for the future, and may be invaluable in helping you stay on track with the actual installation. (See Chapter 8 for help in how to use NetWare

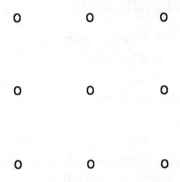

FIGURE 6-2.   Don't limit yourself puzzle

commands to document a server's existing directory and security structure.)

Putting Unnecessary Restrictions On Yourself

With NetWare, you have much more flexibility in designing and installing your internetwork of servers than you may ever have realized. The key to creative, successful planning is not placing unnecessary restrictions on yourself, and not assuming rules for installation design and use that do not exist.

The puzzle in Figure 6-2 illustrates how we too often limit ourselves in seeking solutions to problems. The instructions, listed at the top of Figure 6-2, are quite simple. With four, and only four, straight lines, and without lifting your pencil or pen from the paper, connect all nine dots. Retracing lines is the same as making another line, and is not part of the solution.

After trying this puzzle, turn to Appendix B, which shows the correct answer. Before you protest that the solution violates given limitations, reread the instructions very carefully and think about whose limitations you are violating, that is, who said that you could not go outside the dots?

If you placed that limitation on yourself, you are in good company. Not going outside the dots is a limitation most of us place on ourselves. And it is all too easy to take the familiar (DOS) dots and rules for interconnecting them and unnecessarily apply them to new (NetWare) dots. In designing your NetWare internetwork, do not place unnecessary limitations on yourself. NetWare lets you get outside the DOS dots.

Summary

In this chapter you were introduced to a systematic approach to developing a server installation. Blank copies of forms used in this chapter are provided in Appendix A.

Taking time today to plan on paper an installation will save countless hours tomorrow. And, if you inherit an existing server installation, taking time to develop the documentation discussed in this chapter for your existing server(s) will help you toward a clear understanding of your current plight as LAN manager.

Part II of this book is directed toward helping you, as a user, take advantage of the server directory and security structure you have designed and installed. If you need assistance in planning that structure, take time to reread this chapter. Or refer back to Chapters 4 and 5 for guidance on how to put your plans into effect on a NetWare server.

NETWARE SESSION
MANAGEMENT

IPX, NETx, LOGIN, SETPASS, ATTACH,
AND LOGOUT
MAP
How WordPerfect 5.0 Uses NetWare Pointers
Other NetWare Session Commands
The SESSION Menu
More Permanent Session Mappings
Borrowing User Scripts as SUPERVISOR
Changing the System Login Script
Summary

This chapter introduces you to NetWare tools for managing
your *session* on the network—the time you spend doing
activities. NetWare includes several commands and a menu, the
SESSION menu, which will help you establish and use your
workstation environment.

You can change your working environment at any time by using the commands and menu discussed in this chapter. But it is preferable to have the same working environment set up automatically when you log in to a server. This is accomplished through NetWare *login scripts*. Default, user, and system login scripts are discussed in this chapter. You are shown how to create your own user login script. Also reviewed is SUPERVISOR access to, and use of, the system login script.

IPX, NETx, LOGIN, SETPASS, ATTACH, AND LOGOUT

Several of NetWare's session commands were discussed in Chapter 2 and are only briefly reviewed here.

IPX (Internetwork Packet Exchange)

The IPX.COM command is issued from the workstation prompt, or as part of a workstation AUTOEXEC.BAT file. It is used to load NetWare's Internetwork Packet Exchange protocols at the workstation, in preparation for logging into a server (see Chapter 2).

NET2, NET3, and NET4

NET2.COM, NET3.COM, and NET4.COM load at the workstation the resident NetWare shell program for, respectively, DOS versions 2, 3, and 4. Also available from Novell is an OS/2 Redirector shell program. Along with IPX.COM, the appropriate shell file must be loaded before you log into a server (see Chapter 2).

LOGIN

The LOGIN command provides access to a specific server on the network. A valid, server-specific user name must be provided, along with a valid password, if a password is established.

The general format for the LOGIN command is

```
LOGIN 1st_parameter, 2nd_parameter, 3rd_parameter,
```

For a single-server environment, the LOGIN command format can be issued without any parameters:

```
LOGIN
```

NetWare will prompt you for a valid user name, and password if required.

On a multiserver LAN, issuing LOGIN by itself results in NetWare trying to log you into the server to which you were automatically attached when you issued the IPX.COM command. This server is whichever is closest and available to you at that moment. Since *closest* is not always *available,* NetWare may pick a server on which your user name and account does not exist.

To ensure that you point to the correct server when logging in, include the server name along with the LOGIN command. Appropriate internetwork LOGIN command formats include these:

```
LOGIN servername
LOGIN servername username
```

LOGIN can be issued with additional parameters other than servername or username, and this additional information is used within login scripts to create a customized work environment. An example of such a LOGIN command is

LOGIN username CUSTOMER

This login command allows use of CUSTOMER in login scripts, in IF-THEN statements.

SETPASS

SETPASS allows you to change your password. To use SETPASS, NetWare at your logged in server must be configured to allow users to change their own passwords, and you must be logged into the server and mapped to the directory PUBLIC. You must type the new password twice, with the same spelling, for the new password to be accepted. As a security feature, what you type is not displayed on screen.

ATTACH

On a network of linked (bridged) NetWare servers, you can log into one server and attach simultaneously to several others, thereby gaining controlled access to those other servers' resources. The format of the ATTACH command is

ATTACH servername/username;password.

Include a server name when you issue the ATTACH command.

If you do not specify a user name, NetWare will automatically attach you as the user GUEST (unless the user GUEST has been deleted for security reasons from that server's list of named users).

If you attach as a named user other than GUEST, and that user's account has a password, you are prompted for the password, unless you provided the password as the third parameter in the ATTACH command.

LOGOUT

This command is used to terminate, to log out of, a session on the server. Always issue it when you leave your workstation.

MAP

The MAP command allows you to define, redefine, delete, and view NetWare drive mappings. The MAP command is integral to operating on the network and is discussed in detail here.

Working Through the Examples

Your ability to do the MAP command examples discussed here depends on the setup of your server—whether your server includes the volumes, directories, and subdirectories used in the examples in this section. (Follow the directory structure shown in Figure 6-1 of Chapter 6, except that the directory APPS is included under the volume SYS:, rather than SYS1:.)

If you do not know what directories or subdirectories exist on your server, nor their exact spelling, you will find it difficult to do the MAP commands as demonstrated. You may wish just to read through this section of Chapter 7. As it happens, NetWare has a menu, SESSION, which allows you to do mappings, even when you do not know your directory structure all that well. This menu is discussed later in this chapter. In the meantime, an attempt is made to not only show you the format of commands, but also the consequences you would see if you issued those commands as illustrated.

If you choose to try the MAP statements contained here, you should know that any mapping changes you make from the prompt

or through the SESSION menu are *not* permanent. When you log
in again, your former mappings are restored intact.

Default Mappings
From Default Login Scripts

When you log in to a server devoid of any *customized* login scripts,
you receive minimal NetWare mappings, and their exact nature
depends on whether you log in as SUPERVISOR or as another
user. An example of default script mappings for a user other than
SUPERVISOR is shown here:

```
Drive A    maps to a local disk.
Drive B    maps to a local disk.
Drive C    maps to a local disk.
Drive D    maps to a local disk.
Drive E    maps to a local disk.
Drive F := FS1/SYS:VENESSA
Drive Y := FS1/SYS:PUBLIC
_____
Search1 := Z:. [FS1/SYS:PUBLIC/IBM_PC/DOS/V2.0]


F:>\
```

If you have created user home directories immediately below
the volume SYS—for instance, SYS:VENESSA—you will receive a mapping like that just shown for the F: drive. If you do not
use this directory structure, or have failed to create a home directory under SYS for the user logging in, drive pointer F: will point
to (server-name)/SYS:. Similarly, drive pointer Z: will point to
SYS:PUBLIC/IBM_PC/DOS/V2.0 only under these conditions:

- Your directory structure includes IBM_PC/DOS/V2.0.

- These directory names are embedded in the DOS shell used at your workstation or in a SHELL.CFG file included on your boot disk.

If these conditions are not met, Search Drive 1 will just point to PUBLIC.

Notice that NetWare will provide initial mappings to local drives A: through E:, regardless of whether these drives actually exist at your workstation. Those that do not actually exist at your workstation drop out of your map listing when you call that list from the prompt, as shown in other listings here. You may view your current mappings by typing **MAP** at the prompt and pressing `ENTER`.

Managing NetWare Drive Mappings

There are two types of NetWare mappings: plain, network drive mappings and search drive mappings. To use files defined through a network mapping you must point to that drive (make it your default drive) or, in some instances, your application (WordPerfect 5.0, for example) just needs to know of that mapping. In either case, a mapping must exist as part of your workstation session environment for you or your application to locate files in a specific directory or subdirectory.

ADDING DRIVE MAPPINGS   To create a new network drive mapping, use the following MAP command format:

MAP G:=FS1/SYS1:DATA/USERS/VENESSA

A message tells you that a new mapping has been created. Issue MAP at the prompt and press (ENTER) to see how NetWare has added that mapping to your current mappings.

```
Drive A    maps to a local disk.
Drive B    maps to a local disk.
Drive F := FS1/SYS:
Drive G := FS1/SYS1:DATA/USERS/VENESSA
Drive Y := FS1/SYS:PUBLIC

Search1 := Z:. [FS1/SYS:PUBLIC]


F:>\
```

You must provide a drive pointer letter (G, H, and so on) as part of the MAP command statement, followed by a colon and an equal sign. The rest of the mapping includes server, volume, directory, and subdirectory names. The server name and volume name do not have to be included if you are on a single-server LAN. On an internetwork, including server and volume names ensures that you map yourself to correct locations.

NetWare is friendly as to the direction of the slash delimiter. The slash can be either forward (/) or backward (\). The colon delimiter, separating volume from directory name, is mandatory. You can use any letter, from A: to Z:, to point to any directory or subdirectory on the server, though normally you will follow NetWare's lead and reserve A: through E: as drive pointers for workstation locations.

Deleting a Mapping

You cannot delete a drive pointer while it is your default drive. To delete F:, you must first change directory pointers—to G:, for instance. Having switched to G:, you can then delete the F: mapping:

MAP DEL F:

Press (ENTER) and you receive the message "Definition for drive F: has been removed."

But, you say, F: is needed to point to the directory LOGIN. In fact, a pointer to LOGIN is *not* necessary once you have logged on to a server. Your default F: mapping to the directory LOGIN can be deleted, or you may choose to map F: to some other directory, to the READONLY directory, for example:

MAP F:=FS1/SYS1:DATA/SHARED/READONLY

REDEFINING AN EXISTING MAPPING   When you establish a regular network drive mapping, you decide which drive pointer to use. If you happen to reuse an existing drive letter, the first mapping is overwritten by your new mapping. For illustration, map F: to point to READWRIT as follows:

MAP F:=FS1/SYS1:DATA/SHARED/READWRIT

Type **MAP** and press (ENTER) to see your new map list:

```
Drive A    maps to a local disk.
Drive B    maps to a local disk.
Drive F := FS1/SYS:DATA/SHARED/READWRIT
Drive G := FS1/SYS1:DATA/USERS/VENESSA
Drive Y := FS1/SYS:PUBLIC
_____
Search1 := Z:. [FS1/SYS:PUBLIC]


G:>\
```

F: now points to READWRIT, and there is no pointer to READONLY. To retain a pointer to READONLY, you must use an undefined drive letter in your mapping to READWRIT.

Search Drive Mappings

Search drives are very special types of drive pointers in two respects:

- Executable, command, and batch files contained in a (sub)directory pointed to with a NetWare search drive pointer can be accessed automatically, even though you are pointing to another directory as your default drive.

- NetWare assigns for you the drive pointer used to point to a (sub)directory location, beginning from the bottom of the alphabet and working upward through unused drive pointers.

Type **MAP** and press (ENTER) again and look for Z:. Z: probably points to the directory PUBLIC, and NetWare tells you this is Search Drive 1. This holds true if PUBLIC was the first search drive defined and Z: was not already in use. If Z: points to PUBLIC but not as a search drive, it may be because a system or user login script plays when you log in and redefines the Search Drive 1 mapping.

CREATING A SEARCH DRIVE MAPPING   To create a second search drive, use the following MAP command format:

MAP S2:=FS1/SYS:APPS/WP50

Pointing to the APPS root directory (FS1/SYS:APPS) does not make executable, command, or batch files in subdirectories available to you. You must point to each specific subdirectory as a separate search drive.

REDEFINING A SEARCH DRIVE MAPPING   You reuse an existing search drive to point to a new location. For instance, to redefine Search Drive 2, type

MAP S2:=FS1/SYS:APPS/PARADOX3

and press (ENTER). Type **MAP** at the prompt and press (ENTER) to see the changes in their entirety:

```
Drive A    maps to a local disk.
Drive B    maps to a local disk.
Drive F := FS1/SYS:DATA/SHARED/READWRIT
Drive G := FS1/SYS1:DATA/USERS/VENESSA
Drive X := FS1/SYS:APPS/WP50
Drive Y := FS1/SYS:PUBLIC


Search1 := Z:. [FS1/SYS:PUBLIC]
Search2 := W:. [FS1/SYS:APPS/PARADOX3]


G:>\
```

The new Search Drive 2 (S2) is identified by the first available, unused letter, selected in reverse alphabetical order. And, interestingly, your existing S2 pointer is bumped to network drive status (see X: pointing to WP50), rather than disappearing altogether. NetWare is friendly to you when you redefine search drives. In contrast, when you reuse a regular network drive pointer, the previous mapping is altogether lost.

INSERTING A SEARCH DRIVE MAPPING   You usually do not want to redefine existing search drives, until you reach the limit allowed (16 with version 2.1 of NetWare, 10 with version

2.0a). But you may find it useful to have among the first of your defined search drives those directories that contain your most frequently used programs. NetWare searches sequentially through the search drives: S1, S2, S3, and so on. SYS:PUBLIC contains frequently used NetWare commands, and file access time may be reduced if your first search drive is to PUBLIC.

This advantage is somewhat obviated by file caching (see Chapter 2). And NetWare will execute the MAP command for you even if SYS:PUBLIC is your sixteenth search drive. It could just take a little longer.

Should you decide a search drive needs to be placed somewhere within a list of existing search drives, and you do not want to lose any of those existing search drives, you can use an INSERT parameter with the MAP command. For example:

MAP INSERT S2:=FS1/SYS:APPS/WP50

Press (ENTER); then type **MAP** and press (ENTER) and you will see that Search Drive 2 now points to WP50, with the former Search Drive 2 pointer to PARADOX3 now redefined as Search Drive 3.

MAPPING ALL SEARCH DRIVES AS S16   Another way to avoid losing an existing search drive mapping is to map your new search drive as though it were the maximum available in NetWare, 16. Using S16, NetWare adds the new search drive to the bottom of the list of existing search drives, in numerical order. For instance:

MAP S16:=FS1/SYS:APPS/LOTUS

Type **MAP** and press (ENTER) and you see that the S16 mapping to APPS/LOTUS was added not as S16 but as Search Drive 4, the next available search drive number.

```
Drive A    maps to a local disk.
Drive B    maps to a local disk.
Drive F := FS1/SYS1:DATA/SHARED/READWRIT
Drive G := FS1/SYS1:DATA/USERS/VENESSA
Drive X := FS1/SYS:APPS/WP50
Drive Y := FS1/SYS:PUBLIC

_____
Search1 := Z:. [FS1/SYS:PUBLIC]
Search2 := V:. [FS1/SYS:APPS/WP50]
Search3 := W:. [FS1/SYS:APPS/PARADOX3]
Search4 := U:. [FS1/SYS:APPS/LOTUS]


G:>\
```

Get in the habit of using S16 to create new mappings, and you will run little risk of losing existing search drive mappings.

 The list of drive pointers contains multiple mappings to FS1/SYS:APPS/WP50. *Multiple mappings to the same location do no harm.* If you want, you can use MAP DEL X: to delete the duplicate network (non-search) drive pointer. (You want to retain the search drive pointer to WP50 so WP50 program files can be found by NetWare, regardless of which directory you point to as your default directory.)

Mappings to Other Servers

You may map yourself to directories or subdirectories on any server on an internetwork, *after you first attach to that server.* For instance:

```
ATTACH FS3/GUEST
ATTACH MIS/JOHN;Whataguy
MAP L:=FS3/DATA:DATABASE/INVENTORY
MAP S16:=MIS/APPS:DBASEIV
```

In these examples, you remain logged into server FS1, but use L: to point to server FS3, the volume DATA, the subdirectory INVENTORY under DATABASE. You have also created a NetWare search drive mapping to a dBASE IV program subdirectory under the volume APPS of server MIS (the Management Information System department's server).

You may be able to use dBASE IV. NetWare drive mappings are a necessary, but not sufficient condition for your doing things in the directories pointed to. You must have *effective rights* to do things in a directory (see Table 4-1 in Chapter 4).

HOW WORDPERFECT 5.0 USES NETWARE POINTERS

It is instructive to consider what mappings you need in order to use a particular application. WordPerfect is an example. Typical of many other application programs, WordPerfect can use multiple network drive pointers to locate application-specific files, but search drives are also used in a WordPerfect installation. Search drives offer convenience, flexibility, and power beyond what you might expect, as you will see later.

Placing WordPerfect 5.0 Program Files on a Search Drive

First, you use a NetWare search drive to point to the directory in which WordPerfect executable and command files are located. You can now find and load to your workstation executable and command files while pointing to a default directory other than APPS/WP50. This is the simple, straightforward use of a NetWare search drive.

Network Pointers

Typically, you will do your word processing in a working directory pointed to with a network drive pointer. This could be your home directory, for example, DATA/USERS/VENESSA. Network drive pointers are defined for other purposes as well. For instance, you may define a mapping to a macro directory:

M:\FS1\SYS:APPS\WP50\MACROS

For WordPerfect 5.0 to locate files in this directory, both Word-Perfect 5.0 and NetWare must know about it.

Through WordPerfect 5.0 installation procedures, you designate a directory for macros, and the same or other directories for other special WordPerfect files: dictionary files, keyboard layout files, and so forth. These special WordPerfect directories do not have to be search drives, but a network drive path must be defined within both NetWare and WordPerfect. The same, identical drive letter and path specification must be used in both the WordPerfect and the NetWare map definitions.

That done, WordPerfect knows how to find files using these joint WordPerfect-NetWare drive mappings, even when your current default drive is pointing to your home directory.

WordPerfect can find macro files in APPS/WP50/MACROS while you point to DATA/USERS/VENESSA, but that does not mean it will always go to the MACROS directory for the called macro file. In practice, WordPerfect looks first to your default directory for the requested file. If you press (ALT-M) to invoke a WordPerfect macro file named ALTM.WPM, WordPerfect looks in your current default directory for ALTM.WPM and executes it from there, if it is present. Only if there is no ALTM.WPM in that directory will WordPerfect look to the directory you have defined (within WordPerfect 5.0) as the location for macros: APPS/WP50/MACROS.

The implication is that you can define more than one version of ALTM.WPM: a generally available ALTM.WPM (for users who have not defined their own ALTM.WPM macro) and work directory versions of ALTM.WPM (available when you are working in the directory in which the macro file resides).

Extending WordPerfect Functionality Through NetWare Search Drives

Suppose there was no ALTM.WPM file in either your current, default directory nor in the APPS/WP50/MACROS network directory. What would happen?

Interestingly, NetWare might find an ALTM.WPM file and send it to your workstation, if a named ALTM.WPM file is located in any of your NetWare defined search drives. *Even though the macro file has a .WPM extension—not an .EXE, .COM, or .BAT extension—NetWare finds the WordPerfect 5.0 .WPM file from NetWare search drives.*

If there is an ALTM.WPM file in more than one search drive, it is the first encountered version of the file that is sent to your workstation for execution (all this assuming you have effective Read, Open, and Search rights in the search drive in question). This is the added functionality and power of NetWare search drives.

To summarize this section:

- WordPerfect will always look first to whatever default directory you are pointing for a requested macro. If you press (ALT-M) while you are pointing to your home directory, it is the version of ALTM.WPM located in your home directory that will be invoked.

- If you do not have an ALTM.WPM file in your default home directory (though you may have other macros there), WordPerfect 5.0 will look to the directory you defined within WordPerfect 5.0 as the location for macro files (to APPS/WP50/MACROS).

- In practice, you can define a permanent WordPerfect 5.0 macro directory, and temporarily override this default during your use of WordPerfect, though this is a level of complexity not alluded to in the previous discussion.

- If ALTM.WPM is not in the WordPerfect 5.0 reserved macro directory (as currently defined by you in WordPerfect), *NetWare will look through each search drive for an ALTM.WPM file (and will invoke the first occurrence of ALTM.WPM it encounters).*

The ability of applications to use multiple network drive pointers to locations where special-purpose files are located, combined with NetWare's ability to search for various types of files within defined search drives opens up all sorts of options for creative directory and work place structures. An example is summarized in Table 7-1.

OTHER NETWARE SESSION COMMANDS

Other NetWare session commands help you know who you are on the network and what your effective rights are. Still others tell you who else is on the network and allow you to communicate with those other users.

Mapping	Use
Search drive mapping to FS1/SYS:APPS/WP50	WordPerfect program files located in this directory, including the main dictionary file. Users who have only Read, Write, and Search rights will not be allowed to modify these files.
Search drive mapping to FS1/SYS:APPS/WP50/MACROS	Located here will be macros and keyboard layout files for use by any user. This directory will be defined within WordPerfect as the global default for these files. While not required to be a search drive, this setup allows named files in this directory to be used even if the WordPerfect default for macros and keyboard layouts is changed temporarily (see below).
Network drive mapping to FS1/SYS1:DATA/CLIENT	In this location will be special word processing macro and keyboard layout files used by word processing service bureau staff. After entering WordPerfect, these word processing specialists will change the default for macro and keyboard layouts to this directory (or to other client specific directories where such files are located). While pointing within WordPerfect to DATA/CLIENT as the default for macros and keyboard layout files, macros and keyboard layout files may be accessed from WP50/MACROS. Long filenames for these macros are not duplicated in DA-TA/CLIENT (or other temporary default locations).

TABLE 7-1.   Creative Use of Multiple Network and Search Drive Pointers

Network drive mapping to FS1/SYS1:DATA/CLIENT/IPS	Like the DATA/CLIENT directory, this directory can be made the WordPerfect temporary default location for macro or keyboard layout files used while word processing in a subdirectory under CLIENT/IPS on a specific project for client IPS.
Network drive mapping for a project to ...CLIENT/IPS/MANUAL ...CLIENT/IPS/PROPOSAL	
Search drive mapping to FS1/SYS:APPS/WP50/PS	Location for WordPerfect printer setting default files.

TABLE 7-1.   Creative Use of Multiple Network and Search Drive Pointers (*continued*)

RIGHTS

To find out your effective rights in a mapped directory you can do either of the following:

- Change your default drive to the directory for which you wish to know your effective rights (at the prompt, type **Z:** and press (ENTER), for instance); then issue the RIGHTS command (type **RIGHTS** and press (ENTER)).

- Issue the RIGHTS command with a drive pointer specified (**RIGHTS Z:**).

Your current, effective rights are displayed on the screen.

In NetWare you do not have to include the path when issuing the RIGHTS command. The path is defined explicitly through your previous mapping of a pointer to a specific directory. This same principle applies when you change drive pointers at the prompt.

If you are unable to perform some activity from within an application, use the RIGHTS command to check your effective rights in the directories in which you are working.

USERLIST

To see a list of other users on the network who are currently logged in, at the prompt type **USERLIST** and press (ENTER). To learn additional information about users, include an /E or /A flag:

USERLIST/E   (To see your effective rights in the directories to which you are mapped)
USERLIST/A   (To see all available personal user information)

To print a hardcopy of this information, issue USERLIST with a DOS print reroute parameter as follows:

USERLIST/A >LPT1:

The information obtained with USERLIST/A will be rerouted to either the local printer attached to your workstation's first parallel port (LPT1) or to a network printer, if you previously told NetWare to reroute your printing from LPT1 to a NetWare print queue. (See Chapter 9 for a discussion of use of the CAPTURE command.)

SEND

With NetWare Internetwork Packet Exchange protocols loaded, you can send short, peer-to-peer messages to other logged in network users. Here are some examples of the SEND command:

```
SEND "Type a message of 40 characters or less." TO Venessa
SEND "Maybe send a message to a named group." TO EVERYONE
SEND "Or be selective in sending messages." TO Venessa, Sam
```

If you are sending a message to users or groups on another server, you must include the server name with the user or group name. For example:

```
SEND "Server down in 10 minutes!" FS1/EVERYONE,FS2/EVERYONE
```

A message like this may also be sent through use of the server BROADCAST Console command (see Chapter 10). Quotation marks must surround the message.

The SEND command interrupts whatever else the user receiving the message is doing at his or her workstation. Imagine yourself in the middle of spell checking a long document, and a short message suddenly and unexpectedly appears at the bottom of your screen. "Hi, you buying lunch today? FROM DOUG."

NetWare uses a terminate-and-stay-resident procedure in sending the message to a workstation, interrupting workstation activity and allowing immediate display of the SEND message on the screen. Press (CTRL-ENTER) to clear the message from your screen, and resume your work. If more than one message is queued to you, you must press (CTRL-ENTER) until all message interruptions are cleared.

CASTOFF and CASTON

You can block receipt of SEND command messages with CAST-OFF. To reinstate receipt of SEND messages, issue the CASTON command.

Any messages transmitted with the SEND command while you are CASTOFF are lost to you. Unlike E-Mail packages, SEND does not place messages in user mailboxes. *CASTOFF does not block your receiving of messages sent via means of the server BROADCAST Console command.* While CASTOFF you will receive a BROADCAST "Server down in 10 minutes!" message. (See Chapter 10 for Console command instructions.)

WHOAMI

The NetWare WHOAMI command queries NetWare for information about yourself, that is, about the user you are logged in as on a server. Several flags can be used with WHOAMI:

WHOAMI/G (to see to what groups you belong)
WHOAMI/S (to see to whom you are a security equivalent)
WHOAMI/R (to list your effective rights, **in the default**
            directory to which you are pointing when you
            issue the WHOAMI command**)**
WHOAMI/A (to obtain all of the above information)

A hardcopy of information about yourself can be printed through inclusion of a DOS reroute parameter.

WHOAMI/A >LPT1:

You can also use WHOAMI to see if someone logged in under another user name while you were away from your workstation.

SYSTIME

Issue the SYSTIME command and NetWare tells you the current day of the week, the time of the day, and the date, as it knows it from your default server. Your workstation's date and time are also automatically synchronized with the server.

If no one changed the time on the server when daylight savings time came or went, the server will be off by an hour.

MENU

MENU allows you to call a customized work menu to the screen, and simultaneously invokes those NetWare menu programs necessary to use the custom menu.

For MENU to function, you must

- Be pointing to a default directory in which you have at least Create and Write effective rights.

- Have created a named, unformatted menu text file, with .MNU as the filename extension.

- Either have the named file located in a NetWare search drive directory or in a network directory to which you are pointing when issuing the MENU (textfile) command.

You can call any NetWare menu (SYSCON, FILER, SESSION, and so on) from a customized menu named MAIN.MNU. At the prompt, type **MENU MAIN** and press (ENTER). If you meet the requirements just stated, you should now see the menu shown in Figure 2-3 of Chapter 2. You can now enter NetWare's SESSION menu by selecting **1. Session Management.**

THE SESSION MENU

Remembering all of the commands just discussed is difficult. And to use the MAP command from the prompt, you must know and correctly type the names of subdirectories, directories, and, possibly, volumes and servers. Because of this, Novell included an optional method of issuing SESSION commands, through the NetWare SESSION menu.

To call up the SESSION menu, at the prompt type **SESSION** and press (ENTER). The SESSION main menu is displayed on the screen (see Figure 7-1).

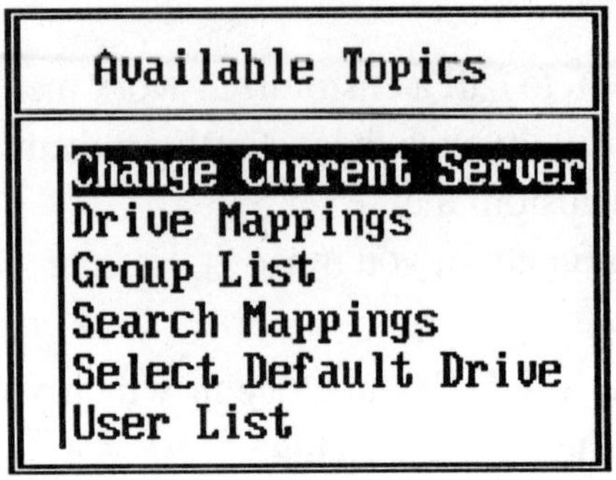

```
┌─────────────────────────────────┐
│     Available Topics            │
├─────────────────────────────────┤
│┌───────────────────────────────┐│
││Change Current Server          ││
││Drive Mappings                 ││
││Group List                     ││
││Search Mappings                ││
││Select Default Drive           ││
││User List                      ││
│└───────────────────────────────┘│
└─────────────────────────────────┘
```

FIGURE 7-1.   SESSION Available Topics menu

If you are not familiar with NetWare menus, refer back to the section "About NetWare Menus" in Chapter 3 and the "Changing the Current Directory Path" and "Creating the Directories APPS and DATA" sections of Chapter 4.

Change Current Server

The first option within SESSION allows you to attach to additional servers. With the cursor over the **Change Current Server** item, press (ENTER). NetWare displays the current server to which you are logged in, and any additional servers to which you have already attached yourself.

If you have not attached to additional servers, only your logged into server name (and your user name) will be shown (see Figure 7-2).

ATTACHING TO ADDITIONAL SERVERS   As with other NetWare menu lists, you may add to a list by pressing (INSERT), highlighting the item you wish to add, and pressing (ENTER). In this instance, pressing (INSERT) shows you what additional servers are

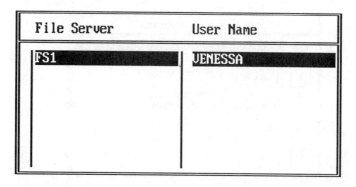

File Server	User Name
FS1	VENESSA

FIGURE 7-2.   List of attached servers

active on your network, if any. You may place the highlight bar over any one of the listed servers and press (ENTER) to add that server to the list of servers available to you. Your effective rights on the server are equivalent to those of the user as whom you attached.

CHANGING THE SERVER   If you are on a network with only one server, you will never need to change the current server. On a multiserver network, selecting Change Current Server will display more than one server (in the screen shown in Figure 7-2) if you have attached to those additional servers. But do you really need to change the server to which you are pointing? Seldom.

The most common use of SESSION is to establish or change network or search mappings. You do *not* need to select Change Current Server to create mappings to other servers, once you have attached to those servers and added them to the list shown in Figure 7-2. Why then did the SESSION main menu not just say "Attach to Additional Servers"?

The answer is that SESSION *can* be used to send messages to other users on the network. To send messages through SESSION

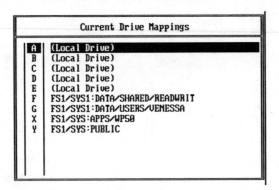

```
┌──────────────────────────────────────────────────┐
│              Current Drive Mappings                │
├──────────────────────────────────────────────────┤
│ █A█  (Local Drive)                                 │
│  B   (Local Drive)                                 │
│  C   (Local Drive)                                 │
│  D   (Local Drive)                                 │
│  E   (Local Drive)                                 │
│  F   FS1/SYS1:DATA/SHARED/READWRIT                 │
│  G   FS1/SYS1:DATA/USERS/VENESSA                   │
│  X   FS1/SYS:APPS/WP50                             │
│  Y   FS1/SYS:PUBLIC                                │
│                                                    │
│                                                    │
│                                                    │
└──────────────────────────────────────────────────┘
```

FIGURE 7-3.   Existing drive mappings

to users logged into servers other than the server you are logged into, you must first change the current server.

Drive Mappings

From the SESSION Available Topics menu, highlight **Drive Mappings** and press (ENTER). A list of your current network drive mappings is displayed (see Figure 7-3).

ADDING A NEW NETWORK MAPPING   To add to this list, press (INSERT). The suggested network drive letter is displayed. You may accept NetWare's choice of drive letters (it is the first available from the top of the alphabet down, excluding A through E), or you may backspace over the letter shown and provide your own choice. You are *not* allowed to use a drive letter already in use.

Press (ENTER). You will see a space in which to either type or insert a directory path for the drive letter you selected. If you know the path, including correct spellings, just type the path (including server and volume names). Be sure to place a colon between the server name and the first directory name.

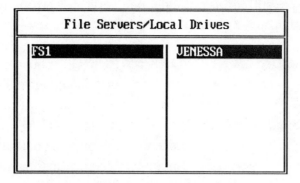

FIGURE 7-4.   List of available servers for mappings

Alternatively, you can press (INSERT). You will see a list of servers available to you (the one to which you are logged in, and any additional servers to which you have already attached) as shown in Figure 7-4.

If you have not previously attached to a server to which you wish to create a mapping, you can do so now. Press (INSERT) and, from a list of available servers, select the server to add to your list of available servers.

Highlight the server name for the path you are defining, and press (ENTER). You now see a list of volumes (at least the volume SYS:). Highlight the volume name for the path you are defining and press (ENTER). Continue selecting directory and subdirectory names, from lists provided, until you have the complete path defined. (If you did not do so earlier, you may chose to map yourself to FS1/SYS:APPS/WP50/MACROS, if this directory structure exists on your server.)

Now press (ESC) and then (ENTER). Your new network drive pointer is added to the list of existing drive pointers. Why (ESC) and then (ENTER)? (ESC) takes you out of Insert mode. Pressing (ENTER) without (ESC) deletes the last portion of your selected path.

You are still in Insert mode, but NetWare performs a "de-insert" function.

DELETING A NETWORK MAPPING   You may delete an existing mapping by highlighting that mapping and pressing the (DELETE) key, followed by the appropriate verification that the deletion is to occur. You are not, however, allowed to delete the drive to which you are currently pointing, the default directory to which you are pointing and to which you are to be returned when you exit the SESSION menu.

Select Default Drive

To change your default drive from within SESSION, highlight **Select Default Drive** and press (ENTER). All of your currently defined drive pointers are listed (see Figure 7-5). Highlight one of them, and press (ENTER). You have changed your current default drive. When you leave the SESSION menu, you will be pointing to the directory you selected.

While you are still viewing the list of current drive mappings, you may display your current effective rights by pressing (ENTER) (having first highlighted the appropriate drive pointer). This is equivalent to issuing the RIGHTS command at the prompt.

Search Mappings

To add to a list of search drive mappings, in the SESSION Available Topics menu highlight **Search Mappings** and press (ENTER). You may add or delete search mappings using the same procedures discussed under "Drive Mappings." The one difference is that NetWare does not allow you to pick the drive pointer to be used.

```
┌─────────────────────────────────────────┐
│           Select Default Drive            │
├───┬───────────────────────────────────────┤
│ A │ (Local Drive)                         │
│ B │ (Local Drive)                         │
│ C │ (Local Drive)                         │
│ D │ (Local Drive)                         │
│ E │ (Local Drive)                         │
│ F │ FS1/SYS1:DATA/SHARED/READWRIT         │
│ G │ FS1/SYS1:DATA/USERS/VENESSA           │
│ H │ FS1/SYS:DATA/SHARED/READONLY          │
│ U │ FS1/SYS:APPS/LOTUS                    │
│ W │ FS1/SYS:APPS/WP50                     │
│ X │ FS1/SYS:APPS/PARADOX3                 │
│ Y │ FS1/SYS:APPS/WP50                     │
│ Z │ FS1/SYS:PUBLIC                        │
└───┴───────────────────────────────────────┘
```

FIGURE 7-5.   Directory list of mappings

Nor may you redefine an existing search drive (or network drive). In SESSION you can only delete or add drive pointers. In this way, NetWare discourages you from simply redefining existing mappings by using a DOS change directory type procedure.

As discussed previously, you need to get out of the habit of using the DOS CD\ command, except as it applies to local drive pointers (A: through E:). If you use CD\ to change the /APPS/WP50 search drive to /APPS, you are no longer pointing to the WP50 subdirectory. And you cannot access WordPerfect executable and command files from the subdirectory WP50 while pointing to the directory APPS. By prohibiting you from redefining an existing search drive mapping in SESSION, NetWare is helping ensure that you do not accidentally delete a needed search drive pointer.

User List and Group List

Highlight **Group List** and press (ENTER). A list of groups set up on your logged into server (or the server to which you changed using

```
Message: From VENESSA[3]:  Are payables ready to be printed?
```

FIGURE 7-6.   SESSION menu SEND command format

---

the Change Current Server option) is displayed. Highlight a user group and press (ENTER). A space is provided in which to type a short message of up to 40 characters. The message is to be sent to all currently logged in members of the group you highlighted. You do not have to place quotation marks around the message when SENDing the message from within SESSION (only when you use the SEND command at the prompt).

From whom the message derives is defined by who *you* are on the server to which you are pointing when you send the message. In the example in Figure 7-6, VENESSA is preparing to send a message to the group ACCOUNTING. The "(3)" after "VENESSA" indicates the station from which the message is sent. This helps tie down exactly who sent the message, since NetWare allows more than one individual to log in under the same user name. (An exception is when Limit Concurrent Connections for that user is set to one. See Chapter 3 for how to use Limit Concurrent Connections, and why *not* to set concurrent connections to one.)

You may send a message to several users by following these steps:

1. Highlight **User List** in the SESSION Available Topics menu and press (ENTER).

2. Highlight and use the (F5) key to mark each user to whom the message is to be sent.

3. Press (ENTER), type the message, and again press (ENTER).

With several users marked, the only option presented to you is to send a message to the marked users. If you highlight a single user and press (ENTER), you are presented with an Available Options menu. You can select the **Display User Info** option and press (ENTER) to view additional, but not very useful, information (see Figure 7-7).

You cannot change this information, even if it is your user name you highlight. The single line around the user information box indicates that the information is for display only. (As indicated previously, NetWare uses double lines around those menus or options where you *can* provide information or perform an action.)

```
Full Name:        (No Full Name Specified)
Object Type:      User
Login Time:       Monday  November 6, 1989   4:02 pm
Network Address:  00000003
Network Node:     00000000000e9
```

FIGURE 7-7.   User information available in SESSION

MORE PERMANENT SESSION MAPPINGS

Any server attachments or mappings you create during a SESSION on the network disappear when you log out of the server. Having to reissue map commands to re-establish drive pointers each time you log in is a real inconvenience.

Fortunately, NetWare allows you to establish for yourself a *user login script,* containing your commonly used SESSION commands.

Many users are not aware that NetWare allows them to create and change their own user login script. The next section explains the process of creating a login script for yourself. However, your user script is only one of three scripts that may exist. Before proceeding to create your own login script, you need to know

- How these three scripts interact with each other

- What statements need to be in a login script

- The format for login script statements

Default, User, and System Login Scripts

Three types of login scripts may exist in NetWare: a default login script, a system login script, and a user login script. No more than two of these scripts ever play when you log in, and only one may play.

As illustrated in the left column of Table 7-2, anytime you do not have a user log in script, the default login script plays. If no system login script exists, only the default login script plays. At the beginning of this chapter you saw the mappings you receive through the default login script. This script includes one mapping you *must* have to work on the server, a mapping to SYS:PUBLIC.

USER SCRIPT EXISTS?

		NO	YES
	NO	Only default login script plays	Only user login script plays
SYSTEM SCRIPT EXISTS?	YES	Default login script plays, followed by system login script	System login script plays, followed by user login script

TABLE 7-2.   Relationship Among Default, System, and User Login Scripts

User login scripts residing on a particular server (stored in user mailbox directories) are associated with a particular user name, and are played by NetWare at the time you log in to that specific server. Some of the script statements a user requires are common to all users on the network. Because the existence of a user login script causes the default login script not to play, all users will need a mapping to SYS:PUBLIC, the directory in which NetWare user commands are located. This mapping to PUBLIC can be included in each individual user login script, or it can be included once in the system login script.

The system login script plays every time a user logs in, in conjunction with either the default login script or, if one is present, the user login script. The system login script will play either after the default login script or before the user login script. It is in the system login script that you will want to place those script statements common to all users.

While a mapping to PUBLIC is included in the default script, the default does not play if you have any user script statements. *If you forget to define a search drive mapping to SYS:PUBLIC in your user login script, and no system login script mapping to PUBLIC exists, you will not be able to do any network activity, not even change your user login script.*

SUPERVISOR Access to PUBLIC

If you are not careful, you can lock out the user SUPERVISOR from effective use of server commands. This happens if you somehow fail to have a mapping to PUBLIC created when SUPERVISOR logs into the server. *To prevent this unhappy state of affairs, it is strongly suggested you place a mapping to SYS:PUBLIC in the user login script of the user you setup as a backup supervisor (see Chapter 3). Also, place a mapping to SYS:PUBLIC in SUPERVISOR's user login script, and leave it there.* When and if you place a mapping to SYS:PUBLIC in the system login script, the user SUPERVISOR will receive a second mapping to PUBLIC. This is by far the preferable circumstance.

Be sure your mapping to PUBLIC in the backup supervisor's user menu works properly before attempting to create a similar mapping in SUPERVISOR's user login script.

You must be logged in as SUPERVISOR or a supervisor-equivalent user to create or change a server's system login script. Some guidance on doing this is provided toward the end of this chapter. Remember that the system script helps define your workstation environment. It is not used to configure the server. A

Command	Use
ATTACH	To attach to additional servers on an internetwork.
MAP	To create network or search drive mappings.
WRITE	To send a text message directly from the login script to the workstation screen.
PAUSE	To pause screen scrolling and display the DOS "Press any key to continue" message.
DISPLAY	To call a saved, unformatted text file from a directory to the workstation screen. (Use FDISPLAY to call a formatted text file to the screen, for unformatted display.)
REMARK	To create login script documentation. REMARK statements appear only as login script text.
FIRE PHASERS *x* TIMES or FIRE *x*	To fire your workstation phaser sound the number of times specified, up to nine times per FIRE command.
#	To temporarily leave the login script and execute a named batch, command, or program executable file: #CAPTURE or #WP.
EXIT or EXIT (filename)	To end playing of the login script(s) and exit to the workstation prompt, or directly to a named program executable, command, or batch file: EXIT C:\RUN.BAT.
IF..THEN, BEGIN	To direct the flow of the login script based on the outcome of a conditional test.
DRIVE	To change the default drives: DRIVE H:.
COMSPEC	To tell your workstation where to look for the DOS COMMAND.COM file: COMSPEC=S2:Command.com.
BREAKON	To allow a user to interrupt login script execution. The default of BREAKOFF is usually preferable.
DOS BREAKON	To allow use of (CTRL-BREAK) after login scripts have finished executing. The default is DOS BREAKOFF.
DOS SET name="value"	Used like the DOS SET command to manage the workstation DOS environment, but with values placed in parentheses: DOS SET PROMPT PG.

TABLE 7-3.   Available Login Script Commands

DOS VERIFY ON	To invoke the DOS verify function when copying data to a local drive. The DOS default is DOS VERIFY OFF.
INCLUDE (filespec)	To process subscripts—mini login script files called into the current script: INCLUDE Z:\PUB-LIC\PARADOX3.MAP
COMPATIBLE or PCCOMPATIBLE	To call a filename while working on an IBM PC-compatible computer (and using a long machine name in a SHELL.CFG file). Used in conjunction with EXIT.

TABLE 7-3.   Available Login Script Commands (*continued*)

separate AUTOEXEC.SYS file is used by SUPERVISOR to configure the server.

Login Script Command Formats

You can include NetWare commands and some DOS command statements within login scripts. In some instances, commands must be capitalized. To ensure you follow proper syntax, turn on the (CAPS LOCK) key and type all login scripts in capital letters.

If used with other commands or as part of conditional tests (IF..THEN statements), the NetWare or DOS command must be placed in quotation marks. While the NetWare command MAP can be typed into a login script just as you would type it at the prompt, other commands (CAPTURE, for instance) must be preceded with a pound sign (#) or Exit command (more on this later).

Some of the statements you can use in a login script are summarized in Table 7-3. Table 7-4 shows a sample login script.

MAP S16:=FS1/SYS:PUBLIC

MAP S16:=FS1/SYS:PUBLIC/DOS

MAP G:=FS1/SYS1:DATA/USERS/%LOGIN_NAME

COMSPEC=S2:Command.com

MAP S16:=FS1/SYS:APPS/WP50

MAP S16:=FS1/SYS:APPS/PARADOX3

MAP H:=FS1/SYS1:DATA/SHARED/READONLY

MAP F:=FS1/SYS1:DATA/SHARED/READWRIT

REMARK The following takes the user into an
REMARK electronic mail program, if he or she
REMARK has "unopened" mail in his or her user
REMARK mailbox (the subdirectory under SYS:MAIL).

IF NEW_MAIL="yes" THEN BEGIN

  WRITE "You have new mail, %LOGIN_NAME."
  #MAIL

 END

REMARK If not a member of the group EXECUTIVE, the
REMARK user is exited from the login script to NetWare's
REMARK MAIN user menu, without a mapping to DATA/EXECUTIV
REMARK being created. If a member of the group EXECUTIVE,
REMARK the user receives a mapping to DATA/EXECUTIV and a
REMARK different custom user menu: EXECUTIV.MNU.

TABLE 7-4.   Sample Login Script

IF NOT MEMBER OF "Executive" THEN BEGIN

#MENU Main.mnu

END
EXIT

MAP M:=FS1/SYS1:DATA/EXECUTIV

#MENU Executiv.mnu

TABLE 7-4.   Sample Login Script (*continued*)

COMMANDS ISSUED AS IF AT THE PROMPT   Commands
that can be typed as though you were issuing the command at the
workstation prompt include the following.

MAP is probably the most used login script command. You type
it exactly as you would at the prompt. WRITE allows you to send
text statements to your screen. PAUSE is used to keep that text
from scrolling off the screen.

You can have an ASCII text file displayed on screen using the
DISPLAY command. For DISPLAY to work, you must have
already created a mapping to the directory that holds the file to be
displayed. Also, you must have done one of the following:

- mapped the directory along a search drive

- used the DRIVE command to switch your current default drive
  pointer to the text file directory (before issuing DISPLAY)

- included the drive pointed to as part of the DISPLAY command

To document your login script, use the REMARK command.

Your workstation can probably make noises, besides the familiar beep. Using FIRE PHASERS you can include a very rudimentary attention getter within your scripts.

CONDITIONAL LOGIN STATEMENTS   You can temporarily leave your login script and execute a DOS batch file by preceding the batch filename with a pound sign (#). You can also use the pound sign to temporarily exit to a program and, when exiting the program, be returned to the same place within your login script (for example, #123).

EXIT is similar to the pound sign, but it exits you permanently from your login script. Any login script statements that appear after an executed EXIT will never play. As with the pound sign (#), you may exit to a named command or to an executable or batch file. For files invoked through either the pound sign (#) or EXIT to execute, you must have first created a mapping to their directory location.

IF..THEN statements allow you to test for a condition, and to play or not play additional login scripts depending on the test's outcome. Relationships that may be tested for in IF..THEN statements include the following:

```
=  or  EQUALS
IS NOT or DOES NOT EQUAL or NOT EQUAL TO
>  or  IS GREATER THAN
<  or  IS LESS THAN
>= or  IS GREATER THAN OR EQUAL TO
<= or  IS LESS THAN OR EQUAL TO
<> or  IS LESS THAN OR GREATER THAN
```

You may create compound conditionals using commas or the word AND. IF..THEN statements are most often used with special NetWare identifier variables.

NETWARE IDENTIFIER VARIABLES   NetWare *identifier variables* extract information from the server or from your workstation and substitute that information within login script statements. A list of available NetWare identifier variables is provided in Table 7-5.

To be distinguished from usual typed words, identifier variables are preceded by a percent (%) sign. For instance, within a WRITE statement, which sends a message to the screen, you could use the following identifier variables:

```
WRITE "Good %GREETING_TIME."
WRITE "The time is %HOUR:%MINUTE %AM_PM."
WRITE "You are logged in to workstation %STATION."
PAUSE
```

The identifier variables are shown in boldface. What you will see when you log in is

```
Good afternoon.
The time is 4:33 pm.
You are logged in to workstation 3.
Strike any key when ready . . .
```

Required or Recommended
Login Script Statements

Following are some login script statements you will find especially useful, along with some that are required.

MAPPING TO SYS:PUBLIC   You must be mapped to PUBLIC to issue NetWare commands and use the server. To find PUBLIC commands no matter where you are pointing with your default drive, make your mapping to PUBLIC a search drive. If there is already a mapping to PUBLIC in the system login script, and you include a second in your user script, you will have created

Identifier Variable	Value or Variable Substituted
HOUR	Server hour of the day or night (1 - 12).
HOUR	Server hour in 24-hour clock format (00 - 23).
MINUTE	Server minute in 60-minute format (00 - 59).
SECOND	Server seconds in 60-second format (00 - 59).
AM_PM	AM or PM time modifier.
GREETING_TIME	Morning, afternoon, or evening.
MONTH	Server month number (01 - 12).
MONTH_NAME	Server month name
DAY_OF_WEEK	Server day of the week (Sunday - Saturday).
DAY	Day number (01 - 21) for server month and day.
NDAY_OF_WEEK	Server weekday number (1 - 7; Sunday = 1).
YEAR	Server year, fully formatted (1970, 2010).
SHORT_YEAR	Server year, last two digits (70, 10).
LOGIN_NAME	User's LOGIN name (Venessa, Doug) from server.
FULL_NAME	Server full name, if defined (see SYSCON).
MEMBER OF "group"	Name of group, used in IF..THEN tests.
NEW_MAIL	Test answer is YES or NO, depending on whether files have been placed in user's mailbox directory which the user has not yet accessed.
STATION	Workstation number, from server station count.
P_STATION	Physical station hexidecimal number, from workstation NIC (network interface card).
SHELL_TYPE	Shell type number (from workstation shell).
OS	The workstation's operating system, as known from the workstation shell or SHELL.CFG file, e.g., IBM_DOS, MS_DOS, OS/2.
OS_VERSION	The version of the workstation's operating system—V2.0, V2.1, etc.—as known from the workstation shell or SHELL.CFG file. Note: revision number (V2.12) is never specified.
MACHINE	The workstation machine name as specified in the workstation shell or SHELL.CFG file, e.g., IBM_PC, COMPAQ, KAYPRO.
SMACHINE	The short machine name specified in the workstation shell or SHELL.CFG file, e.g., IBM.
ERROR_LEVEL	A number representing no errors (0) or the presence of errors (any number other than 0).

TABLE 7-5. NetWare Identifier Variables for Use in Login Scripts

two search drive mappings to PUBLIC. However, this is preferable to no mappings. *Always include a mapping to PUBLIC in your user login script, until you know for sure there is a system script that does this job for you.*

MAPPING TO DOS ON THE SERVER   If you are supporting DOS on the server (perhaps as a subdirectory under SYS:PUBLIC), you can have all DOS commands available to you by creating a search drive mapping to DOS. If you support only one version of DOS on the server, appropriate for all workstations on your LAN, your DOS mapping may be as simple and straightforward as shown in line 2 of Table 7-4. A more complicated version of a DOS mapping, appropriate for a system login script, is discussed briefly at the end of this chapter.

COMSPEC   It is important that your workstation knows from which drive and directory to reload your DOS COMMAND.COM file. DOS would normally look to your current, default drive, and then along a DOS path. Since you will not want to use the DOS PATH command—it tends to get confounded when you also use search mappings—you need to use COMSPEC to define the location of COMMAND.COM. The COMSPEC statement can point to any of your workstation server directories as the designated location for COMMAND.COM. Here are some examples of COMSPEC statements:

```
COMSPEC=S2:Command.com
COMSPEC=Y:Command.com
COMSPEC=C:Command.com
```

These statements are valid only if COMMAND.COM resides in the location specified.

COMSPEC=Y:Command.com is equivalent to COMSPEC=S1:Command.com, but the former is preferable. Even if you inadvertently redefine Search Drive 2, it remains a network drive. Pointing with Y:, COMMAND.COM would be reloaded, even if it was not on a search drive. NetWare used the pointer, not the search drive approach, to finding COMMAND.C0M. Of course, this assumes you know that Y: is the pointer assigned to Search Drive 2.

Creating a User Login Script

To create a user login script like that shown in Table 7-4, you must be logged into a server, either as SUPERVISOR, or under the user name whose script you wish to create.

Type **SYSCON** at the prompt and press (ENTER) to call up the NetWare SYSCON menu. (Or issue the MENU MAIN command and select **4. System Configuration**.)

Within SYSCON, highlight **User Information** and press (ENTER), move the cursor down to the user name under which you logged in and press (ENTER). A User Information submenu is displayed (see Figure 3-11 in Chapter 3). Type **L** to select **Login Script** (or move the cursor down to **Login Script**) and press (ENTER).

If you currently do not have a login script, you will see a blank screen. If a user login script already exists, consider whether you really wish to change it. If you wish to develop your own script, be sure to start with a correct mapping to SYS:PUBLIC, or you may be locked out of the server.

Keep in mind that what you see happen as you develop a login script will be different depending on whether there is an existing system login script.

Rest assured on one point: changing your own personal login script will not destroy the network, nor will it affect other users logged into the network. Try typing in login statements one at a time. To see the consequence of your script addition, exit back to the prompt and log in again. For instance:

1. In the login space provided, use the MAP command to map SYS:PUBLIC as a search drive:

   MAP S16:=(servername)/SYS:PUBLIC

2. Press (ESC) to save your user script.

3. Press (ALT-F10) to quickly exit from SYSCON.

4. LOG IN again under the same user name. You do not have to log out to log in.

5. Re-enter SYSCON and add login statements of your choosing.

Repeat steps 2 through 4 after each login statement is added to see the effects of your work.

There are simple editing tools available to help you develop the scripts. Press (F1) twice to get help on what keys you may use in NetWare menus. Once you have completed the previous exercise, try this:

1. Go to the first line in the left corner of your login script. This should be your MAP S16:=(servername)/SYS:PUBLIC mapping.

2. Press the (F5) (Mark) key.

3. Press the (END) key, to highlight the entire first line of your login script.

4. Press the (DOWN) arrow key once (or more to include other login script statements within the highlighted area).

5. Press the (DELETE) key to delete the highlighted (marked) text.

6. Move down to the bottom of your login script.

7. Press (INSERT).

You should have just moved part of your login script to the bottom of the entire script. However, login script statements that appear before your mapping to PUBLIC will not execute. They reside in PUBLIC, and PUBLIC does not exist until mapped. Before ending this user login script session, use the (F5) (Mark) key to cut and paste your PUBLIC mapping back to the top of your user login script.

For additional instruction on use of login scripts, see Appendix A of the Novell NetWare *Supervisor Reference* manual.

BORROWING USER SCRIPTS AS SUPERVISOR

You will find this section both instructive and helpful if you are the user SUPERVISOR and are responsible for accuracy and usefulness of all user login scripts.

If a user on the server does not yet have an existing user login script, you may copy another user's script, in its entirety, into the login script space of the first user. You must be logged in as SUPERVISOR or a supervisor-equivalent user to accomplish this.

1. In SYSCON, select **User Information** and highlight a user name for whom no login script yet exists.

2. Press (ENTER) to view the User Information submenu, and then select **Login Script**.

3. Press (ENTER) and you will see the screen shown in Figure 7-8.

4. Press (INSERT) NetWare shows a list of all users on the server.

5. Move the cursor to the user whose script you wish to copy and press (ENTER) twice.

```
┌─────────────────────────────────────────────────┐
│            Login Script Does Not Exist            │
├─────────────────────────────────────────────────┤
│ Read Login Script From User:   VENESSA            │
└─────────────────────────────────────────────────┘
```

FIGURE 7-8.   "Login Script Does Not Exist" prompt

You have just copied a user login script. Note that this procedure does not exist in some earlier versions of NetWare.

You can cut and paste all or parts of one user's login script to another user's login script. This works only on versions of Net-Ware that do not clear the cut and paste buffer when you exit a user login script.

The procedure is as follow:

1. Through **SYSCON, User Information**, etc, go to the first user's login script, the one you wish to use in whole or in part.

2. Use the (F5) (Mark) and cursor keys to highlight the portion of the login script you wish to "borrow."

3. Press (DELETE). This places the highlighted portion of this first user script into the NetWare edit buffer.

4. *This next step is very important. Before you do anything else, press* (INSERT) once to add the borrowed login script (or portion of login script) back into the original user's script.

5. Press (ESC) until you are back at the User Names list.

6. Highlight the user into whose script the copied script statements are to go. Press (ENTER) and select **Login Script** from the User Information list.

7. Press (ENTER) to view the existing script for this second user.

8. Move the cursor to the location where you want to insert the copied script and press (INSERT). (If no user script yet exists for this second user, press (ENTER) twice. Then press (INSERT).)

The ability to borrow or copy one user's login script to another user's script makes your job of SUPERVISOR easier. However, the greater simplification comes in use of the system login script to define those script statements that apply to all users.

CHANGING THE SYSTEM LOGIN SCRIPT

You must be logged in as SUPERVISOR or a supervisor- equivalent user to view or change the system login script. Within **SYSCON**, go to **Supervisor Options** and press (ENTER); then select **System Login Script**. When you press (ENTER), you will see a screen just like the one in which you enter user login scripts. The difference is that what you place in the system login script screen will always play before any user login script statements and will play regardless of what user is logging in.

 It is highly recommended that you include in the system login script a search drive mapping to the directory PUBLIC.

If DOS is supported from you server, you may also chose to include a search mapping in the system login script to DOS and the COMSPEC statement.

If you support more than one version of DOS from the server, where the DOS version in use must be specific to a particular machine, you may chose to create your DOS search drive mapping using NetWare %MACHINE, %OS, and %OS_VERSION identifier variables. The mapping would look something like this:

MAP S16:=FS1/SYS:PUBLIC/%MACHINE/%OS/%OS_VERSION

Your server name might not be FS1, and your DOS versions need not have been included under the PUBLIC directory. Similarly, one or another of the identifier variables might not be needed, depending on the nature of your directory structure.

For a mapping to be created automatically, you must

- have a machine name, operating system name, and/or version identifier included within your server directory structure

- have included these directory names, as spelled on your server, either within the actual NetWare shell loaded at the workstation being logged into or in a SHELL.CFG file, which is loaded when the user boots the workstation

For more information on the SHELL.CFG file, see Chapter 10 or Appendix B of the NetWare *Supervisor Reference* manual.

Another statement you may wish to include in the system login script is a mapping to user home directories. You can do this once within the system login script by using the LOGIN_NAME identifier variable as follows:

MAP H:=FS1/SYS1:DATA/USERS/%LOGIN_NAME

While your directory path to the user's named home directory may be different from FS1, SYS1:, DATA, or USERS, the user name logged in with is always substituted in the defined path in place of %LOGIN_NAME.

However, this works only if you have created, at that location within your server's directory structure, a home (sub)directory name that is spelled *exactly* as the name used to log in to the network.

Summary

NetWare SESSION commands from the SESSION menu allow you to customize your work environment (through the LOGIN, ATTACH, and MAP commands) and to learn useful information about your rights (with the RIGHTS command). You may also use the SESSION SEND command (or options under the Group List and User List SESSION Available Topics) to communicate a short message to other users currently logged into the network servers (to which you are attached). CASTOFF and CASTON allow you to control whether you are tied into this direct, peer-to-peer communication network. MENU allows you to call a custom menu for use in organizing and simplifying your session activities.

To avoid having to reissue session commands each time you log into the server, you may place often-used SESSION commands in your user login script. If you are the user SUPERVISOR, you may place scripts that apply to all users in the system login script, or copy or borrow login scripts from one user to another. A mapping to SYS:PUBLIC is required by all users, including SUPERVISOR.

More complex login scripts are discussed in Chapter 10.

NETWARE FILER COMMANDS

NetWare Directory and File-Management Commands
The NetWare FILER Menu
Summary

This chapter introduces you to commands available to you and other users to help you manage files and directories. While many DOS commands are available—DIR and COPY, for instance—NetWare's commands provide added versatility to file- and directory-management tasks.

NetWare also includes a menu, FILER, which is helpful both to new users, who may not know or feel comfortable issuing commands from the prompt, and to any user who must cope with a complex, multilevel, multivolume, and possibly multiple-server directory structure.

To use these commands, you must have effective search rights in the directories toward which you are directing the commands.

An effective search right is the minimum right necessary to retrieve information from a NetWare volume's directory entry table. In the absence of a NetWare search right, directory or file information that may reside in the directory entry table is simply not displayed, and thus not known to a user.

Some commands, NCOPY for instance, require additional rights, appropriate both to the directory *from* which a file is copied and to the directory *to* which the file is copied.

For most of the examples included in this chapter you will log in as a nonsupervisor-equivalent user and will need a mapping to your own home directory, in which you will need all effective rights (Create, Write, Search, Open, Read, Delete, Modify, and Parental). If GUEST is set up on your server with a home directory, this may suffice. Or, if you worked through the exercises in Chapters 4 and 5 you should be able to log in as VENESSA and have the mappings and nearly all the effective directory security rights necessary to complete the examples in this chapter. However, you will find it necessary to add the Parental right back into VENESSA's home directory, and possibly into GUEST's home directory, if you choose to be logged in as GUEST while working through later parts of this chapter. See the "Creating New Directories and Trustee Assignments Through SYSCON: User Home Subdirectories" section of Chapter 4 for guidance on how to add a trustee right back into VENESSA's home subdirectory trustee assignment.

If you are already a user on the network and have your own home directory, with all effective rights, you can log in as yourself in place of VENESSA (though you will need some understanding of your server's current directory structure). Ask your network supervisor or manager for assistance in readying the network for working through this chapter.

NETWARE DIRECTORY AND FILE-MANAGEMENT COMMANDS

NetWare directory and file-management commands provide considerable functionality beyond DOS. To explore these commands, log in as the user GUEST.

LISTDIR and NDIR

LISTDIR and NDIR are NetWare's equivalents to the DOS DIR command. While the DOS DIR command lists subdirectories and files mixed together, the NetWare commands list subdirectories separately from files.

LISTDIR/S/R/D OR LISTDIR/A   Issuing LISTDIR at the prompt without qualification lists the names of the subdirectories that appear immediately beneath the volume, directory, or subdirectory to which you are currently pointing. If you wish to see *all* subdirectory names beneath your default directory, issue LISTDIR with an /S flag.

To see NetWare's required directory structure (and subdirectories) first map yourself to the volume SYS, using a drive letter of your choosing.

MAP K:=(servername)/SYS:

Next, type the chosen drive letter (**K:**) and press (ENTER). Now issue the LISTDIR command with the /S flag: type **LISTDIR/S** and press (ENTER). You will see a directory listing similar to the following:

The sub-directory structure of FS1/SYS:
SYSTEM
 040015
 05001B
 070023
 33001B
 0123
LOGIN
MAIN
 C00DF
 B011F
 1
 20007
 4005D
PUBLIC
DOS
  V2.0
  V3.0

You will notice that the directories SYSTEM and LOGIN are displayed in this directory listing, even though you have no effective rights in these directories. In a friendly gesture, NetWare allows you to always see a directory and subdirectory structure (using LISTDIR), *even if you have no effective Search rights in one or more of the directories listed.*

To print a copy of this directory structure, issue the LISTDIR command with a DOS redirection parameter, for example

K:\LISTDIR/S >LPT1:

The listing will be printed to either a network printer or a local printer attached to the workstation, depending on whether the NetWare CAPTURE command has previously been issued (refer to Chapter 9). Printing the directory structure using the /S flag is a quick way to document a volume's directory structure.

You may use other flags to display the maximum rights mask or creation date of subdirectories beneath your default directory. For instance:

LISTDIR/R	(displays a subdirectory's Maximum Rights Mask)
LISTDIR/D	(displays the date and time a subdirectory was created)
LISTDIR/A	(displays both Maximum Rights Mask and creation date time of all subdirectories beneath a directory)

Issuing the command LISTDIR/A >LPT1: will provide you a complete documentation of your existing directory structure.

NDIR   The NetWare NDIR command is a much more powerful command than DOS's DIR command. The familiar DOS wildcard characters (* and ?) are available to you. However, by using a SUB parameter, you can search for a file (or files) in all directories and all subdirectories of a hard disk volume (for which you have a Search effective right). To do this in DOS would require continually changing directories and reissuing the DIR command.

While pointing to the root volume SYS: of your server, issue the following command:

NDIR *.EXE SUB

Press (ENTER) and after a momentary delay you will see a listing of all executable files beneath your SYS volume, displayed directory by directory. As GUEST, VENESSA, or as yourself on the server, you may not have Search rights in all SYS subdirectories. To the extent this is true the listing you see is incomplete.

However, this SUB flag is very useful in these circumstances:

- You place a file in an incorrect directory and then cannot locate that file.

- You need to remove unused or duplicate copies of files or old unused files from your server hard disk.

In the first instance, issuing NDIR from a root volume, followed by the name of the lost file and the SUB parameter, shows in which directories the file actually resides. You can use a wildcard character in such a search. For example, you might look for all NetWare custom menu files, with this command:

NDIR *.MNU SUB

NDIR will perform a complete search of all directories on the volume pointed to only if you have a Search right in all directories where .MNU files reside. But even as a nonsupervisor-equivalent user, NDIR (filespec) SUB is a useful tool. (If you do not have a Search effective right in a directory, you probably have no rights in that directory, and so would neither have lost a file in that directory location nor have any business working in that location.)

In the second instance, you can print a complete listing of all files in all directories by issuing this NDIR command:

NDIR *.* SUB >LPT1:

With NDIR you can also do the following:

- Exclude files from an NDIR listing: NDIR NOT *.MNU

- Include files by OWNER, the person who created the file originally: NDIR *.MNU OWNER=VENESSA

- Sort files by size, in descending order: NDIR REVERSE SIZE GR 20

- List all files in all subdirectories by their file flag attributes: NDIR RO SUB

FILENAME [NOT]=file	OWNER [NOT]=name
ACCESS [NOT] BEFore I=I AFTer mm-dd-yy	
UPDATE [NOT] BEFore I=I AFTer mm-dd-yy	
CREATE [NOT] BEFore I=I AFTer mm-dd-yy	
SIZE [NOT] GReater than I=I LEss than nnn	
[NOT] SYstem	[NOT] Modified
[NOT] Hidden	[NOT] Indexed
[NOT] ReadWrite	[NOT] ReadOnly
[NOT] SHAreable	[NOT] ExecutableOnly
[NOT] Transactional	
[REVERSE] SORT FILENAME	[REVERSE] SORT OWNER
[REVERSE] SORT ACCESS	[REVERSE] SORT UPDATE
[REVERSE] SORT CREATE	[REVERSE] SORT SIZE
FilesOnly	BRief
DirectoriesOnly	SUBdirectories

TABLE 8-1.   NDIR Command Parameters

Several of the commands listed here use NDIR parameters in combination with each other. A complete listing of available NDIR parameters is shown in Table 8-1.

NCOPY

NCOPY works like the DOS copy command except that NCOPY displays, for each file, the directory from which the file was copied and the directory to which the file was copied, along with the filenames used in each directory. The DOS COPY verify flag (/V) can be included with NCOPY. NetWare performs a DOS-type verification that the copied file is of the same size as the original.

In most instances, the DOS COPY command, with its own verify flag included, will have the same effect as the NetWare

NCOPY command. One difference is that you can use NCOPY to copy a file from one directory to another, even if no mappings currently exist to those directories, for example:

NCOPY /DATA/USERS/DOUG/TESTFILE.DLW /DATA/SHARED/USETHIS

Appropriate effective rights are required in the directories from and to which files are copied. For instance, you can copy files from the directory PUBLIC to your home user directory when you have these rights:

- Search, Open, and Read rights in the PUBLIC directory (the minimum rights required to copy a file from a NetWare directory).

- Create and Write rights in your home directory (the minimum rights required to create a file with a new filename in a directory).

- Search, Open, Read, and Write rights in your home directory (the minimum rights required to write a file to a directory in which the filename is already in use).

COPYING FROM PUBLIC TO YOUR HOME DIRECTORY

To demonstrate the effect of NetWare effective rights on use of the NCOPY command, log in again as a user who is not a supervisor-equivalent for whom a home directory has been established on the server (VENESSA, GUEST, or yourself). (If necessary, go back to Chapter 4 and set up VENESSA on your server as a user with her own home subdirectory, and with all rights in that home subdirectory.)

Issue the MAP command to be sure you are mapped to PUBLIC and to your home directory. (See the previous chapter for guidance on issuing the MAP command to create a mapping to either

PUBLIC or to your home directory, if either does not already exist for you.)

The example provided here assumes Z: is used to point to PUBLIC and G: to point to your home directory. Substitute a different drive letter as appropriate.

Since you are allowed to use drive pointers in issuing the NCOPY command, neither PUBLIC nor your home directory has to be your default drive. From any current drive pointer, issue the following NCOPY command:

NCOPY Z:*.MNU G:*.NEW

You will see a listing of NetWare custom menu files copied from PUBLIC to that other directory, under a new filename, one with a .NEW extension.

Exactly what you see on screen will depend on how many .MNU files are currently in PUBLIC (only one if you are on a newly installed server). But you will see something like the following:

```
From FS1/SYS: PUBLIC
TO   FS1/SYS1:DATA/USERS/VENESSA
     MAIN.MNU            to MAIN.NEW
     MAINMENU.MNU        to MAINMENU.NEW
     ESTIM.MNU           to ESTIM.NEW
     ARNOLD.MNU          to ARNOLD.NEW
     ESTIMATE.MNU        to ESTIMATE.NEW
     EXECUTIV.MNU        to EXECUTIV.NEW
     DOTTIE.MNU          to DOTTIE.NEW
```

DIRECTING COPY TOWARE THE SERVER As previously mentioned, the DOS COPY command can be used to copy files from one server directory to another. Both to demonstrate how the DOS COPY command works, and in preparation for a future exercise, type **COPY Z:*.MNU G:*.BAK** at the prompt and press (ENTER.) You should see a DOS message on screen telling you that one or more .MNU files were copied and saved with the file extension .BAK.

To determine that copying was successful, type **NDIR G:*.NEW** at the prompt and press (ENTER).

Again, assuming G: is the drive pointer to your home directory, to which you just copied one or more files with a .NEW extension, try copying the .NEW files back to PUBLIC. Type **NCOPY G:*.NEW Z:** at the prompt and press (ENTER). As a nonsupervisor-equivalent user, you will receive the following message:

You have no rights to copy files to the specified directory.

The DOS DEL and ERASE Commands And the NetWare SALVAGE Command

NetWare does not provide a specific command for deleting or erasing files from the prompt. However, you can

- Delete files through the NetWare FILER utility (discussed at the end of this chapter)

- Use the DOS DEL or ERASE command to delete files from a server hard disk volume.

As with a DOS workstation hard disk, the deleted or erased file is not really removed. Only the reference to the file in a volume's directory entry table (or file allocation table on a DOS workstation hard disk) is deleted.

Because a file is not actually removed from a hard disk, in a DOS environment you can use special utilities, such as the Norton Utilities to recover deleted or erased files located on the DOS workstation hard disk. To the extent that recovery of files is possible, you can continue to use the Norton Utilities or a similar utility *at your workstation hard disk. However, you cannot use these DOS hard disk utilities on a NetWare server hard disk.*

Fortunately, in certain defined instances, NetWare has provided a means for recovering files you did not intend to delete. You will see how this works after first deleting a file by using the DOS DEL command.

DELETING AND SALVAGING A SINGLE FILE   Probably you are already logged in as a nonsupervisor-equivalent user, perhaps as GUEST or VENESSA. If you are not sure, type **WHOAMI** at the prompt and press (ENTER) and NetWare will tell you who you are on the network.

You do not want to inadvertently erase any NetWare program files. To avoid that risk, log in as GUEST or as another non-supervisor-equivalent user. Then type WHOAMI/A at the prompt and press (ENTER) to check your user status.

Now type **G:** and press (ENTER) to switch to your home directory pointer (or to whichever directory you copied NetWare menu files with the extension .NEW).

At the prompt, type **DEL MAIN.NEW** (being sure to include the .NEW extension) and press (ENTER). You have just deleted the renamed .NEW copy of NetWare's MAIN.MNU file from your home directory, although DOS will not give you a message to that effect. Before doing anything else:

1. Type **SALVAGE** at the prompt.

2. Press (ENTER).

You will see a message telling you that the MAIN.NEW files has been salvaged.

```
Salvaging files on volume FS1/SYS1:
MAIN.NEW      recovered.
```

You are able to recover the deleted file because NetWare has not yet deleted the reference to the file from the server volume directory entry table. Once the reference to the file in the directory entry table is deleted, you are out of luck.

DELETING AND SALVAGING MULTIPLE FILES You also can use SALVAGE to recover multiple file deletions, if the files were deleted as a group.

1. To delete all files, at the prompt type **DEL *.*** and press (ENTER).

2. Confirm your wish to delete all files by typing **Y** and pressing (ENTER).

3. Check that all files were deleted by typing **NDIR** and pressing (ENTER).

4. To recover all deleted files, at the prompt type **SALVAGE** and press (ENTER).

At a minimum, you deleted the files MAIN.NEW and MAIN.BAK (copied to your directory through the instructions given earlier in this chapter) and, because these files were deleted through one delete operation, you recovered both files (and any other files deleted from your directory in step 1).

THE LIMITS TO SALVAGE SALVAGE works only under these conditions:

• You issue SALVAGE prior to deleting or erasing any more files.

• You have not issued the PURGE command.

• You are still logged into the server.

Stated conversely, the reference to a file is deleted by NetWare from a server volume's directory entry table when

• You delete a second file.

• You issue the NetWare PURGE command.

- You log out of the server, log in as another user (thereby automatically logging out of the session on the network during which you deleted a file), or are disconnected from the server.

To demonstrate this complication, while pointing to your home directory, again type **DEL MAIN.NEW** and press (ENTER). Now type **DEL MAIN.BAK** and press (ENTER). You have deleted the MAIN.NEW and MAIN.BAK files one at a time. Type **NDIR** and press (ENTER) to confirm that neither MAIN.NEW nor MAIN.BAK are any longer among your home directory files.

Type **SALVAGE** and press (ENTER). You will see that only the last deleted file (MAIN.BAK) is recovered by NetWare.

If you believe you have deleted a file you need to recover, issue SALVAGE before doing any other activity.

RECOVERING DELETED FILES FROM WITHIN AN AP-PLICATION   Many applications, such as WordPerfect, automatically create and delete files when you enter and leave the application package. If you delete a file while within WordPerfect (or a similar application package) and try to leave the package to recover the file, you will be unsuccessful. WordPerfect's automatic file deletion activity represents a second deletion action subsequent to your own deletion of a file from within WordPerfect.

If you delete a file while within WordPerfect (or any similar application):

1. Stay within the application, do not exit the application.

2. Go to the DOS Shell (available through most application packages).

3. Issue the SALVAGE command from the DOS Shell.

4. Exit back to the application package.

In making this observation about how WordPerfect works, the intent is not to be critical of that package. You will encounter the same type of problem with most, if not all, network application packages. And WordPerfect does allow you to go to the DOS Shell to recover files using the SALVAGE command. The purpose here is to make you aware of the pitfalls, and opportunities, available in using the SALVAGE command to recover deleted files.

PURGE and CHKVOL

PURGE and CHKVOL are used to manage your server volumes' directory entry tables and hard disk space.

PURGE   PURGE is a special NetWare command that allows you to delete from a directory entry table the reference to files deleted with the DOS DELETE or ERASE commands. An implied, PURGE occurs when you log out of the server, so you will not normally need to use the PURGE command. And because PURGE makes deleted files unrecoverable through SALVAGE, PURGE is a command best avoided in usual circumstances.

However, there is one circumstance where PURGE is most useful. If you are running out of disk space, you may delete files to make room for other files that must be stored to disk before you log out. This works fine, as long you have free directory entries in your hard disk volume directory entry table. (See Chapter 2 for a discussion of directory entries.) If you delete files to make room for other files, but do not have any directory entries available, you will not be able to reuse the disk space occupied by the deleted files. Issuing the PURGE command frees up directory entries occupied by the files you have deleted.

CHKVOL   CHKVOL displays information about the following:

- a volume's available disk space

- a volume's available directory entries

- the amount of disk space available to you as a user

The disk space available to you as a user will be all remaining disk space on that volume, unless

- you installed NetWare to allow limits to be placed on the amount of network hard disk storage available to a user

- you invoked restrictions through NetWare accounting (via SYSCON)

At the prompt type **CHKVOL** and press (ENTER). You will see the following type of information displayed

```
Statistics for fixed volume FS1/SYS1:
    57593856 bytes total volume space,
    20074496 bytes in 989 files,
    37519360 bytes remaining on volume,
    37519360 bytes available to user VENESSA,
        2979 directory entries available.
```

If you are supporting more than one volume on your server, you may issue CHKVOL with the named volume specified, for example CHKVOL SYS.

CHKVOL has no purpose other than providing information about the status of your hard disk volumes.

FLAG

You can view information about file attributes (ReadOnly or Read-Write, Shareable or Non-shareable, and so forth) and change file attributes with the NetWare FLAG command. You must have effective Search rights in a directory to view file attributes. To alter a file's attributes you must have effective Parental and Modify rights within the directory in which the file resides.

You will seldom have need of the FLAG command. Effective directory structure and security planning obviates the need to alter file attributes in almost all instances.

VIEWING FILE ATTRIBUTES   While pointing to your home user directory, type **FLAG** at the prompt and press (ENTER). You will see a list of all files in your home directory along with their current file attributes. Here is an example of such a listing.

```
FS1/SYS1:DATA/USERS/VENESSA
    DOTTIE.BAK          Non-shareable Read/Write
    EXECUTIV.BAK        Non-shareable Read/Write
    MAIN.BAK            Non-shareable Read/Write
    ESTIMATE.BAK        Non-shareable Read/Write
    ARNOLD.BAK          Non-shareable Read/Write
    ESTIM.BAK           Non-shareable Read/Write
    MAINMENU.BAK        Non-shareable Read/Write
    DOTTIE.NEW          Non-shareable Read/Write
    EXECUTIV.NEW        Non-shareable Read/Write
    ESTIMATE.NEW        Non-shareable Read/Write
    ARNOLD.NEW          Non-shareable Read/Write
    ESTIM.NEW           Non-shareable Read/Write
    MAINMENU.NEW        Non-shareable Read/Write
    MAIN.NEW            Non-shareable Read/Write
```

CHANGING FILE ATTRIBUTES   The normal attributes of newly created files are Non-shareable Read-Write. To change the attributes of the MAIN.BAK file from Non-shareable Read-Write to Non-shareable ReadOnly, at the prompt type **FLAG MAIN.BAK RO** and press (ENTER).

You will see the following message on the screen:

FS1/SYS1:DATA/USERS/VENESSA
MAIN.BAK   Non-shareable ReadOnly

Because you were not changing the Non-shareable attribute, you did not have to include this attribute as part of your FLAG command. Changing the MAIN.BAK file attributes to ReadOnly ensures that the file will not be changed by other users.

It is possible to use wildcards with the FLAG command, and you can even apply the FLAG command to all subdirectories beneath a directory, though this is not recommended. For instance, by issuing the command FLAG *.MNU RO SUB while pointing at the root directory SYS, you would change the current attributes of all .MNU files to ReadOnly in those directories in which you have effective Modify and Parental rights.

Using the SUB parameter with the FLAG command might do no great harm if you are logged in as a user with minimal rights (in particular, no Parental or Modify rights) in either the NetWare required directories or in shared data directories. But if you use this approach while logged in as SUPERVISOR, or as a supervisor-equivalent, you could easily change file attributes of files you had no intention of changing, and without any awareness of what their previous attribute status had been.

In short, FLAG is a powerful tool, too powerful to use indiscriminately, which is what you are doing when you begin to use wildcards in filenames along with the FLAG SUB parameter.

The DOS MD and CD Commands
And the NetWare RENDIR Command

The RENDIR command allows you to rename a directory or subdirectory. To perform this task you need only Modify effective rights in the volume or directory from which the directory or subdirectory to be renamed branches. To see how this command works, point to your home directory.

MD AND CD   To create a directory beneath your home directory you can use the DOS MD or MKDIR command. You will, however, have to include the entire path when issuing this command. Even though it is a DOS command you are issuing, because you are directing that command toward the server you must have NetWare effective rights appropriate and sufficient to this task.

If you were the user VENESSA on the directory established in Chapter 5, you would type MD\DATA\USERS\VENESSA\ MAKEADIR and press (ENTER). And to change to this new directory, using the DOS CD or CHDIR command, you would type CD\DATA\USERS\VENESSA\MAKEADIR. However, please do not do this just yet. (If you did, switch back to your home directory, type **CD\DATA\USERS\VENESSA** and press (ENTER).)

The DOS requirement that an entire path be defined when using MD\ and CD\ is enough to deter most users from using these commands when pointing to network directories. And this is just as well. Users should be discouraged from indiscriminately using the DOS CD command. CD alters your current, default NetWare mapping. Using CD, you lose the original mapping. This is not always a problem, but it can be a serious problem.

Similarly, users should avoid changing directory and subdirectory names, unless they are well aware of the consequence of their actions. In particular, login script mappings that use existing names remain unchanged when a directory is renamed. In effect, that login script mapping is lost, unless the login script is also appropriately changed. That said, it is time to take a look at the NetWare RENDIR command.

RENDIR   Try now to use the NetWare rename directory command. At the prompt, while pointing to your home directory, the directory from which MAKEADIR branches, type

RENDIR MAKEADIR to ALTERDIR

Now press (ENTER). If you followed the instructions exactly, you have renamed MAKEADIR to ALTERDIR. You will see the message

FS1/SYS:DATA/USERS/VENESSA/MAKEADIR
Directory renamed to ALTERDIR

In this RENDIR command the "to" is optional. You could have typed RENDIR MAKEADIR ALTERDIR.

You will have noticed that you did not have to provide a full path definition when issuing the RENDIR command. Your current, default mapping was already pointing to the directory you wished to rename. In fact, you could have been pointing at the directory to be renamed and used a period in place of the default directory name and the RENDIR command would have worked just fine. To try this, first type **CD\DATA\USERS\VENESSA\ ALTERDIR** and press (ENTER). At the prompt, type **RENDIR . to CHANGED** and press (ENTER).

If you are renaming a directory that is not included as the last directory in your current, default path, you will need to do one of the following:

- issue RENDIR with the entire path specified

- use a / to indicate that the renaming is to occur at the next level down from your current, default directory

To try the latter approach, change back to your home directory. (Type **CD\DATA/USERS/VENESSA** and press (ENTER). Or simply log in again, if by logging in you have a mapping to your home directory automatically created for you.) While pointing to your home directory, at the prompt type

RENDIR /ALTERDIR to THISISIT

Press (ENTER) to complete the RENDIR command procedure.

Use the LISTDIR command to check if you were successful. At the prompt, type **LISTDIR** and press (ENTER). (If the list of subdirectories beneath your home directory does not include THISISIT it may be because you were not initially successful in changing MAKEADIR to THISISIT. Try issuing the command as RENDIR /MAKEADIR THISISIT.)

The RENDIR command is a powerful and useful tool, and is one that NetWare power users will make use of. *However, be sure that your power users do not have Modify rights in directories and subdirectories you would not wish to have renamed. (Or move the RENDIR.EXE command from PUBLIC to the SYSTEM directory, thereby making it unavailable to your users.* This is an extreme measure, and not recommended, but it is an option open to you as SUPERVISOR.)

HOLDON and HOLDOFF

If you wish to keep a file open, and prevent other users from writing to the file while you are working on it, you can type **HOLDON** at the prompt and press (ENTER). This command does not prevent other users from reading a file on which you have placed a hold. It does prevent other users from writing a copy of the file back to its originating directory under its original filename, while the original file is still in use. The phrase "still in use" is a critical qualifier, as the following discussion illustrates.

If one user types **HOLDON** and presses (ENTER) at the prompt, and then enters Lotus 1-2-3, any file he or she creates and saves will have a HOLDON attribute set for it at the time of saving. If it is a new spreadsheet that is saved, no other user will be able to either read or write to that file, until after the first user releases the file (either by leaving Lotus 1-2-3 or by recalling a saved copy of the file back into Lotus 1-2-3). Any attempt to read or write to the file will be met within Lotus 1-2-3 with a "Disk error" message (a cryptic and misleading message).

If it is an existing file that the first user calls into the Lotus 1-2-3 workspace, other users can access that file, and save it back to the same directory under a new filename. And, while the first user is viewing or changing the file, another user cannot write the file back to the same directory under its original filename (the name under which both users retrieved the file into Lotus 1-2-3).

However, once the first user exits Lotus 1-2-3, the second user can save the file under its original name to the same directory with the changes he or she made to the file. And therein lies a problem: the second user is unaware of any changes the first user may have made to the file and saved to disk under the existing filename before exiting Lotus 1-2-3.

In short, HOLDON does not fully resolve your problem of earlier versions of Lotus 1-2-3 not being network, multiuser application packages. Accidental overwriting of each others files is still possible, even with HOLDON activated.

To reverse the effects of HOLDON, type **HOLDOFF** at the prompt and press (ENTER). To be sure that accidental overwriting of files does not occur, purchase well-behaved network application packages. While invoking HOLDON for users when they log in to the network may be a useful aid to avoiding accidentally overwriting files, do not expect HOLDON to entirely solve the multiuser file-locking problem for you.

THE NETWARE FILER MENU

In this section you are guided through the NetWare FILER menu. Through FILER you can perform nearly all of the activities that you can perform through Command-Line commands. There are a few limitations to FILER:

- You can copy only one file at a time.

- You cannot issue the SALVAGE command.

- You can search for files in only one directory or subdirectory at a time.

On the other hand, it is easier through FILER to copy a file from and to directories to which you do have an existing NetWare mapping.

NCOPY allows you to copy files without prior mappings, but you must provide correct path definitions. Network paths can be quite long and difficult to remember. FILER guides you through the directory structure when you are defining paths. That in itself makes FILER especially useful.

The FILER Available Topics Menu

To access FILER, type **FILER** at the prompt and press (ENTER). You will see the FILER Available Topics menu on the screen, a copy of which is shown in Figure 8-1. In the center, second line of the header of the FILER menu, at the top of your screen, you should see a path that points to your home directory. That path will look something like this:

(servername)/SYS1:DATA/USERS/VENESSA.

If you are pointing to some other location, do one of the following:

- Exit FILER back to the prompt, switch to your home directory drive pointer, and re-enter the filer menu.

- Go to **Select Current Directory** and change your current drive to your home directory.

(In Chapter 4 you were taken through the steps involved in selecting a current directory. Refer back to Chapter 4 as necessary to refresh your memory about that topic.)

File Information Menus

Move the cursor down (or up, if you had to change directories) to place the highlight bar over **File Information** and press (ENTER).

```
         Available Topics

 Current Directory Information
 File Information
 Select Current Directory
 Set Filer Options
 Subdirectory Information
 Volume Information
```

FIGURE 8-1.   FILER Available Topics menu

Files

ARNOLD.BAK
ARNOLD.NEW
DOTTIE.BAK
DOTTIE.NEW
ESTIM.BAK
ESTIM.NEW
ESTIMATE.BAK
ESTIMATE.NEW
EXECUTIV.BAK
EXECUTIV.NEW
MAIN.BAK
MAINMENU.BAK
MAINMENU.NEW

FIGURE 8-2.   FILER Files list with MAIN.BAK highlighted

You will see a listing of files in your home directory. At a minimum, the file MAIN.BAK should be listed.

Highlight the file MAIN.BAK (either by paging down to that file or by typing the filename until the file is highlighted), as shown in Figure 8-2. Now press (ENTER) to call up the FILER File Information submenu (shown in Figure 8-3).

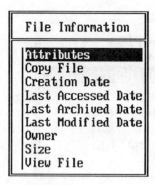

File Information

Attributes
Copy File
Creation Date
Last Accessed Date
Last Archived Date
Last Modified Date
Owner
Size
View File

FIGURE 8-3.   FILER File Information submenu

Many of the features of the File Information submenu simply display information you would see if you issued the NDIR command at a prompt with a file specified. At least one feature, View File, goes beyond what you can do at the prompt.

FILER ATTRIBUTES FOR MAIN.BAK   The Attributes option under the File Information submenu allows you to view current file attributes and, if you have appropriate NetWare effective rights, to modify a file's attributes.

With **Attributes** highlighted, press (ENTER). Because you were pointing to the file MAIN.BAK when you called up the File Information menu, it is the attributes for MAIN.BAK that appear on the right side of your screen. Press (INSERT) to see on the left side of your screen a list of additional file attributes you could attach to the file. Figure 8-4 shows both the current File Attributes and the Other File Attributes screen menu boxes.

File MAIN.BAK's attributes are Modified Since Last Backup and ReadOnly. ReadOnly is an attribute you established above through issuing the FLAG command. Modified Since Last Backup is information maintained by NetWare that lets you know whether you are working with a file for which a NetWare archiving session has been performed, or one for which the current form of the file

```
┌─────────────────────────────┐  ┌─────────────────────────────┐
│     Other File Attributes   │  │       File Attributes       │
├─────────────────────────────┤  ├─────────────────────────────┤
│ Hidden File                 │  │ Modified Since Last Backup  │
│ Indexed                     │  │ Read Only                   │
│ Shareable                   │  │                             │
│ System File                 │  │                             │
│                             │  │                             │
│                             │  │                             │
└─────────────────────────────┘  └─────────────────────────────┘
```

FIGURE 8-4.   FILER File Attributes and Other File Attributes options for MAIN.BAK

will be lost if you make changes to the file and then store it back to the directory from which it derives, using the same filename.

MAIN.BAK is a Non-shareable file. But the Normal attributes of a file (Non-shareable, Read-Write) are *not* separately displayed on the File Attributes screen. You have to know that the normal status of a file is Non-shareable, Read-Write.

Certain attributes are compatible with each other, while other attributes are exclusive. For instance, a file cannot simultaneously be flagged ReadOnly and Read-Write. Nor can it simultaneously be a Shareable and Non-Shareable file. But a file can be Shareable, ReadOnly, and Hidden, for instance.

To make MAIN.BAK a Shareable file, highlight **Shareable** in the Other File Attributes list and press (ENTER). Shareable has now been added to the File Attributes list.

To return MAIN.BAK to a Non-shareable, Read-Write status (the Normal status of a file), delete from the File Attributes list both the ReadOnly and Shareable attributes, by using one of these methods:

• One at a time, highlight the ReadOnly and Shareable attributes, press the (DELETE) key and (ENTER) to remove the highlighted attribute from the list of current File Attributes.

• Use the (F5) (Mark) key to mark both the ReadOnly and Shareable attributes, and press (DELETE) followed by (ENTER) to simultaneously delete both attributes.

To further add to or alter the File Attributes of MAIN.BAK, press (INSERT) to see a list of additional or alternative file flags. Use the (F5) (Mark) key to highlight both the Read-Write and Shareable attributes and press (ENTER).

The File Attributes screen will now look like the right side of Figure 8-5. If you again press (INSERT) you will see the file flag options available to you, as illustrated on the left side of Figure 8-5.

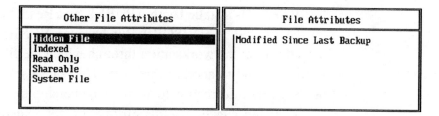

```
┌─ Other File Attributes ──────────┐ ┌─ File Attributes ─────────────────┐
│ Hidden File                      │ │ Modified Since Last Backup        │
│ Indexed                          │ │                                   │
│ Read Only                        │ │                                   │
│ Shareable                        │ │                                   │
│ System File                      │ │                                   │
│                                  │ │                                   │
└──────────────────────────────────┘ └───────────────────────────────────┘
```

FIGURE 8-5.   Modified MAIN.BAK File Attributes and altered Other File Attributes lists

When you are through viewing the File Attributes menu, press the (ESC) key until you are back to the File Information menu (Figure 8-3).

To summarize: Unless you otherwise change a file's attributes, the default attributes will be Normal, meaning Non-shareable, Read-Write. You can alter the attributes through either the FLAG command or the FILER File Attributes submenu.

FILE OWNER   While you are in the File Information submenu, press the **O** key to highlight the **Owner** option. Press (ENTER) and you will see, in Figure 8-6, that the owner of the MAIN.BAK file is VENESSA.

The owner of the original file, MAIN.MNU, is SUPERVISOR, an ownership established by NetWare at the time of NetWare

```
┌──────────────────────────────┐
│ File Owner:   VENESSA         │
└──────────────────────────────┘
```

FIGURE 8-6.   MAIN.BAK file owner

installation on the server. (The file MAIN.MNU comes with NetWare and is installed within PUBLIC as a ReadOnly file owned by the user SUPERVISOR.) But because VENESSA was the named user at the workstation through which the file was copied from PUBLIC to another directory, NetWare uses the NetWare bindery files information to attribute ownership to VENESSA.

Ownership can be useful information for managing files on server hard disks. Using this information, you can produce a list of files for a particular user and ask that user to delete outdated or unused files. The format of the NDIR command that accomplishes this and gives you a hardcopy listing of files is

NDIR OWNER=VENESSA SUB >LPT1:

For the listing to be complete you need to be pointing to a root volume and be logged in as SUPERVISOR or a supervisor-equivalent user.

FILE SIZE You also can see from within FILER (and list through NDIR) the size of a file in bytes. Escape back to the File Information screen, select **Size** and press (ENTER). As displayed on your screen, and shown in Figure 8-7, the MAIN.BAK file takes up 318 bytes of hard disk space.

```
File Size:  318 bytes
```

FIGURE 8-7. MAIN.BAK file size

```
Last Modified Date:  Wednesday  February 3, 1988
Last Modified Time:  5:04 pm
```

FIGURE 8-8.   MAIN.BAK file's last modified date

FILE CREATION, ACCESSED, ARCHIVED, AND MODI-FIED DATES   By selecting **Last Modified Date** within the File Information screen you can see the actual date the file was last modified.

While within the File Information submenu, highlight **Last Modified Date** and press (ENTER). You will see information like that shown in Figure 8-8. Or you can highlight **Creation Date** or **Last Accessed Date** and see information like that shown in Figures 8-9 and 8-10, respectively.

By highlighting **Last Archived Date** and pressing (ENTER) you will see either the date the file was last archived *through use of the NetWare archive command* or a message, like that shown in Figure 8-11, which indicates that the file has not been Archived.

VIEW OPTION   Escape back to the File Information screen and select the **View** option. Press (ENTER) to see a portion of the actual

```
File Creation Date:  Thursday  November 30, 1989
```

FIGURE 8-9.   MAIN.BAK file's creation date

```
┌────────────────────────────────────────────────┐
│ Last Accessed Date:  Thursday  November 30, 1989 │
└────────────────────────────────────────────────┘
```

FIGURE 8-10.   MAIN.BAK file's last accessed date

MAIN.BAK file. This is the same text listing shown and discussed in Chapter 2 under the topic "NetWare Menus". You may page down the screen to view portions of the file that may not currently fit in the display box.

Because MAIN.BAK is a pure ASCII text file, the displayed information is sensible. If the file includes embedded formatting characters (as does a Lotus 1-2-3 spreadsheet file or a highly formatted word processing document), the displayed information may appear as gibberish. FILER's View option does not format a file for display purposes. In that sense it is a crude tool.

On the other hand, this tool has been available for years, unlike more powerful tools that have only recently become available. Again, the purpose of View is to allow you to go somewhat beyond DOS. Novell is leaving it to NetWare Value Added resellers to develop file-management interfaces that will represent the second or third generation beyond what FILER can do for you.

```
┌──────────────────────────────────┐
│          (Not Archived)          │
│   <Press ESCAPE to continue>     │
└──────────────────────────────────┘
```

FIGURE 8-11.   FILER's "Not Archived" message

COPYING A FILE FROM WITHIN FILER   FILER allows you to copy one file at a time from any server directory to any other server directory. It is not necessary for you to have an existing mapping to either of those locations, although you must have appropriate effective rights within each directory.

To use the FILER copy routines, you do have to be pointing at the name of the file to be copied within the directory where that version of the file resides. In this instance, you are already pointing to MAIN.BAK in your home directory and are probably in the File information submenu. If not, escape back to the FILER Available Topics menu, and be sure you are pointing to MAIN.BAK in your home directory; then press (ENTER) to call up the File Information submenu.

You are about to copy the MAIN.BAK file, with a new name, MAIN.WOW, to the subdirectory you created beneath your home directory (the subdirectory THISISIT).

1. Within the File Information submenu, highlight **Copy File** and press (ENTER). A blank Destination Directory path will be displayed.

2. Use the Insert mode to define a path to the subdirectory beneath your home directory:

   a. Press (INSERT).

   b. Highlight the file server to which the file is to be copied (**FS1** in the example in Figure 8-12) and press (ENTER).

   c. Highlight the volume beneath which your home directory resides (**SYS1** in the example in Figure 8-12) and press (ENTER).

   d. Continue highlighting and pressing (ENTER) until you have defined the entire path to the subdirectory THISISIT, beneath your home directory.

```
┌─────────────────────────────────────────────────┐
│                Destination Directory             │
├─────────────────────────────────────────────────┤
│ FS1/SYS1:DATA/USERS/VENESSA/THISISIT             │
└─────────────────────────────────────────────────┘
```

FIGURE 8-12.   Destination directory path for copying the MAIN.BAK file

e. When the complete path appears in the Destination Directory box (Figure 8-12), press (ESC) to go out of NetWare Insert mode and then press (ENTER) to complete the path definition process.

3. At this point you will see a Destination File Name box with the current name of the file included (as shown in Figure 8-13).

4. While NetWare makes the assumption that you will copy the file to a new directory using the existing filename, you can either provide a new filename or modify the existing name.

a. Backspace over the BAK extension to the MAIN.BAK filename.

b. Type a new extension, **WOW**, so that the destination filename becomes MAIN.WOW (as shown in Figure 8-14).

```
┌─────────────────────────────────────────────────┐
│ Destination File Name:   MAIN.BAK                │
└─────────────────────────────────────────────────┘
```

FIGURE 8-13.   Default destination filename (MAIN.BAK)

```
Destination File Name:  MAIN.WOW
```

FIGURE 8-14. Modified destination filename (MAIN.WOW)

5. With the destination filename modified to the name to which you wish to have the file saved, press (ENTER) to complete the copying process.

Check that the file was copied by changing your current directory to THISISIT and listing (from within FILER) files contained in that subdirectory.

1. Escape back to the FILER Available Topics menu and highlight **Select Current Directory**.

2. Press (ENTER) to call up the Current Directory Path box, with the path pointing to the directory from which MAIN.BAK was copied (your home directory, as illustrated in Figure 8-15).

3. Include the subdirectory to which you copied MAIN.WOW either by typing the subdirectory name (**THISISIT**); or by

```
                  Current Directory Path
FS1/SYS1:DATA/USERS/VENESSA
```

FIGURE 8-15. Current directory path to VENESSA's home directory

```
┌──────────────────────────────────────────────────────┐
│                   Destination Directory                │
├──────────────────────────────────────────────────────┤
│FS1/SYS1:DATA/USERS/VENESSA/THISISIT                    │
└──────────────────────────────────────────────────────┘
```

FIGURE 8-16.   Current directory path to THISISIT subdirectory

pressing (INSERT) to display a list of subdirectories beneath your home directory, highlighting the subdirectory to **THISISIT** and pressing (ENTER) to include THISISIT in the current directory path, and pressing (ESC) to exit from Insert mode.

4. With the completed path in the Current Directory Path Definition box (Figure 8-16), press (ENTER) to make THISISIT the current path to which FILER is pointing.

5. Move the cursor down to File Information in the FILER Available Topics menu (or just press **F** to skip to that choice) and press (ENTER).

The FILER Files menu box with MAIN.WOW listed will appear on the screen, as illustrated in Figure 8-17.

While NCOPY has the advantage that groups of files can be copied using DOS wildcard characters, FILER is a very handy tool for copying a single file on the fly, particularly in the light of the extended path names that must be used in a network environment.

Subdirectory Information

If you completed the examples in Chapter 4, you already know how to create directories and subdirectories using FILER. Only a brief review of that topic is given here, with attention focused on how to manage subdirectories through FILER. Refer back to

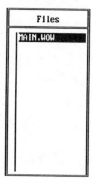

FIGURE 8-17.   Files menu with MAIN.WOW displayed

Chapter 4 if you wish further guidance on actually creating directories (through the Select Current Directory and Subdirectory Information options in the FILER Available Topics screen).

CREATING AND RENAMING SUBDIRECTORIES   To rename, create, or delete a subdirectory, you must be within FILER and pointing to the directory above the subdirectory to be created, renamed, or deleted. At this juncture you are still pointing to the THISISIT subdirectory beneath your home directory. You must move one level back up the directory tree structure.

At the FILER Available Topics menu, highlight **Select Current Directory** and press (ENTER). The current directory path pointing to THISISIT is displayed (as illustrated in Figure 8-16). Now, backspace over /THISISIT to remove that subdirectory from the path definition. (Alternatively, place the cursor on the / in **/THISISIT** and use the (DELETE) key to remove THISISIT from the path definition.) Press the (ENTER) key once to change your current directory path back to your home directory level (as illustrated in Figure 8-15).

FIGURE 8-18.   THISISIT and NEWSUBDIRECTOR placed beneath user's home directory

Move the cursor down through the Available Topics menu until you have highlighted **Subdirectory Information**. Press (ENTER) and you will again see on the left side of your screen the current network directories that appear beneath your home directory. At a minimum you should see THISISIT displayed.

To add a new subdirectory to the list, press (INSERT) and type **NEWSUBDIRECTOR** as the name of the new subdirectory to be placed beneath your home directory. Press (ENTER) and you will see a listing like that shown in Figure 8-18. You should have at least two subdirectories listed, THISISIT and NEWSUBDIREC-TOR.

NEWSUBDIRECTOR is 14 characters in length, the maximum allowed for NetWare directory names. But as mentioned elsewhere in this book, some auxiliary tape backup systems fail to recognize directory names of greater than eight characters, even though they are advertised as fully Novell compatible. If you leave NEWSUB-DIRECTOR named as it is, you could fail to back up files in that subdirectory. With this in mind, rename NEWSUBDIRECTOR to GOODIDEA.

With the highlight bar over **NEWSUBDIRECTOR** in the Network Directories menu (Figure 8-18), press the (F3) key once.

```
┌─────────────────────────────────────────┐
│Edit Directory Name:  EWSUBDIRECTOR│
└─────────────────────────────────────────┘
```

FIGURE 8-19. FILER Edit Directory Name box with
NEWSUBDIRECTOR displayed

(F3) is NetWare's Modify Function key. It is a quirk of NetWare
that it allows 14-character directory names, but only allows 13
characters to be displayed in this edit box (see Figure 8-19).

You can modify the name as you wish. Simply backspace over
NEWSUBDIRECTOR (or go to the beginning of the name and
use the (DELETE) key to remove it) and type **GOODIDEA**, as shown
in the top portion of Figure 8-20. If you do not change the initially
displayed directory name, but simply press (ENTER) while pointing
to the Edit Directory Name box, you will receive a message (as
shown in the bottom portion of Figure 8-20) that you cannot
rename a directory to its existing name.

Having changed the name, when you now press (ENTER) you will
see that NEWSUBDIRECTOR has been changed to GOODIDEA,
as illustrated in Figure 8-21. This procedure is equivalent to using
the RENDIR command at the DOS prompt.

```
        ┌─────────────────────────────────────────┐
        │Edit Directory Name:  GOODIDEA        │
        └─────────────────────────────────────────┘

┌───────────────────────────────────────────────────┐
│ Unable To Rename Directory GOODIDEA to GOODIDEA.    │
│             <Press ESCAPE to continue>              │
└───────────────────────────────────────────────────┘
```

FIGURE 8-20. FILER Edit Directory Name box with
GOODIDEA entered and "Unable to Rename"
message displayed

FIGURE 8-21. Subdirectories listing with GOODIDEA and THISISIT directories

DELETING EMPTY SUBDIRECTORIES   To delete a directory or subdirectory is quite easy if you have Parental and Delete effective rights. While still in the Network Directories submenu of FILER (Figure 8-21), place the highlight bar over **GOODIDEA** and press the (DELETE) key. The highlight bar will be resting over the Delete Subdirectory's Files Only option (see Figure 8-22). Having just created GOODIDEA, you know there are no files in this subdirectory. Therefore, place the highlight bar over **Delete Entire Subdirectory Structure** and press (ENTER).

NetWare will ask you to confirm that you wish to delete the entire directory structure, including all subdirectories and files

```
 Delete Subdirectory Options
 Delete Entire Subdirectory Structure
 Delete Subdirectory's Files Only
```

FIGURE 8-22.   Delete Subdirectory Options menu

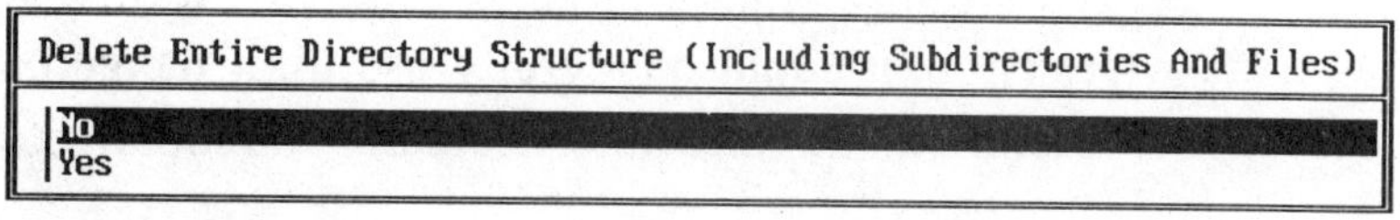

```
Delete Entire Directory Structure (Including Subdirectories And Files)
No
Yes
```

FIGURE 8-23.   Delete Entire Directory Structure menu

beneath the directory being deleted. As shown in Figure 8-23, NetWare assumes the answer to this question is No. Place the highlight bar over **Yes** and press (ENTER). You should have deleted the directory GOODIDEA and your screen will display only the THISISIT directory, along with any subdirectories that existed before you began this exercise.

Deleting a subdirectory is quite easy. But what if there had been files in the subdirectory GOODIDEA? Or what if beneath GOODIDEA you had created additional subdirectories with files contained in those subdirectories?

Under DOS you are required to remove files from a directory or subdirectory before you can delete the directory or any subsidiary subdirectories. Does NetWare follow this same principle?

DELETING DIRECTORIES WITH RESIDENT FILES   When you are working at the prompt, DOS continues to require you to delete all files from a directory before you can use the DOS RD (remove directory) command to delete a directory. While using the RD command you must empty and delete each subdirectory before any higher level directory can be removed from the directory structure.

This is one instance where DOS has a certain built-in logic to it. By requiring these step-by-step procedures DOS helps ensure that files and subdirectories are not accidentally deleted. But when you are managing a large, complex hard disk volume directory structure, it could be awfully useful, if dangerous, to be able to delete entire subdirectory structures and subdirectory-resident files all at once.

In fact, NetWare allows you to do this through FILER.

1. Within the Subdirectories menu, highlight **THISISIT** and press the (DELETE) key once.

2. In the Delete Subdirectory Options menu (Figure 8-22), highlight **Delete Entire Subdirectory Structure** and press (ENTER).

3. Confirm that **yes**, you do wish to Delete Entire Directory Structure (Including Subdirectories and Files) and press (ENTER) (Figure 8-23).

You have just deleted THISISIT while it contained the resident file MAIN.WOW. You can simultaneously delete a directory and all the files in it. If you are not careful, you can delete entire subdirectory structures, and all the files in those subdirectories.

There are, however, two features of NetWare that offer some protection. First, you can change the FILER options to require confirmation of file deletions, on a file-by-file basis, as will be demonstrated later. NetWare will still allow you to follow the directory deletion procedure just outlined, but if the directory to be deleted has resident files you will be asked whether each file is to be deleted, and you will not be allowed to delete the directory until you have deleted each individual file.

Unfortunately, Confirm File Deletions is not the default setting for FILER, and helps only if a user thinks to change the default each time he or she enters FILER.

The more important preventive measure is not to allow a user to have Parental rights in a directory that, if deleted, would cause loss of needed files (in that directory or subdirectories beneath it). Again, the solution to the subdirectory deletion option offered in

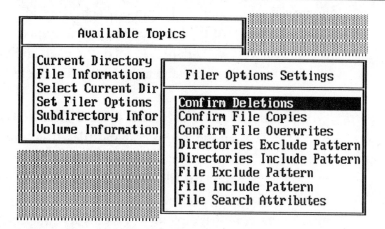

FIGURE 8-24.   FILER Options Settings menu

FILER is not to restrict your users from using FILER, but to carefully plan your directory and user security structure (as discussed in Chapters 4, 5, and 6).

Set Filer Options and the Filer Options Settings Menu

Just as you can perform complex directory and file searches from the DOS prompt using NetWare's LISTDIR and NDIR commands, you can set options within FILER to sort through a directories list of files and subdirectories.

From the FILER main Available Topics menu, highlight **Set Filer Options** and press (ENTER). You will see the Filer Options Settings menu shown in Figure 8-24.

CONFIRM DELETIONS   If you choose to have FILER require confirmation when you delete files, leave the highlight bar over **Confirm Deletions** and press (ENTER). When you are prompted

prompted with Confirm Delete of Each File Individually, select **Yes** and press (ENTER). The next time you attempt to delete any file (or directory) you will be required for each individual file to confirm that yes, you intend to have that file deleted.

CONFIRM FILE COPIES AND FILE OVERWRITES   You will have noticed that when copying files from one directory to another, NetWare performs the copy without question (either at the prompt or within FILER). This is true whether the file is copied to a directory using a new file (a create file process) or a filename already in use in that directory (a file overwrite process).

You can choose to have either file copies (new creations) or file overwrites (copying of files to an existing filename) confirmed before they take effect. For one or the other option, simply select **Confirm File Copies** or **Confirm File Overwrites**, select **Yes**, and press (ENTER).

CHANGING THE FILE INCLUDE OR EXCLUDE PATTERN
You will use the Filer Options Settings more often to manage files than directories. For this reason, and because the Directories Exclude Pattern and Directories Include Pattern options work the same as their File Pattern cousins, the discussion that follows focuses strictly on file management.

Highlight **File Include Pattern** and press (ENTER). You will see displayed an Include File Patterns box with an asterisk in it, as shown in Figure 8-25. The single asterisk is equivalent to the DOS *.* wildcard pattern. It is the "*" in this field that results in all files in a directory or subdirectory being displayed when you select File Information from the FILER Available Topics main menu.

No files will be displayed if

- the FILER File Include Pattern is set to blank

- the FILER File Exclude Pattern is set to "*"

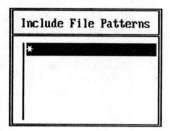

FIGURE 8-25.   FILER Include File Patterns box

(If you wish you can confirm that the FILER default File Exclude Pattern is set to blank by pressing (ESC) once, highlighting **File Exclude Pattern**, and pressing (ENTER). If you do so, return to the File Include Patterns screen before continuing.)

You can specify multiple File Include Patterns or combinations of File Include and File Exclude Patterns. While you are in the Include File Patterns screen, press (INSERT) once to display the New Pattern box. Type ***.BAK** (see Figure 8-26) and press (ENTER). *.BAK now appears among the Include File Patterns, as shown in Figure 8-27.

If you return to the FILER Available Topics menu, select File Information, and press (ENTER), you will *not* see listed only those files in your home directory that have a .BAK extension. You will still have all files listed because all include and exclude file patterns work in conjunction with each other. In this case, *.BAK is limiting, but * is still equivalent to the DOS *.* wildcard search.

New Pattern: *.BAK

FIGURE 8-26.   FILER New Pattern box with ***.BAK** typed

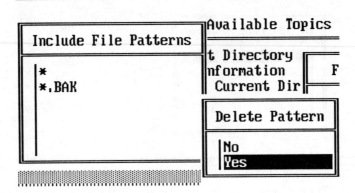

FIGURE 8-27.   FILER Include File Patterns box with * and
*.BAK

FILER uses both file include patterns in its search and lists all files contained in your home directory.

To search only for files with a .BAK extension, you must delete the "*" file include pattern. From within the Include File Patterns box, highlight the "*" pattern and press (DELETE). Now only *.BAK should be displayed in the Include File Patterns box. When you escape back to the Available Topics menu and select File Information, FILER should list only .BAK extended filenames.

MULTIPLE FILE INCLUDE AND EXCLUDE PATTERNS

You can use multiple file include patterns and multiple file exclude patterns simultaneously. To demonstrate this, go to Set Filer Options, select **File Include Pattern**, and change the *.BAK pattern back to "*" as follows:

1. Highlight the *.BAK pattern.

2. Press (F3) to call up the *.BAK pattern for editing.

3. Backspace over the .BAK extension, so that only the "*" is shown in the edit box.

4. Press (ENTER).

Next, create a *.BAK file exclude pattern as follows:

1. Highlight the **File Exclude Pattern** option within the FILER Options Settings menu and press (ENTER).

2. Press (INSERT) to call up the New Pattern box.

3. Type ***.BAK** and press (ENTER.)

Now escape key back to the Available Topics menu, select **File Information**, and press (ENTER). You should see displayed all files in your home subdirectory except those with a *.BAK extension.

FILE SEARCH ATTRIBUTES   The statement that the single asterisk, "*", allows you to list all files in a directory is not entirely true. Specifically, files flagged as either System or Hidden will not be listed. However, with appropriate rights, it is possible to search for and then view files that have the System and Hidden attributes attached to them—files that would otherwise not be included among the files listed when you select File Information from the FILER Available Topics menu.

File Search Attributes works like the File Include Pattern feature with these exceptions:

• When you select File Search Attributes and press (ENTER), you see a blank Search File Attributes screen.

• When you press (INSERT) to create a search pattern, the available patterns are displayed for you.

The screen you will see if you follow these procedures is shown in Figure 8-28. The File Search Attributes feature will not be of use to most users.

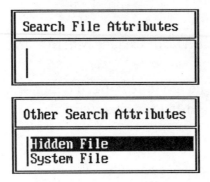

```
┌──────────────────────────────┐
│ Search File Attributes       │
├──────────────────────────────┤
│                              │
│                              │
└──────────────────────────────┘

┌──────────────────────────────┐
│ Other Search Attributes      │
├──────────────────────────────┤
│ Hidden File                  │
│ System File                  │
└──────────────────────────────┘
```

FIGURE 8-28.   FILER Search File Attributes and Other Search Attributes screens

Volume Information

Selecting the Volume Information option is equivalent to issuing the NetWare VOLINFO command at the prompt. While you are in the FILER Available Topics menu, press the letter **V** to highlight **Volume Information**, and then press (ENTER). You will see infor-

```
┌─────────────────────────────────────────────┐
│              Volume Information              │
├─────────────────────────────────────────────┤
│ Server Name:                  FS1           │
│ Volume Name:                  SYS1          │
│ Volume Type:                  Fixed         │
│ Total Bytes:                  57,593,856    │
│ Bytes Available:              37,523,456    │
│ Maximum Directory Entries:        3,968     │
│ Directory Entries Available:      2,980     │
└─────────────────────────────────────────────┘
```

FIGURE 8-29.   FILER Volume Information screen

mation for your current server default volume information like that shown in Figure 8-29.

If you wish to see volume information for another server, you must first switch to a drive path that includes that volume within it. You do not have to be pointing to the volume as your default to have the information in Figure 8-29 displayed. It is only necessary that the volume you wish to know about is part of the current default path.

Summary

In this chapter you have explored NetWare file- and directory-management commands and the NetWare FILER menu.

NetWare provides powerful new tools for managing a large number of files within a potentially complex directory structure. Knowledgeable use of these tools, within the constraints of a well-planned directory system and user security structure, provides a road to effective file and directory management.

chapter **9**

NETWARE
PRINT MANAGEMENT
COMMANDS AND MENUS

The ability to share printers is a fundamental consideration in many network software and hardware purchases. This chapter reviews NetWare print management commands and menus. NetWare does not directly support sharing locally attached printers, but it does allow up to five printers to be attached to any one server.

On an internetwork, you can share printers attached to servers other than the server to which you log in. As an open operating system, NetWare also allows for third-party Value Added Processes (VAPs) to be installed on the server, including print VAPs that extend the basic NetWare print service functions.

Also reviewed briefly in this chapter is the process for installing printers on a NetWare server, and the opportunity that may exist for installing application software that recognizes the existence of NetWare-installed server-attached printers.

You may be using a server running NetWare version 2.0a, either as a single server or on an internetwork of servers. Equivalent NetWare version 2.0a commands will be mentioned but not explored in detail in this chapter.

Avoiding the pitfalls of network printing begins with an understanding of what actually occurs when you print a job at the workstation and send it to a network printer.

NETWARE PRINT MANAGEMENT FUNDAMENTALS

When you print to a network printer, the print job is handled as illustrated in Figure 9-1. The job will most likely be sent from within an application running at your workstation. Rather than going directly to a local printer connected to your workstation, the NetWare shell *reroutes* the job over the network cables to a server *print queue*. The server print queue collects jobs and keeps them in the server's RAM, or sends them for storage to hard disk if the server is shut down prior to your job being serviced by a printer. Each job waits its turn for servicing by the specific printer to which the queue of print jobs is assigned. The server will normally release jobs to a printer on a first-into-the-queue, first-out-of-the-queue basis.

If more than one queue is assigned to the same printer—as illustrated with PRINTQ_0 and LOW_PRIORITY in Figure 9-1—

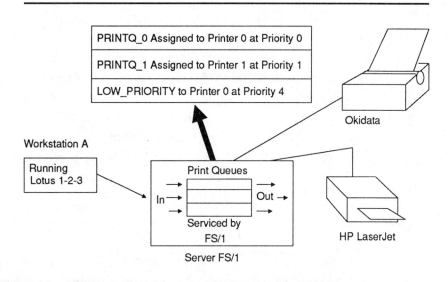

FIGURE 9-1. Diagram of network print job routing

all jobs in the higher-priority queue that are not on hold or delayed to a later time and date will be serviced before any jobs in the lower-priority queue.

Even this simplified picture of network printing presents several complications. Successful printing no longer depends on proper cabling and setup between your workstation and a locally attached printer. Network cabling and server setup and services also play a role.

Successful management of this complex environment begins with an understanding of several NetWare print management fundamentals.

Numbered Printers

To be recognized by the NetWare operating system, printers attached to a server must be installed using NetWare installation or system-maintenance procedures. How to install a printer is discussed at the end of this chapter.

At the time of installation, each printer is assigned a printer number, 0 through 4. This printer number is used in several NetWare printer commands. You are well advised to document the number assigned within NetWare to each particular server-at-tached printer. Among other possibilities, consider placing a label on the printer that includes the NetWare printer number and the names of any queues assigned to that printer.

Named Print Queues

At the time a printer is first installed, a default NetWare print queue is automatically established and assigned to that printer. The name is always PRINTQ_x, where x represents the number of the printer. Thus, printer 0 will initially have associated with it a print queue named PRINTQ_0, printer 1 a queue named PRINTQ_1, and so on.

However, NetWare version 2.1 and later support multiple named print queues. Additional named print queues may be established by the user SUPERVISOR through the PCONSOLE menu. Follow the procedures outlined here to create a new print queue named LOW_PRIORITY.

MANAGING PRINT QUEUES WITH PCONSOLE   While at the DOS prompt, type PCONSOLE and press (ENTER). The PCONSOLE Available Options menu will appear on the screen (as shown in Figure 9-2). The NetWare 2.0a version of this menu is named QUEUE. If you are running NetWare version 2.0a you are limited in the print management tools available to you through NetWare, but you can nevertheless type **QUEUE**, press (ENTER), and read this section with the QUEUE menu options in front of you.

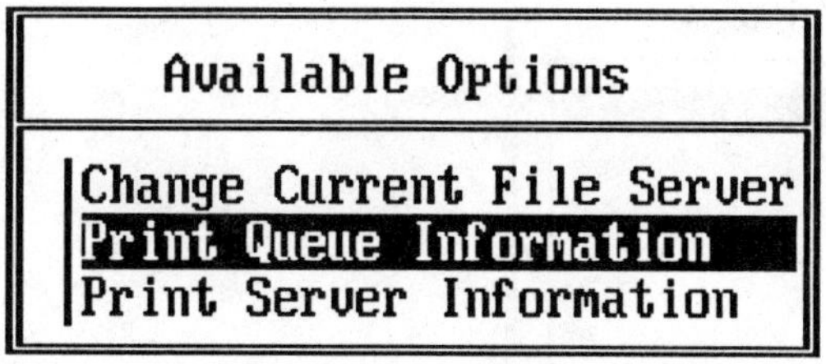

```
┌─────────────────────────────────────┐
│        Available Options             │
├─────────────────────────────────────┤
│ Change Current File Server           │
│ Print Queue Information              │
│ Print Server Information             │
└─────────────────────────────────────┘
```

FIGURE 9-2.   PCONSOLE Available Options menu

As with other NetWare menus, the second line of the menu header provides important information about your current status on the network. In the PCONSOLE menu header, displayed at the top of the PCONSOLE screen, you are informed of who you are on the network, to what server you are currently printing, and your connection number—for example, User SUPERVISOR On File Server FS1 Connection 2. On an internetwork of servers, you may temporarily point to another server to inspect print queues of that server.

PRINT QUEUE INFORMATION FOR THE CURRENT SERVER   When you enter PCONSOLE, NetWare places the highlight bar over the **Print Queue Information** choice. (This is a change from NetWare version 2.0a, where the highlighted choice is to change file servers.)

Press (ENTER) and you will see a list of print queues known to the server to which you are currently pointing (as indicated in the header of the PCONSOLE menu). Figure 9-3 shows only two print queue names, the default queues established by the NetWare operating system during installation or maintenance for each of two server-connected printers.

FIGURE 9-3.   PCONSOLE Print Queues listing

CREATING A NEW PRINT QUEUE   You may have more or fewer print queues on your server, and the default queues may have been renamed. For later reference (when you are working at the prompt) take a moment to write down the names of the existing print queues for your server. You are not required to spell print queue names in capitals, but you must use "0" for the number zero, not the letter "O." Any underscores must be included in the queue name. (On most keyboards, the underscore is the uppercase character on the hyphen key.)

To create a new print queue, from the Print Queues screen press (INSERT). A new queue name box is presented in which you can type the name of the new queue. Type **LOW_PRIORITY** into the space provided and press (ENTER). The queue name is added to the list of queues created on the server to which you are currently pointing.

For these queues to become operative, you must define who can use that print queue (the default is EVERYONE), assign the queue to a particular printer (at a service priority), set up or train users to use the named queue, and designate one or more individuals to be queue operators (unless you are going to personally manage the queue as SUPERVISOR).

These newly created, named print queues can be used in place of or in addition to the default print queues (PRINTQ_0 and so forth). Or, the default queue names can be changed (to HP_QUEUE, OKIDATA, and so on). In either instance an appropriate server assignment Console command must be issued before a user is allowed to place a print job into the queue. These assignment Console commands must be reissued each time the server is booted.

Named Queue Users

You must be set up as a queue user before you can place a job in a print queue. Specifically, you must either

- have the user name with which you logged in to the server listed among the queue's queue users

- or hold membership within a group which is listed among the queue's users.

(With NetWare version 2.0a, all users automatically have access to the one print spooler created for each printer.)

NetWare places the group EVERYONE in the list of queue users for either the default print queues or queues you create through PCONSOLE. Accordingly, all users on the server are allowed to place print jobs in PRINTQ_0, PRINTQ_1, and so forth, unless you choose to restrict use of these print queues (as discussed later).

Follow the instructions provided here to make the user VENESSA (and yourself, if you are set up on the server) the sole users of the LOW_PRIORITY print queue.

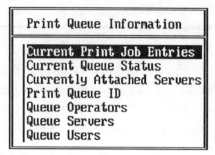

FIGURE 9-4.   PCONSOLE Print Queue Information menu

PRINT QUEUE USERS   Highlight the **LOW_PRIORITY** print queue name and press (ENTER). You will see a Print Queue Information menu as shown in Figure 9-4. Within the Print Queue Information menu, highlight **Queue Users** and press (ENTER). As illustrated in Figure 9-5, the group EVERYONE is the sole entry in the list of queue users.

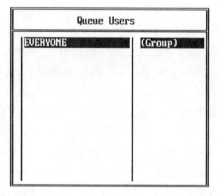

FIGURE 9-5.   PCONSOLE Queue Users listing

```
┌─────────────────────────────────────┐
│     Queue Operator Candidates        │
│ ┌─────────────────────────────────┐ │
│ ▲│JAMESS         (User)           │ │
│  │JEFF           (User)           │ │
│  │JERRY          (User)           │ │
│  │JIMMY          (User)           │ │
│  │JUDY           (User)           │ │
│  │LEV            (User)           │ │
│  │MARK           (User)           │ │
│  │OPERATIONS     (Group)          │ │
│  │PAT            (User)           │ │
│  │PROJECTS       (Group)          │ │
│  │SECRETARY      (Group)          │ │
│  │TIM            (User)           │ │
│ ▼│VENESSA        (User)           │ │
│ └─────────────────────────────────┘ │
└─────────────────────────────────────┘
```

FIGURE 9-6.   Queue Operator Candidates listing with VENESSA highlighted

Because the group EVERYONE is listed, you and all other users can access the print queue LOW_PRIORITY (once other setup procedures are completed, as discussed later).

DELETING EVERYONE AS A LOW_PRIORITY QUEUE USER   To restrict access to the LOW_PRIORITY queue, you must delete the group EVERYONE. Highlight the name **EVERYONE** and press the (DELETE) key once, confirm that you do wish to delete this group from the list of queue users, and press (ENTER).

ADDING VENESSA AS A QUEUE USER   To add a user to the list of queue users, press (INSERT). A list of all users and groups set up on the server (who are not current users of the queue) is displayed. Move the cursor down this list, or type as much of the user name **VENESSA** as necessary, until the highlight bar rests over the user VENESSA, as illustrated in Figure 9-6. Press (ENTER) and VENESSA will be added as a user of this print queue.

You can use the (F5) (Mark) key to add or delete several users or groups at once. Press (INSERT) again, use the cursor and (F5) key to mark several users for inclusion in the LOW_PRIORITY queue user list (including your user name on the server), and press (ENTER). Delete any group or user from the LOW_PRIORITY queue user's list to whom you wish to deny access to the LOW-PRIORITY print queue.

Print Queue Operators

Each named print queue can have one or more assigned queue operators. A print queue operator can do the following:

- set a queue flag to allow or disallow users placing jobs in the queue
- set a queue flag to allow or disallow servicing of queue jobs by a server
- delete any print job in the queue
- place a print job on hold
- delay printing of a job to a specific day and time
- change print job parameters, such as the form number associated with the print job
- change the sequence in which print jobs will be serviced

The queue operator can perform these tasks only under these conditions:

- the print job is in the queue for which he or she is manager
- the print job has not already been released, in whole or in part, to the printer

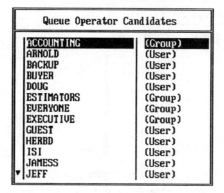

Queue Operator Candidates

ACCOUNTING	(Group)
ARNOLD	(User)
BACKUP	(User)
BUYER	(User)
DOUG	(User)
ESTIMATORS	(Group)
EVERYONE	(Group)
EXECUTIVE	(Group)
GUEST	(User)
HERBD	(User)
ISI	(User)
JAMESS	(User)
JEFF	(User)

FIGURE 9-7.   Queue Operator Candidates listing

The one exception to the last rule is that a queue operator can delete a job released to a printer, as long as the entire job has not yet been released.

The user SUPERVISOR, or a user with supervisor-equivalent rights, can manage any job in any print queue. He or she does not need to be designated as a queue operator to perform print queue job-management activities through PCONSOLE.

CREATING A QUEUE OPERATOR FOR LOW_PRIORITY

To designate a queue operator for the LOW_PRIORITY queue, escape back to the Print Queue Information screen, highlight **Queue Operators**, and press (ENTER).

For a new queue, the Queue Operators list is blank; no users have yet been designated as queue operators. Add yourself as manager of this queue. Press (INSERT) to see a list of all users and groups set up on your default server (see Figure 9-7). Highlight your user name and press (ENTER). You have been added as a queue operator.

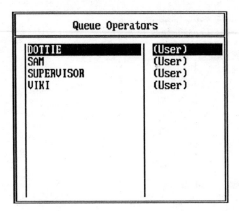

FIGURE 9-8.   PCONSOLE Queue Operators listing

**VIEWING AND CHANGING OTHER QUEUE INFORMA-
TION**   To see who is a queue operator or queue user of an existing
print queue, escape back to the list of available queues, highlight
the queue about which you wish to learn additional information
(PRINTQ_0, perhaps), and press (ENTER).

Within the Print Queue Information screen, highlight **Queue
Operators** and press (ENTER). You may see that several users have
been designated as queue operators, as illustrated in Figure 9-8.
Note, however, that inclusion of SUPERVISOR as a queue operator is an unnecessary redundancy. By virtue of SUPERVISOR's
status on the network, he or she can manage jobs in any print queue.

Current Queue Status

Over the years, NetWare print management options have become
more sophisticated. NetWare now allows SUPERVISOR or a

```
┌─────────────────────────────────────────────────────┐
│                Current Queue Status                   │
├─────────────────────────────────────────────────────┤
│Number of entries in queue:                    2       │
│Number of servers attached:                    1       │
│                                                       │
│Operator Flags                                         │
│   Users can place entries in queue:          Yes      │
│   Servers can service entries in queue:      Yes      │
│   New servers can attach to queue:           Yes      │
└─────────────────────────────────────────────────────┘
```

FIGURE 9-9.   PCONSOLE Current Queue Status box

queue manager to set queue flags to allow or disallow users placing a job in a queue or to allow or disallow a server servicing the queue.

To check the current queue status of a named print queue, highlight that item in the Print Queue Information screen and press (ENTER). A screen like that shown in Figure 9-9 will appear. It is the Operator Flags section of this screen that is of particular interest. As shown in Figure 9-9, the queue's Operator flags are set such that users can place entries in the queue, one or more servers can service entries in the queue, and new servers can be attached to the queue.

If either of the first two flags—Users can place entries in queue, and Servers can service entries in queue—is set to No, the named queue will be of little use. The default setting when a queue is installed is Yes on all three flag counts.

User and Server Operator flags being set to Yes is a necessary condition for using a queue. However, this is not a sufficient condition; you must also be a queue user.

PCONSOLE on an Internetwork

NetWare allows, in theory, for any user to access the print queues and printers of any server on an internetwork, within the security limits set by network supervisors.

On an internetwork, you can view information about any print queue on any server, but you must first attach to the appropriate server for print queues you wish to examine.

USING PCONSOLE TO ATTACH TO OTHER SERVERS

Re-enter the PCONSOLE menu, and from the Available Options menu select **Change Current File Server** and press (ENTER). If the server to which you wish to attach is not listed, press (INSERT), highlight the server name, and press (ENTER). You must then provide a user name through which to attach to the selected server. If you are not set up as a user on that server, you may type **GUEST** and press (ENTER) to attach as GUEST. If the GUEST account on that server is password protected, you will be prompted to provide the required password.

USING PCONSOLE TO LEARN ABOUT PRINT QUEUES ON OTHER SERVERS   Once you have included additional servers among your list of available servers, you can point to a server and examine its print queues.

From the PCONSOLE Available Options menu, highlight **Change Current File Server** and press (ENTER). Highlight the server to which you wish to point and press (ENTER). The second line header of the PCONSOLE menu informs you of which server you are pointing to, and the user name through which you are attached to that server (the user name determines which, if any, of the server's print queues you can use).

Having reviewed the alternative usable print queues, press (ALT-F10) and exit from PCONSOLE.

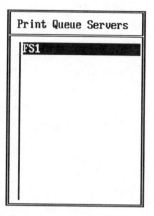

FIGURE 9-10.   Print Queue Servers box

PRINT QUEUE ID AND QUEUE SERVERS   To determine what servers are currently available to you to service a queue, from within the Print Queue Information screen (Figure 9-4) highlight **Queue Servers** and press (ENTER). In all likelihood you will see only your current server name listed in this screen, as illustrated in Figure 9-10. This means that network print services currently available to you are probably entirely through the auspices of NetWare at the server.

However, Novell developed NetWare as an open system to encourage third-party development of NetWare add-on packages. If there are any third-party print VAPs active on your server, they will be listed in the Print Queue Servers screen. These print server VAPs can be selected, or information about them explored, through this screen.

To see print server VAPs installed but not currently active for you, press (INSERT). A Queue Server Candidates List is displayed. If there are no print VAPs installed on your default server, the screen will be blank, as illustrated in Figure 9-11.

FIGURE 9-11.   Queue Server Candidates box

You can also see a list of installed third-party print servers from the PCONSOLE Available Options menu. As envisioned by Novell, print servers can be specialized network servers, devoted to servicing print jobs in ways that go beyond the services available through NetWare.

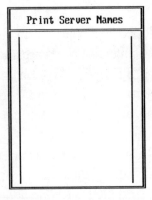

FIGURE 9-12.   Print Server Names box

Escape back to the PCONSOLE Available Options menu. Highlight **Print Server Information** and press (ENTER). If there are no
print servers known to NetWare through PCONSOLE, the Print
Server Names screen will be blank, as illustrated in Figure 9-12.

You can install new print server names by first pressing (INSERT).
This takes you to a Queue Server Candidates screen, which may
also be blank, as illustrated in Figure 9-11. Press (INSERT) again,
type a new print server name (**DOUG**) in the space provided, and
press (ENTER). You are now in the Queue Server Candidates listing.
Highlight the print server name you created (**DOUG**) and press
(ENTER) to add that print server name to the Print Server Names list.

With a new named server (which probably does not exist on
your network) added to the list of available print servers, you could
further configure that server on your internetwork by password
protecting access to the named print server. To do this, highlight
the server name (**DOUG**) in the Print Server Names list and press
(ENTER). A Print Server Information screen is displayed as shown
in Figure 9-13. Highlight **Change Password** and press (ENTER) and

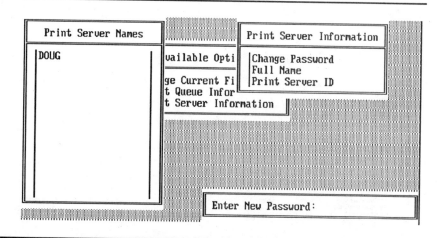

FIGURE 9-13.   DOUG queue server setup

you are provided a place in which to type the password that will protect the DOUG print server from unauthorized access.

Since you probably do not care about establishing a DOUG print server, escape back to the Print Queue Information screen.

Highlight the **Print Queue ID** option and press (ENTER). Net-Ware uses an alphanumeric code to uniquely identify this print queue. Including a queue ID number in NetWare's bindery files allows third parties to develop Value Added Processes (VAPs) that can access NetWare's print queues.

Workstation Versus Server Console Control

With version 2.15 of NetWare many print management activities can be performed either through the workstation (using PCONSOLE) or through commands issued at the server console. Whenever possible, you will want to manage jobs through a

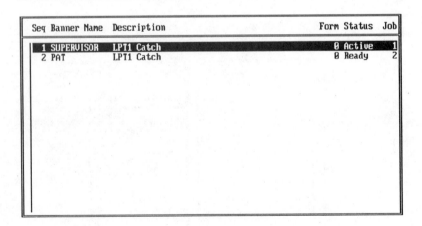

Seq Banner Name	Description	Form Status	Job
1 SUPERVISOR	LPT1 Catch	0 Active	1
2 PAT	LPT1 Catch	0 Ready	2

FIGURE 9-14.   PCONSOLE Print Queue Jobs listing

workstation. The fewer persons who have access to the server keyboard, the better your server security.

CURRENT PRINT JOB ENTRIES   To see what jobs are currently in the print queue, place the highlight bar over **Current Print Job Entries** within the Print Queue Information screen and press (ENTER). A screen like that shown in Figure 9-14 will appear. Figure 9-14 illustrates a print queue jobs listing with two jobs in the queue. The first job in the queue, (Seq 1), is as follows:

- for the user SUPERVISOR

- named LPT1 Catch (a default job name used in the absence of a user-defined name)

- using form 0 (zero)

- an active job, meaning that it is being released to the printer (whether or not the printer is on-line and operating)

- job number 1

In contrast, the second job in line for servicing (Job 2) is for the user PAT and, carrying a status of Ready, is not printing and will not be released for printing until the first, *active* job (for SUPERVISOR) is disposed of.

Later, you will learn when and how to manage jobs from a PCONSOLE print queue listing like that shown in Figure 9-14. For now, examine the jobs screen for the queue you plan to use in doing the exercises suggested later in this chapter. If there are numerous jobs listed, you may want to either send your jobs to a less active queue or defer completing the exercises in this chapter to a less active printing time.

In selecting a print queue to which to send jobs, you will also need to answer these questions:

- Are you a qualified user of the selected print queue?

- Is the queue status set such that you can place jobs in the queue?

- Is there a server actively servicing that queue?

SERVER CONSOLE PRINT COMMANDS   Certain tasks *must* be performed through server Console commands, including the following:

- Stopping or restarting a print job.

- Rewinding pages of a print job when you encounter a paper jam and want to reprint part of a document (for which the print job is still in the server print queue).

- Mounting a specific form, a special instance of restarting printing, after the server has provided you an opportunity to change the printer paper or form.

Someone must have access to the server keyboard for some network print management purposes. If this is a problem for you, the need for server access may be obviated in these ways:

- By use of workstation application software that includes advanced print management capabilities at the workstation that go beyond those found in NetWare's PCONSOLE menu.

- By installation of specialized print management software, at the server and or workstation, that provides specialized print-management capabilities (perhaps allowing network users to access printers attached locally to other workstations).

Because of the importance of server Console commands to network print management, and because of the need to use one of these commands to complete your set up of the LOW_PRIORITY queue server, Console commands are discussed here.

CONSOLE CONTROL OF PRINT JOBS

Once a print job is in a queue, it may still need to be managed. You have some control over print job management through the PCONSOLE menu, as will be discussed later. But the greatest control is provided through the server keyboard.

Server keyboard commands are referred to as *console commands*. If you are working on a nondedicated server, on which you may be running a DOS session, you may toggle between Console mode and DOS mode by typing **CONSOLE** or **DOS** at, respectively, the DOS (\:>) or NetWare console (:) screen prompt.

When you are in server Console mode, the printer and print queue management commands listed in Table 9-1 are available.

Viewing a List
Of Installed Printers

To view a list of printers installed on your server, in Console mode from the server keyboard type **PRINTERS** and press (ENTER). You will see a listing like the following:

```
FS1 is configured for 3 printers.
Printer 0: Running On-Line Form 0 mounted Servicing 1 Queues
Printer 1: Running On-Line Form 0 mounted Servicing 1 Queues
Printer 3: Running On-Line Form 0 mounted Servicing 0 Queues
```

If you do not have a server printer installed, turn to the last section of this chapter (and to the *NetWare 286 Maintenance* manual) for guidance on printer installation.

Version 2.1 Command	Version 2.0a Command
PRINTER *nn* STOP	STOP PRINTER *nn*
PRINTER *nn* START	START PRINTER *nn*
PRINTER *nn* MOUNT FORM *xx*	(No such command)
PRINTER *nn* REWIND *xx* PAGES	REWIND PRINTER *nn* *xx* (*xx*=PAGES)
PRINTER *nn* FORM FEED	(No such command)
PRINTER *nn* MARK TOP OF FORM	FORM CHECK *no.*
PRINTER *nn* ADD QUEUE *name* AT PRIORITY *nn*	(No such command)
PRINTER *nn* QUEUES	QUEUE *no.*
PRINTERS	(No such command)
QUEUES	(No such command)
QUEUE *name* JOBS	QUEUE
QUEUE *name* DELETE JOB *xx*	KILL QUEUE
QUEUE *name* DELETE JOB *	KILL PRINTER
QUEUE *name* CHANGE JOB *nn* TO PRIORITY *xx*	CHANGE QUEUE *nn* JOB *nn* TO PRIORITY *xx*
QUEUE *name* CREATE	(No such command)
QUEUE *name* DESTROY	(No such command)

TABLE 9-1.   Console Commands for Printer and Queue Management

Q and Q *queuename* JOBS

At the server keyboard in Console mode, type **Q** and press (ENTER) to see a list of all print queues created for this server.

```
FS1 Print Queue:
PRINT Q_0          0 queue jobs     serviced by 1 printers.
LOW_PRIORITY       0 queue jobs     serviced by 0 printers.
PRINTQ_1           0 queue jobs     serviced by 1 printers.
```

To view a list of jobs in a particular print queue, type **Q** *queuename* **JOBS** and press (ENTER). If there are any jobs in the queue, you will see a listing like the following:

```
Jobs currently in Print Queue PRINTQ_0:
    Priority      User    File   Job   Copies   Form
       1          SAM     LST:    1      1        0
```

Other Console commands are issued in just this way through the server keyboard.

Stopping and Starting a Printer

You can stop or start a printer through the server. In Console mode on the server, issue the following command to stop a printer:

P *xx* STOP

For the *xx,* substitute the number of the network printer to which your job was sent and press (ENTER). To restart the printer, type **P *xx* START** and press (ENTER).

Assigning a New Print Queue To a Printer

If you created a new queue while in PCONSOLE as the user SUPERVISOR, you can now assign that queue for servicing by one or other of the printers attached and installed to your server. To assign that queue to a printer, at the server in Console mode, type

P *nn* ADD *newqueue* AT PRIORITY 04

For *nn* substitute the number of the printer on your server to which you wish the queue assigned. In place of *newqueue* type the name of the print queue you created, probably LOW_PRIORITY.

You should see a message on the server screen confirming that the queue has been added at priority 04. The reason for using priority 04 is that at least one other queue is probably already assigned at priority 01. You cannot assign to two queues the same priority status to a printer. If you wanted to assign your named queue at priority 01, you would first have to reassign the current priority 01 queue to a lower priority.

Print queue assignment commands must be issued each time a server is booted. This is an inconvenience for which NetWare provides a solution.

Placing Console Print Commands In a Server AUTOEXEC.SYS File

To avoid having to issue routine commands each time a server is booted, Novell includes as a NetWare feature a file called AUTO-EXEC.SYS. This is equivalent to a workstation file called AUTO-EXEC.BAT.

The AUTOEXEC.SYS file is accessed through SYSCON. You must be logged in as SUPERVISOR (or a supervisor-equivalent user) to create, view, or alter the AUTOEXEC.SYS file.

From the prompt, type **SYSCON** and press (ENTER). Within the Available Topics menu, select **Supervisor Options** and press (ENTER). If you are not allowed into the Supervisor Options menu, it is because you did not log in as SUPERVISOR or a supervisor-equivalent user.

Within the Supervisor Options menu (Figure 9-15), highlight **Edit System AUTOEXEC File** and press (ENTER). On a newly installed server, the System AUTOEXEC File screen will be blank. Simply use this screen as you used the System Login Script and User Login Script screens (in Chapter 7), inserting those repetitive Console commands that you would otherwise need to issue through the server console keyboard upon booting the server.

```
┌─────────────────────────────────────────┐
│            Supervisor Options            │
├─────────────────────────────────────────┤
│ Default Account Balance/Restrictions     │
│ Default Time Restrictions                │
│ Edit System AUTOEXEC File                │
│ File Server Console Operators            │
│ Intruder Detection/Lockout               │
│ System Login Script                      │
│ View File Server Error Log               │
└─────────────────────────────────────────┘
```

FIGURE 9-15.   SYSCON Supervisor Options menu

 The server contains its own boot routines, so an AUTOEXEC.SYS file does not have to be created, except to supplement the normal NetWare boot routines.

Figure 9-16 lists some of the types of Console print-related commands that might go into a server's AUTOEXEC.SYS file. While NetWare automatically creates default print queues, such as PRINTQ_0 and PRINTQ_1, you may find it necessary to make these queues known to installed printers. The P 0 add printq_0 and P 0 add printq_1 commands accomplish this. Note that capital letters are not required.

The two SPOOL commands in Figure 9-16 hark back to earlier versions of NetWare. As it happens, the server from which this screen was extracted is supporting an accounting package that does not know how to access NetWare named print queues. Instead, the program accesses *print spoolers*. How queues, print spoolers, and printers interact is not normally of importance, but you should be

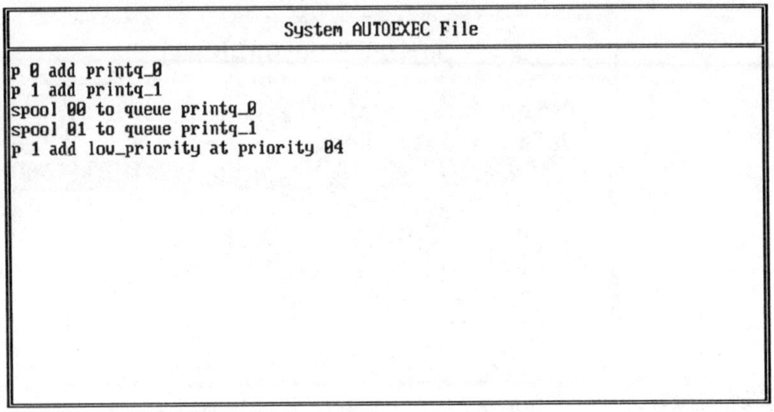

```
                        System AUTOEXEC File

p 0 add printq_0
p 1 add printq_1
spool 00 to queue printq_0
spool 01 to queue printq_1
p 1 add low_priority at priority 04
```

FIGURE 9-16.   Server AUTOEXEC.SYS screen with
Console print commands

aware that print spoolers (which are like but not the same as print queues) are supported in NetWare and can be assigned to specific printers.

The last line of the AUTOEXEC.SYS file shown in Figure 9-16 represents the LOW_PRIORITY queue assignment statement you issued through the server console following earlier instructions in this chapter. With this statement in the AUTOEXEC.SYS file, you will not need to issue this statement each time the server is booted. NetWare will play the AUTOEXEC.SYS file when the server boots, and thereby perform this task for you.

To exit an AUTOEXEC.SYS file without saving changes to it, press (**ALT-F10**), select **Yes**, and press (**ENTER**) to directly exit SYSCON. If you create or make changes to an AUTOEXEC.SYS file and wish the changes saved, escape out of the System AUTO-EXEC.SYS File screen.

NETWARE PRINT MANAGEMENT COMMANDS

In this section you will log in as VENESSA or as the user you logged in as when completing the exercises in Chapter 8. If you were logged in in Chapter 8 as GUEST, log in again under that user name. If you logged in under a user name that is not currently included among the list of queue users for the print queue to which you will be sending print jobs, you will have to add that name to the list, as explained previously under the "Print Queue Users" subheading.

PSTAT (Q in Version 2.0a)

To quickly confirm the existence and status of network printers, from the DOS prompt type **PSTAT** and press (ENTER). A listing of printers like that shown here will be displayed on your screen. (The analogous command for NetWare Version 2.0a is **Q**.)

```
Server FS1: Network Printer Information
Printer      Ready        Status      Form: number, name
---------    ---------    ---------   -----------------------------
0            Off-Line     Active      0, plain
1            Off-Line     Active      0, plain
2            Off-Line     Active      0, plain
```

NPRINT

The quick way to print a file is through use of the NetWare NPRINT command. To try this command, first switch to your user home directory (type **G:** and press (ENTER) if you are set up as VENESSA as shown earlier in this book). Now type **NDIR** and press (ENTER) to see a list of files in your home directory. MAIN.BAK should be included among that listing, if you worked through the NCOPY procedures in Chapter 8.

To print MAIN.BAK (or another file of your choosing, preferably a small file), at the prompt type something like the following:

```
NPRINT G:MAIN.BAK Q=LOW_PRIORITY B=NPRINT_MAIN
```

The Q= names the print queue to which you wish the job sent for servicing. Substitute another queue name after the Q= if you are using a queue other than LOW_PRIORITY.

The B= parameter prints the words following the equal sign as a banner in the lower half of a print job cover page. Banners may be up to twelve characters and cannot contain blanks.

Blanks are used in NetWare commands to separate command parameters, or modifiers. The underscore is used in both the queue name and the banner title so as not to confuse parts of a filename or banner with NPRINT parameters.

A list of available NPRINT parameters is shown in Table 9-2. These parameters are not discussed in detail here, for two reasons. First, unless you include the Job= parameter as part of your NPRINT command, you will find your file is printed unformatted. Normally, you will use an application's print services to print your file properly formatted. Second, most of these parameters can also be used with the CAPTURE command, which is discussed in detail later.

Take a moment now to issue the NPRINT command as just shown (substituting a correct queue name after Q=). Press (ENTER) to have the typed command executed. If the NPRINT command is successfully executed, you will see a message like this:

```
Queuing data to Server FS1, Queue LOW_PRIORITY
FS1/SYS1:DATA/USERS/VENESSA
        Queuing file MAIN.BAK
```

SERVER=*servername*
JOB=*job*
PRINTER=*n*
QUEUE=*queuename*
FORM=*formname* or *n*
COPIES=*n*
TABS=*n*
NoTabs
NAME=*name*
BANNER=*banner*
NOBANNER
FORMFEED
NOFORMFEED
DELETE

TABLE 9-2. NPRINT Parameters

There will be some delay while the server prepares to send MAIN.BAK to the queue you selected and on to the printer to which that queue is assigned. (If the queue is not assigned to a printer, your job will not be placed in the named queue. Or, if the printer is not turned on, not loaded with paper, and so forth, the job will simply sit in the named queue.)

CAPTURE and ENDCAP
(SPOOL or ENDSPOOL in Version 2.0a)

NetWare assumes you have a printer attached to your local workstation to which you will send print jobs. To send a job to a server print queue, you must reroute the job from the workstation to the server, to a specific print queue. The CAPTURE command accomplishes this rerouting. (In NetWare version 2.0a, the equivalent command is SPOOL.)

The NetWare CAPTURE command opens a door to a server print queue for receipt of a print job from a workstation. Think of this as the front door to a designated server print queue. Print jobs released from a print queue exit through the back door of a server's queue, figuratively speaking.

The mechanics of NetWare's print services requires a server queue's front door be closed before the back door leading to the printer can be opened. This description of queue operations is an analogy only, not an exact description of what happens. But it may help you to understand why the CAPTURE command by itself does not result in a print job being released from the server queue to a designated printer. CAPTURE only opens the front door.

To open the back door, through which a print job exits the server to the printer, an actual or implied ENDCAP (end capture) command must be issued. (In NetWare version 2.0a, the equivalent command is ENDSPOOL.)

PRINTING A JOB WITH AN EXPLICIT ENDCAP   To see how this works, issue a CAPTURE command like the following at the prompt and press (ENTER).

```
CAPTURE Q=LOW_PRIORITY
```

You will see a message indicating that print jobs are to be rerouted to the server from your workstation LPT1 port.

```
Device LPT1: re-routed to queue LOW_PRIORITY on server FS1.
```

Create a print job by pressing the (PRTSC) key. You should see a line flicker down your computer screen. However, if you are working on a nondedicated NetWare server in DOS mode, the (PRTSC) key is disabled. Try working from a workstation.

You can now wait, and wait, and wait. Your job will not be printed. CAPTURE only opens the front door to a print queue for receipt of a print job.

This is appropriate. It is possible you are sending a print job to the server in parts, and you want to keep the queue front door open until all the pieces of your print job are received into the queue.

Using the CAPTURE command as just described leaves under your control the opening and closing of the front and back doors to the print queue (figuratively speaking). Type **ENDCAP** and press (**ENTER**) to complete your print job, to close the front door on that job and open the queue's back door through which the job can be released to a printer. Depending on whether your print job is the first in the server queue, your job will print immediately or after some delay.

Notice, however, that when you issue ENDCAP, you receive a message that the printer default is returned to your local printer.

Device LPT1: set to local mode.

Thus, to reroute another job to a server queue you have to issue another CAPTURE command.

PRINTING A JOB WITH AN IMPLICIT ENDCAP   NetWare
issues an ENDCAP for you in two instances:

- When you exit an application program (for example, Lotus 1-2-3 or WordPerfect).

- When you log out of the server (or log in again; an implied LOGOUT situation).

Any print jobs created and rerouted to a server print queue will be released to the printer (if the printer is ready and you have not placed a hold or delay on the print job in question).

While this implicit ENDCAP feature frees you from having to remember to issue an ENDCAP command, it has the disadvantage that you must leave the application or log out of the server before the implicit ENDCAP takes effect. Exiting to a DOS shell from within an application and issuing ENDCAP from there is not a much better procedure, as you must also reissue the CAPTURE command before sending any additional print jobs to the server. Fortunately, NetWare offers a TIMEOUT= parameter you can use with CAPTURE (or with SPOOL, if you are working on a NetWare version 2.0a server), which gets around this inconvenience.

CAPTURE Parameters

CAPTURE command parameters are listed in Table 9-3. These parameters can be used in combination, as will be demonstrated. Only the more commonly used parameters are discussed here.

QUEUE=*QUEUENAME* (Q=)   The QUEUE= parameter lets you specify to which server queue a print job is to be sent. If no queue is specified and no printer is specified, the job is sent to PRINTQ_0.

If you followed the instructions earlier in this chapter, you have already used the QUEUE= parameter in a CAPTURE command, using the shortened version of this parameter: Q=.

[If you are working on a NetWare Version 2.0a server, substitute PRINTER=*n* (or P=) for the QUEUE parameter.]

TIMEOUT=*SECONDS* (TI=)   The TIMEOUT=*seconds* parameter provides control over when an implicit ENDCAP command is issued. TIMEOUT has the additional advantage that the CAPTURE command previously issued stays in place, unaltered.

The number placed after TIMEOUT= (or TI=, if you use the shortened version of this command) represents a delay measured in seconds. TIMEOUT delay measurement begins at any point the server ceases receiving print job information from your workstation. If the specified TIMEOUT seconds elapse before more print

SHOW
AUTOENDCAP
NOAUTOENDCAP
TIMEOUT=*n*
LOCAL=*n*
SERVER=*server*
JOB=*job*
PRINTER=*n*
QUEUE=*queue*
FORM=*formname* or *n*
COPIES=*n*
TABS=*n*
NOTABS
NAME=*name*
BANNER=*banner*
NOBANNER
FORMFEED
CREATE=*filespec*
KEEP

TABLE 9-3.   CAPTURE Parameters

job information is received at the server from your workstation, the server will assume the print job is complete and ready to be sent to a printer.

Try this parameter by typing at the prompt a CAPTURE command like the following:

```
CAPTURE Q=LOW_PRIORITY TI=15
```

Now press the (PRTSC) key to send a print screen to the server. Count off 15 seconds, and if there are not other print jobs spooled to your printer, your print job should begin printing.

If you send an additional print screen prior to 15 seconds passing, that second print screen will be included with the first and the two screens treated as a single print job by the server. After 15 seconds the job is ready for release from the print queue, and any subsequent print screens (or other print jobs) will be treated as separate print jobs.

By using the TIMEOUT= parameter, you can stay in an application (such as Lotus 1-2-3) and send countless print jobs without having to leave the application (an implied ENDCAP being issued) or going to the application's DOS shell (through which you previously would have issued an explicit ENDCAP).

To how many seconds should TIMEOUT= be set? There is not one answer. For most jobs, five or ten seconds is sufficient. For large print jobs, where there may be breaks in your workstation sending the job to the server, a longer timeout period may be required for the entire job to be included in the queue.

For instance, when you are printing a long, heavily formatted WordPerfect job from disk, a timeout of 120 seconds, or longer, may be appropriate. WordPerfect at the workstation goes through a process of compiling a set of pages (about 20) for sending to the server queue. After the first set of pages is sent, a second set must be compiled, and this can be a lengthy process. If the timeout period is set too low (10 seconds), the timeout period will expire and the server will assume the job is complete before the next set of WordPerfect document pages is readied and sent to the print queue. Only your first 20 or so pages will print. (In an interesting quirk, the remaining pages never get queued or printed. They just disappear to electronic thin air.)

The same kind of problem can occur with a database where a search for specific records is occurring simultaneously with printing of those records. You may only receive a printout of the first set of records if timeout is set too low.

How long is too long and too short a time? There is no single answer. A general guideline is to set timeout long enough to ensure that all of a job is received in a queue, but not so long that a user must wait at the printer for his or her print job to be released.

NO BANNER (NB)   NetWare normally prints a *banner page* as a cover page to each print job. The banner page helps identify the print job. This is especially useful if a large number of jobs are printing or your organization is large. The banner page can help route the printing to the correct user.

In a small office, or where a printer is serving only a few users in proximity to each other, you can dispense with the banner page being printed by including a NoBanner (or NB) parameter as part of your CAPTURE command.

NOFORMFEED (NFF)   When your print job ends, NetWare will normally issue a form feed command to your printer. This helps ensure that the last page, only partially printed on, is ejected from the printer before the next print job starts.

Most application packages issue their own form feed command at the end of a print job. If NetWare also issues its own form feed (the default CAPTURE setting) an extra blank page is printed at the end of each print job. If you do not want this blank page to be printed, use the NFF parameter in your CAPTURE command.

On the other hand, Lotus 1-2-3 does not issue a form feed to your printer, unless you explicitly press (PGUP) while you are in the Print submenu. (This is so you can print one or more spreadsheets, or portions of a spreadsheet, as part of a single print job.) In this instance, you may wish to include NFF (and a sufficiently long TIMEOUT) in your CAPTURE command to ensure that Lotus 1-2-3 has the opportunity to send all parts of the job to the printer as one job.

On the other hand, issuing CAPTURE without NFF ensures that the last page of a Lotus 1-2-3 print job ejects from the printer, which is a great benefit to other users if you forget to issue a Lotus 1-2-3 (PGUP) command. (If you forget the Lotus 1-2- 3 (PGUP), the next user's print job will most likely begin on the last page of your Lotus spreadsheet print job.)

COPIES=*N* (C=)   If you want multiple copies of a print job printed, you can include a COPIES= parameter in your CAPTURE command statement. If your application package allows you to specify the number of copies, as does WordPerfect Version 5.0, it is unnecessary to do so in your CAPTURE command.

FORM=*NUMBER OR NAME* (F=)   A particularly troublesome problem is how to ensure that paper is changed in a printer before a print job requiring special paper (letterhead) or a special form is released from a print queue.

The answer to this puzzle is to do one of the following:

- Include a FORMS= parameter in your CAPTURE command.

- Use a software application package (WordPerfect 5.0) that allows you to manage forms internal to the application.

Even if your applications manage form changes for you, you will be advised to have a clear understanding of how NetWare handles form change information.

In its simplest version, you can begin with a list of form types, with numerals assigned to each form type (0 through 9). For instance, you might use this list:

```
0 = Plain White 8 1/2" by 11" paper
1 = Plain White legal size paper
2 = First page of company letter stationery
3 = Second page of company stationery
4 = Purchase Order forms
9 = Other (to be used with NetWare Made Easy book only)
```

There is no special significance to the numbers themselves, except that when the server boots, NetWare always assumes form zero (0) is loaded in a printer, unless it is explicitly told otherwise. And the default for a CAPTURE command is FORM=0. If you boot your server with company letterhead in a printer tray, but the first print job to that printer either comes without a form type specified, or with type zero (0) specified, the job will print on the company letterhead.

 NetWare has no way of knowing what paper is actually loaded in a printer. All it can do is keep track of the form number for each print job and pause in its releasing of jobs to a printer whenever the form number changes.

With form zero (0) assumed by NetWare at time of server booting, jobs will continue to be relased to a printer (all other things being equal) until the form number associated with a print job (through the CAPTURE command) changes to, say, form 5. At this point, the server stops releasing jobs to the printer, giving you (or whomever is in charge of that printer) an opportunity to mount the correct paper.

When the correct paper is placed in the printer, NetWare again has no way of knowing this. You must tell it to resume releasing print jobs by issuing an appropriate printer Console command. Having completed a print job for form 5 (to, one hopes, form 5), NetWare now inspects the next job in the queue for its form number, which is zero (0) if not otherwise specified through a FORM= parameter. If the next job is also for form 5, that job is released to the printer, on the assumption that correct form is already mounted in the printer. If the form number is different from 5, NetWare pauses again to allow you an opportunity to change the printer paper or form, after which you must again issue the appropriate printer Console command to resume release of the next print job to the printer.

A SUMMARY EXAMPLE   An example of how some parameters, including FORM=, might be used in a single CAPTURE command is shown here. Do not proceed with this example unless you have access to the server. If you place a print job in a queue for which there is a form change, it may result in the server ceasing to send print jobs to the printer. This will cause considerable consternation for others, particularly if no one in your organization knows how to issue the proper Console command to resume printing, or if the server keyboard is inaccessible.

If you are able and prepared to follow through on the action your are about to take, at the prompt type the following CAPTURE command and press (ENTER). Substitute for PRINTQ_0 in the Q= command the server queue to which you wish your job to be sent.

CAPTURE Q=LOW_PRIORITY TI=15 NB COPIES=2 FORM=9

Do not include the NoFormFeed (NFF) parameter in the command. When you test this CAPTURE command by pressing (PRTSC), a form feed is not issued by DOS as part of the printscreen routine. You need NetWare's default of FORMFEED to ensure that your print job ejects from the printer.

MOUNTING A NEW FORM AT THE SERVER IN CONSOLE MODE

In the last CAPTURE command you issued, you sent a print screen job to a queue using a FORM=9 parameter. The result of this is that when your job becomes active, ready for releasing to the printer, NetWare will cease sending any jobs to that printer. (Unless the preceding job also just happened to use form 9, which is probably not the case.)

Unfortunately no message is sent to any workstation telling users that a network printer needs to have a different paper or form mounted in it. You will, however, see such a message on the *server's* screen, and it will probably look like this:

Mount form 9 (UNKNOWN) in printer 0. Then use PRINTER 0 MOUNT FORM 9.

Since you really do not care about what paper your job is printed on, if the paper in the printer is plain white paper, just leave that paper in place. To restart the printer *from the server keyboard*, as instructed by the on-screen message, type **PRINTER 00 MOUNT FORM 9** and press (ENTER). When you have used the correct form of this command, you will see the following message:

:
Printer 0 Form 9 mounted.
:

Once your print screen job has printed, again restart the printer and tell the server (through the command just listed) that form *xx* is mounted in the printer (*xx* representing the form number corresponding to the paper actually in the printer). Monitor the server screen to be sure the next job sent to the printer executes correctly.

NETWARE WORKSTATION MENUS

The three workstation print menus available in NetWare are PCONSOLE, PRINTDEF, and PRINTCON. The latter menus are not going to be discussed in detail in this book. Users on a network typically use application software to control their network printing and find little need for PRINTDEF or PRINTCON services. Moreover, if you fail to use these menus appropriately, particularly PRINTCON, you may inadvertently lock out your users from the network printers. However, a brief discussion follows.

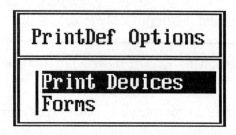

FIGURE 9-17.   PRINTDEF Options menu

Using PRINTDEF and PRINTCON
To Control Print Modes

The purpose of PRINTDEF is to allow the network SUPERVISOR to define modes of operation for network print devices. For instance, users sometimes want to print in condensed mode, but have difficulty remembering what escape codes to issue or how or where to place them in their application file to accomplish this task.

PRINTDEF provides a means to create (edit) the appropriate escape code sequence that tells a specific make and model of printer to print in condensed mode (see the Print Devices option in Figure 9-17). If print devices are already set up on other servers on an internetwork, you can choose to import those definitions to your server (or export those you create to other servers). Figure 9-18 shows the PRINTDEF submenu through which you approach these tasks.

With print definitions set up, PRINTCON (or NPRINT or CAPTURE) can be used to send this sequence of escape codes to the printer ahead of the actual file to be printed. PRINTCON is not discussed here, for several reasons which may already be apparent. But the PRINTCON Available Options main menu is shown in Figure 9-19.

```
┌─────────────────────────────────────┐
│                                      │
│   Print Device Options               │
│                                      │
├─────────────────────────────────────┤
│ ▌Edit Print Devices                  │
│  Import Print Device                 │
│  Export Print Device                 │
│                                      │
└─────────────────────────────────────┘
```

FIGURE 9-18.   PRINTDEF Print Device Options submenu

Why not use PRINTDEF and PRINTCON to define and use
print devices? First, even if you take the time through PRINTDEF
and PRINTCON to define print job modes, your efforts may be in
vain. Many application programs (WordPerfect, for instance) send
a reset escape code to a printer at the beginning of a print job.
If your application does this, the escape codes sent through
PRINTCON, NPRINT, or CAPTURE are nullified. Again,
PRINTDEF and PRINTCON are tools, not necessarily solutions.

Second, use of PRINTDEF and PRINTCON takes considerable
knowledge of printer operations and how these interact with

```
┌──────────────────────────────────────────────┐
│            Available Options                   │
│                                                │
├──────────────────────────────────────────────┤
│ ▌Edit Print Job Configurations                 │
│  Select Default Print Job Configuration        │
│  Supervisor - Copy Print Job Configurations    │
└──────────────────────────────────────────────┘
```

FIGURE 9-19.   PRINTDEF Available Options main menu

application packages, and many application packages allow you to accomplish the same type of task as easily within the application software. Finally, it is quite possible by using PRINTCON to confound your printing efforts and create a situation where you cannot use your usual NetWare network printing arrangements.

All of this is not a recommendation to not use PRINTDEF and PRINTCON, but it is a caution. For more on how to use PRINTDEF and PRINTCON to define network print device modes, see the NetWare *Menu Utilities* manual.

Using PRINTDEF to Create Form Types

There is one use for PRINTDEF that you may wish to install. This feature is the creation of a forms list, internal to NetWare, that users can access to ensure they issue the CAPTURE command with an appropriate FORM= parameter (where that is necessary). However, before doing this, be aware that named form types apply to all queues and all printers equally. The number 2 and the name LETTERHEAD are only nominal categories, having no direct influence on what form actually is placed in a printer, but associating the numeral 2 with a form type name LETTERHEAD means that LETTERHEAD will be listed on the screen as form type 2 whenever a user calls up a forms listing.

Get some agreement in your organization about what numbers to associate with form types before proceeding. And consider reserving one number, perhaps 9, as an "Other" form category. (Other can cause some confusion if it is used by different users for different forms, but it gives a user some category to hang his or her hat on if they do not see the form type they plan to use listed among the defined forms.)

To create form types through PRINTDEF, you must log in and access PRINTDEF as the user SUPERVISOR. After logging in, at the prompt type **PRINTDEF** and press (ENTER).

FIGURE 9-20.   PRINTDEF Forms list

You will see the PRINTDEF Options menu, as illustrated in Figure 9-17. Highlight **Forms** and press (ENTER). A Forms listing screen will appear. If any form types have already been defined, as illustrated in Figure 9-20, they will be listed; otherwise, this screen will be blank.

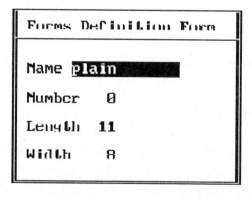

FIGURE 9-21.   PRINTDEF Forms definition form

To define a new form type, press (INSERT). A Forms Definition form like that shown in Figure 9-21 will be displayed. Use this form to define a new form type, providing a name, an associated form number (not already in use), and the length and width of the form measured in inches. When you have completed the definition, press (ENTER) to have the new form added to the current Forms listing.

To leave PRINTDEF, press the (ESC) key until you see the "Exit PRINTDEF" prompt. Select **Yes** and press (ENTER) to leave PRINTDEF. A list of form types is now established for your server.

Using PCONSOLE to Manage Print Jobs: A User's Perspective

In this section, you will log in as a user of the print queue you established earlier through PCONSOLE and assigned to a printer through a server console assign command. It is important that the print jobs you create remain in the print queue in question. This can best be assured if the printer to which the queue is assigned is left turned off, which means you may have to complete the exercises given here during a nonpeak network use period.

In the examples that follow, VENESSA is the assumed user login name. At the prompt, type a CAPTURE command like the following:

```
CAPTURE Q=LOW_PRIORITY TI=5 NB
```

Now press the (PRTSC) key several times, waiting at least five seconds between each keypress to ensure that multiple jobs are created and sent to your LOW_PRIORITY queue.

Next, type **PCONSOLE** and press (ENTER) to access the PCONSOLE menu. From the Available Options menu, select **Print Queue Information** and press (ENTER). Highlight **LOW_PRIORITY** (or the queue where you sent your print screen

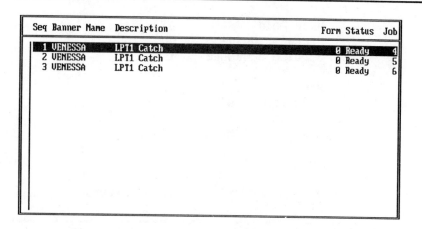

```
  Seq Banner Name  Description                        Form Status  Job

    1 VENESSA      LPT1 Catch                            0 Ready    4
    2 VENESSA      LPT1 Catch                            0 Ready    5
    3 VENESSA      LPT1 Catch                            0 Ready    6
```

FIGURE 9-22. LOW_PRIORITY queue jobs listing

jobs) and press (ENTER). You will see listed the several jobs you
sent to the print queue, as illustrated in Figure 9-22.

As a user, you can manage each of your own print jobs in a
variety of ways. To see just how, highlight any of the print jobs

```
                      Print Queue Entry Information

Print job:          4                File size:       2052
Client:             VENESSA[2]
Description:        LPT1 Catch
Status:             Ready To Be Serviced, Waiting For Print Server

User Hold:          No               Job Entry Date:  December 5, 1989
Operator Hold:      No               Job Entry Time:  1:11:03 pm
Service Sequence:   1

Number of copies:   1                Form:            plain
File contents:      Text             Print banner:    No
Tab size:           8                Banner name:
Suppress form feed: Yes              Banner file:

Defer printing:     No               Target date:
                                     Target time:
Target server:      (Any Server)
```

FIGURE 9-23. Print job 4 print queue entry information
screen

```
User Hold:          Yes
Operator Hold:      No
Service Sequence:   1

Number of copies:   1
File contents:      Text
Tab size:           8
Suppress form feed: Yes

Defer printing:     No

Target server:      (Any Server)
```

FIGURE 9-24.   Left portion of the print queue entry
information screen

and press (ENTER). A Print Queue Entry Information screen like that
shown in Figure 9-23 will be displayed, with the information for
the print job you highlighted before pressing (ENTER).

You cannot alter some of the information in this screen. For
instance, you cannot even move the cursor up to the print job
number. And if you move down a line from the Description line,
your cursor skips over the Status line. In fact, NetWare allows you
to highlight only those items a user is allowed to change or manage,
in this instance skipping down to the User Hold item.

To aid in our discussion, Figure 9-24 highlights a portion of the
left side of the Print Queue Entry Information screen.

PLACING A JOB ON HOLD   Jobs are normally placed in a
queue ready to be serviced. If you want to indefinitely delay
printing of a job, change the User Hold option to Yes. The job will
now remain in the queue until such time as you (logged in under
your user name), the user SUPERVISOR, or the queue operator
for this queue sets User Hold back to No.

One complication is that you must enter PCONSOLE to set
HOLD to Yes. If the queue is otherwise empty when your job is

added, and your TIMEOUT parameter is set to only a few seconds, your job could be released to the printer before you have time to enter PCONSOLE and change HOLD to Yes. There is no solution other than

- using a longer TIMEOUT in your CAPTURE command

- turning off the printer temporarily

- using a server Console command to stop the printer

None of these solutions is elegant, but they work.

NUMBER OF COPIES With the highlight bar on User Hold, press the (DOWN) arrow key once. You will notice that the highlight bar skips over the Operator Hold and Service Sequence options (unless you are a queue operator for this queue or a supervisor-equivalent user) and lands on the Number of Copies field. The number in that field is 1, the default copies number for the CAPTURE command, or a higher figure, if you used the COPIES= parameter in your CAPTURE command.

You may change the Number of Copies figure from within PCONSOLE, but you must do this before a job is released to the printer. See the previous discussion under "Placing a Job on Hold" for how to enter PCONSOLE before your job is released from the queue.

FILE CONTENTS, TAB SIZE, AND SUPPRESS FORM FEED Press the (DOWN) arrow key once again, and you are on the File Contents field, which is probably set to Text. If you press (INSERT) once, you see displayed a File Contents submenu (shown in Figure 9-25). You may choose to send your file in Byte stream mode, rather than Text mode. The default setting for the CAPTURE command is Text.

FIGURE 9-25.   File Contents submenu

You may continue to move the cursor down the Print Queue
Entry Information screen and change the NetWare default Tab Size
and Suppress Form Feed parameters. The default tab size is 8, but
this default will have no effect on most of the files you print, where
tabs are set inside the file being printed.

Suppress Form Feed defaults to No, so that NetWare normally
issues its own form feed. If Suppress Form Feed is set to Yes, it is
because you used the NoFormFeed (NFF) parameter as part of a
CAPTURE command before sending this job to the print queue.

DEFERRING A JOB TO A SPECIFIC DATE AND TIME

You may encounter a situation where you want to defer printing a
job to a later time and date. This might be a lengthy print job that
can be deferred to the evening, or even the early hours of the
morning, when no one is using the network.

To defer printing, highlight **Defer Printing** and change from
the default of No to **Yes**. (You need only press the **Y** key.) As
illustrated in Figure 9-26, NetWare provides a suggested target
date and target time. Automatic placement of the highlight bar over
the Target Date field is on the assumption you may wish to change
one or both of these date and time parameters.

```
┌──────────────────────────────────────────────────────────────────┐
│                    Print Queue Entry Information                   │
│ Print job:         4               File size:       2852           │
│ Client:            UENESSA[2]                                      │
│ Description:      ▐LPT1 Catch                       ▌              │
│ Status:            Ready To Be Serviced, Waiting For Print Server  │
│                                                                    │
│ User Hold:         No              Job Entry Date:   December 5, 1989│
│ Operator Hold:     No              Job Entry Time:   1:11:03 pm     │
│ Service Sequence:  1                                               │
│                                                                    │
│ Number of copies:  1               Form:             plain         │
│ File contents:     Text            Print banner:     No            │
│ Tab size:          8               Banner name:                    │
│ Suppress form feed: Yes            Banner file:                    │
│                                                                    │
│ Defer printing:    No              Target date:                    │
│                                    Target time:                    │
│ Target server:     (Any Server)                                    │
└──────────────────────────────────────────────────────────────────┘
```

FIGURE 9-26.   Print queue entry information for print job 4 with Defer Printing set to Yes

Type a new date and time. NetWare will recognize several different date and time formats: January 9, 1990, or 01/09/90, for instance.

The deferred job will be released from the queue for printing as soon after the target date and time as the server is powered on and the printer available (powered on, loaded with paper, and any already active print jobs completed).

If you down the server before queued print jobs are released from the queue, those jobs are saved to disk. The jobs are not lost if the server is properly shut down using the Console DOWN command.

To set Defer Printing back to No, with the highlight bar on the **Target Date** field, press the (LEFT) arrow key once, and change Yes to **No**.

TARGET SERVER   Because, in theory, multiple servers can service a single print queue, you are provided with a Target Server

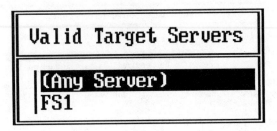

FIGURE 9-27.   Valid Target Servers options

option. The NetWare default is Any Server. Highlight this item and press (INSERT) to see the valid target servers to which you might wish to assign this specific job for servicing. As illustrated in Figure 9-27, you may have only one target server available to you, in which instance Any Server and the available server are always the same.

Unless you are on an internetwork with complex internetwork printing options established, you normally will not need to change the NetWare target server default. In fact, attempting to do so may only confound your printing efforts and unnecessarily complicate your life.

CHANGING A JOB'S ASSOCIATED FORM NUMBER OR TYPE   As a user, you can change the default or specified form number or form type for your print job. To accomplish this, place the highlight bar over the **Number of Copies** choice and press the (RIGHT) arrow key. You should land on the Form option.

Press (INSERT) to see a list of currently defined valid forms types (see Figure 9-28). If you did not use PRINTDEF to define a form type, a form number will be displayed, which you can change to any number between 0 and 9.

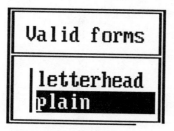

FIGURE 9-28.   Valid Forms submenu within PCONSOLE

Having completed your inspection of the Print Queue Entry Information screen, press (ESC) to return to the Jobs Listing screen (shown in Figure 9-22).

DELETING A JOB FROM A QUEUE   It is common for a user to place a job in the queue and then decide not to print the job. Less common, but most troublesome, is a user placing the same job in a queue multiple times. This usually occurs when the user fails to see the job exit from the network printer, for any number of reasons (including the user expecting the job to print to a printer other than the printer to which that queue is assigned, meaning the user probably specified the wrong queue in his or her CAPTURE command).

If you enter PCONSOLE and inspect your jobs in the queue, you can choose to delete one or all of them. To delete a single job, place the highlight bar over that job (number 4 in Figure 9-22) and press the (DELETE) key once. A Delete Queue Entry screen will be displayed (Figure 9-29). Confirm that, **Yes**, you wish to delete the entry, and press (ENTER). If the job was not already active, it will be deleted.

If you are attempting to delete an already active print job—one being released to the printer—you will be asked a second time to

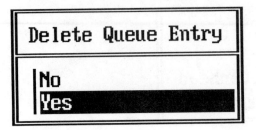

FIGURE 9-29.   Delete Queue Entry box

confirm that you wish to delete active job number such and such. Select **Yes** and press (ENTER) and the active job is deleted from the queue.

You may use the (F5) (Mark) key to highlight several print jobs for deleting. When you press (DELETE), you will see the Delete All Marked Queue Entries screen as shown in Figure 9-30. Select **Yes** and press (ENTER) to delete the group of marked jobs.

Should you try to delete a job that is not yours, and you are not a queue operator or supervisor-equivalent user, you will be informed that you are not allowed to delete that print job item.

```
┌──────────────────────────────────────┐
│ Delete All Marked Queue Entries        │
├──────────────────────────────────────┤
│ No                                      │
│ Yes                                     │
└──────────────────────────────────────┘
```

FIGURE 9-30.   Delete All Marked Queue Entries box

Delete all of your jobs from the LOW_PRIORITY print queue (or whichever queue you are using), and then press (ALT-F10) to quickly exit out of the PCONSOLE menu.

Using PCONSOLE to Manage Print Jobs: The SUPERVISOR and Queue Operator Perspective

A user cannot normally delete any jobs except those that he or she created. Only a queue operator or SUPERVISOR can change the order in which jobs will be serviced.

The examples discussed here illustrate this point. No attempt is made to walk you through this process. However, if you set up yourself and VENESSA earlier in this chapter as users of the queue LOW_PRIORITY and you made VENESSA a queue user, you can log in under your usual user name and place jobs in the LOW_PRIORITY print queue; then log in as VENESSA and see how VENESSA, as a queue operator, can manage your own user jobs.

This section illustrates how to change a job's service sequence. Having logged in under the user name for a queue operator or supervisor equivalent user, call up the PCONSOLE menu. With the cursor over **Print Queue Information**, press (ENTER). Highlight the queue you wish to manage (perhaps **LOW_PRIORITY**) and press (ENTER).

(You must have several jobs in the queue to manage the job sequence. As required, exit back to the prompt and issue the proper CAPTURE command to allow you to place additional jobs in the print queue.)

Place the cursor over the last print job in the list of jobs; then press (ENTER). Figure 9-31 shows a Print Queue Entry Information screen for a Print Job numbered 319 (line 1, upper-left corner). The Service Sequence (line 7 on the left side of the figure) is currently number 3. (In this example there are only three jobs in the queue.)

```
┌──────────────────────────────────────────────────────────────────┐
│                  Print Queue Entry Information                     │
├──────────────────────────────────────────────────────────────────┤
│Print job:        319            File size:         4104            │
│Client:           DOUG[2]                                           │
│Description:      LPT1 Catch                                        │
│Status:           Ready To Be Serviced, Waiting For Print Server    │
│                                                                    │
│User Hold:        No             Job Entry Date:    December 5, 1989 │
│Operator Hold:    No             Job Entry Time:    1:09:17 pm       │
│Service Sequence: 3                                                 │
│                                                                    │
│Number of copies: 1              Form:              plain           │
│File contents:    Text           Print banner:      No              │
│Tab size:         8              Banner name:                       │
│Suppress form feed: No           Banner file:                       │
│                                                                    │
│Defer printing:   No             Target date:                       │
│                                 Target time:                       │
│                                                                    │
│Target server:    (Any Server)                                      │
└──────────────────────────────────────────────────────────────────┘
```

FIGURE 9-31.   Print Queue Entry Information screen for print
job 319

Move the cursor down to **Service Sequence** and change the
current sequence number to **1**. Press (ESC) once to return to the list
of queue jobs. As illustrated in Figure 9-32, job 319 has been
moved to the head of the queue and is first in line for servicing.

 If a current job 1 is active, you must change a later job to job 2, so
that it will print after the currently active job.

PCONSOLE is a useful tool for managing network print jobs
from workstations. You can reduce your network management
responsibilities considerably by

- creating queue operators (other than yourself) who will be
  responsible for managing specific server print queues

- training users (particularly queue operators) in how to use
  PCONSOLE

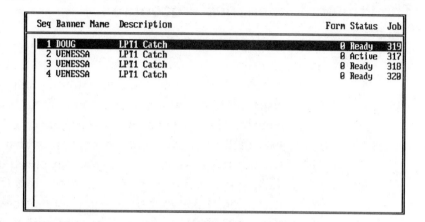

Seq	Banner Name	Description	Form	Status	Job
1	DOUG	LPT1 Catch	0	Ready	319
2	VENESSA	LPT1 Catch	0	Active	317
3	VENESSA	LPT1 Catch	0	Ready	318
4	VENESSA	LPT1 Catch	0	Ready	320

FIGURE 9-32.   Job 319 placed at the head of the queue

INSTALLING NETWORK PRINTERS

It is often the case that an initial NetWare server setup does not include any network printers or includes only one. It is not necessary to reconfigure all of NetWare to add or change existing printer setups. However, you must use a NetWare system maintenance procedure to add to or alter network printer configurations. The discussion that follows assumes you have a floppy disk drive on your server and that maintenance will be accomplished on the server.

If you are installing a serial printer, you will need to know several pieces of information about how your server and printer will communicate with each other. Default values for these items are available in NetWare. They are as follows:

Baud Rate:	9600
Word Length:	8 bits
Stop Bits:	1 bit
Parity:	None
XON/XOFF Protocol:	No

The Printer Maintenance Procedures

Following is a simplified outline of the procedures to use to install network printers. It is strongly recommended that you carefully read your NetWare documentation before attempting the procedures listed here. If you are in any doubt about how to proceed, rely on the manuals that came with your version of NetWare.

Be especially attentive to the prompts provided about how to *accept* a definition or choice. While you may press (ENTER) to select a highlighted menu choice, you must often press (ESC) to keep a setup definition. Take your time, and read the screens carefully. And keep your NetWare installation and maintenance manuals close at hand.

Also, always work with backup, working copies of your Net-Ware diskettes (which must already have been created for you to be doing a maintenance activity).

In brief outline, this is the procedure for installing network printers:

1. Be sure the printer being installed is physically connected to the server. A printer may be attached through either a server parallel or serial port, but the printer cable coupler must be appropriate to the server port, and the printer of a make and model appropriate for parallel or serial printing. (Some printers can work in either parallel or serial mode, though you may have to set printer dip switches to select the correct mode.)

2. Begin a NetWare operating system maintenance session using the following steps:

   a. Down your server.

   b. Place a DOS boot disk appropriate for your server in the server A:\ drive and power on (reboot) the server.

   c. You must have on your DOS boot disk a DOS CON-FIG.SYS file that includes the lines:

```
FILES = 20
BUFFERS =15
```

The server is now running DOS, not NetWare.

d. Place a *working copy* (not the original) of your **NETGEN** diskette into the server disk drive A.

e. At the prompt, type **NETGEN** and press (ENTER). (NETGEN command flags are available; refer to your NetWare documentation. But be sure *not* to use the N flag. This would put you into a new system generation mode. You are trying to update the system, not recreate it from scratch.) You will be prompted to insert additional (working copies) of diskettes into the server disk drive(s) as they are needed.

f. From the NetWork Generation Options menu, select **NetWare Installation** and press (ENTER).

g. NetWare will verify hard disk information, but you will not want to alter the current information. Eventually, you should see an Installation Options submenu.

h. Within the Installation Options submenu, highlight **Select Custom Installation Options** and press (ENTER). This should take you to the Custom Installation submenu.

i. From within the Custom Installation submenu, highlight **Miscellaneous Maintenance** and press (ENTER). You are finally at the Miscellaneous Maintenance submenu.

3. Within the Miscellaneous Maintenance menu, highlight **Printer Maintenance** and press (ENTER). You should now see a list of spooled printers. (If you do not see this list, exit this NetWare maintenance session and refer to your NetWare system installation and maintenance books.)

4. A list of parallel (LPT) and serial (COM) devices installed on your server will appear on the screen, along with a definition

of any printers already installed to a device. Note that if no printer has been installed (defined) as attached to a particular serial or parallel port, "Not Spooled" will appear beneath the Spooled Printer # column.

You should also see at the bottom of your screen an Available Printer Definition Operations submenu. Use the items in this submenu to

a. edit (SELECT or MODIFY) an existing printer setup definition

b. delete a printer setup definition ((DELETE))

c. exit the maintenance process ((ESC))

This discussion assumes you wish to add a new printer definition.

5. To add a new printer definition to the server, highlight an unused COM or LPT port and press (ENTER). A Printer Definition form will appear on your screen.

a. If it is a parallel (LPT) device you selected, the printer definition form will be something like this:

   Spooled Parallel Printer
   Device: LPT3
   Spooled Printer #: 4

   To accept the default printer number and definition, just press (ESC) once. (If the definition proves to be incorrect, use the (DELETE) option to remove the definition and start over.)

b. For a serial (COM) device, you will see a Printer Definition screen something like the following:

```
          Spooled Serial Printer
       Spooled Printer:           0
       Baud Rate:                 9600
       Word Length:               8 bits
       Stop Bits:                 1 bit
       Parity:                    None
       Xon/Xoff Protocol:         No
```

You may either accept the default values provided by Net-Ware or change any of the values. When you have made whatever changes are necessary, press (ESC) to accept the printer definition.

6. When you are satisfied with your printer definitions, press (ESC) to exit the printer installation process. (Pressing (ESC) a second time will take you back into the Changing the Spooled Printer List screen.)

   Pressing (ESC) just once, you will be prompted with "Use New Printer Definitions?" If you want to abandon your changes, select **No**. By selecting **Yes**, you will be returned to the Miscellaneous Maintenance submenu with the definitions recorded.

7. In the Miscellaneous Maintenance submenu, select **Return to Previous Menu** and press (ENTER). This returns you to the Custom Installation menu.

8. In the Custom Installation menu, highlight **Return to Previous Menu** and press (ENTER). This takes you back to the Installation Options menu.

9. In the Installation Options menu highlight **Continue Installation** and press (ENTER). You will now be prompted with "Install Networking Software on Filer Server?" If you want your new network printer configuration installed, select **Yes**. (If you

select **No**, you will be asked to confirm abandonment of the changes.)

Having selected **Yes**, routines on your NetWare NETGEN diskette take over the process of installing your network printer changes. A message will appear on the screen asking you to be patient as the installation process can take several minutes.

Once the installation maintenance process is complete, remove your NETGEN (and DOS) diskette from the server drives and reboot the server (first place a required boot diskette in the A drive on a nondedicated server).

INSTALLING AN APPLICATION
TO A NETWORK PRINTER

Increasingly, network application software includes network printing services that operate transparently to the user. For example, WordPerfect Version 5.0 can be installed so that server-attached printers are listed among available printers within WordPerfect print-management menus.

Making network printers available from within application software is an application software responsibility and problem, not a NetWare problem. As an open operating system, NetWare allows for and encourages such application development. But application software must be written to make network printers transparently available to users. How an application arranges for access to network printers (if at all) is an important consideration in any network application software purchase decisions.

Once purchased, application software will not automatically know of network printers. The software must be configured and installed to make it aware

- that it is running on a NetWare server

- of what network printers (up to five) are installed on and attached to the NetWare server

See your application software documentation for guidance on how to make your application aware of network printers.

THE PITFALLS
OF NETWORK PRINTING

You have a network printer attached to your server and you want to send a print job to it. Whether your printing effort will bring joy or disappointment depends on knowing and avoiding the pitfalls of network printing.

"What can go wrong will go wrong." The corollary to that truism is, "If you know what can go wrong, you can make it go right." Understanding the pitfalls of network printing gives you important insight into how to make printing go right.

Proper Print Driver Selection

In the world of printers, all printers are not created equal. A room full of printers is analogous to a room full of United Nations delegates. While there may be one or two semi-standard languages—English and French for U.N. delegates, IBM and Epson for printers—no one language is spoken or understood by all. And even the same language is spoken with different accents.

Most application software, whether installed on the server or at the workstation, allows you to define printer defaults. These defaults include one or more *print drivers*. A printer driver is a special file that acts as a translator between the electronic copy of your print job and the printer that produces the hardcopy version. A printer driver, like a conscientious U.N. translator, will do its best to translate your electronic print job into a language understood by your printer. But if you select an incorrect printer driver, one that does not know your printer's standard language (or the accent it uses in speaking a semi-standard printer language), the best you can hope for is a hardcopy of your print job that approximates what you developed on the screen.

Your network users may understandably be unaware of the importance of printer drivers to accurate printing. They may be used to printing jobs to the one and only printer attached to their local workstation. They may be unaware that a print job configured for, say, a workstation-attached Okidata Microline printer will not print properly to an HP laser printer, whether the HP is attached to the server or to a local workstation.

If your network print jobs have unexpected characters embedded, do not format quite as you expected, or just simply "hang up," check the printer driver being used in conjunction with your print job. In selecting application software for the network, look for software that is flexible in allowing you to install printer drivers, and that allows for users to temporarily select default printer drivers.

Fonts and Special Formatting

Some printers, particularly laser printers, allow you to use a variety of fonts (type styles) within a document. Fonts are a special case of special formatting instructions. Special formatting can include escape codes embedded in a document (such as a Lotus 1-2-3 setup string in a spreadsheet file print job).

For print jobs that use special fonts, you need more than just the correct printer driver. If your application uses fonts other than *internal hard fonts* (fonts always resident in the printer itself) you must have either of the following:

- A *font cartridge* physically inserted in the printer (the cartridge containing the required fonts).

- Downloaded *soft fonts* from a computer file to the printer.

Some application programs allow you to include codes in the document that will download soft fonts automatically, as part of the print job activities controlled through the application. In other instances, you may have to download the desired fonts before sending the job to the printer. In either case, these fonts have to be resident on some storage medium.

One alternative is to place these fonts in a server hard disk directory. For the fonts to download, a user will need a mapping to the server fonts directory.

 Difficulty in using fonts is more often an application software problem than a NetWare server printing problem.

Is Your Job Rerouted to the Server?

If a user does not have a printer attached to his or her workstation and fails to issue a CAPTURE command prior to printing, application software may direct the print job to a workstation port. The application assumes a local printer is attached. At best, the print job will just not happen and the application will echo a message to the workstation screen indicating there is a problem with the printer. Or, no message will appear, and the print job will just not happen. In the worst case, your application will hang up the workstation.

 You can avoid the "no local printer" problem by including in user login scripts a CAPTURE command that reroutes a user's print job to the appropriate server print queue.

No Actual or Implied End
Of the CAPTURE Command

Sometimes a job just seems not to release from the queue. The problem can be that there was no TIMEOUT parameter issued with the CAPTURE command. If a print job has been sent to the server, to a correct queue, but the job is not yet printing, try issuing the ENDCAP command at the workstation prompt.

Multiple Print Queues
And Multiple Printers

Sometimes a user sends a print job to the server with a proper print driver for the selected network printer, but places that print job in the wrong print queue. Remember:

- You can have up to five installed network printers attached to any one server.

- Multiple print queues can service any one printer.

Having a user automatically captured at log in to a default print queue (through a system or user login script) is fine as long as there is only one printer, or one print queue, to which a user might ever wish to send a print job. But with multiple printers, and the possibility of multiple queues servicing any one printer, a user can easily send a print job to an incorrect queue and printer.

Similarly, local workstation-attached printers may still be used by some users, for at least some print jobs. You need a device for helping a user select the local printer, when desired, and the correct network print queue and printer, when desired. A useful tool is to include in custom menus a submenu of printer choices, with an option to go to the printer submenu before calling up a particular application software package. An example of what these submenu screens might look like is shown in Figure 9-33.

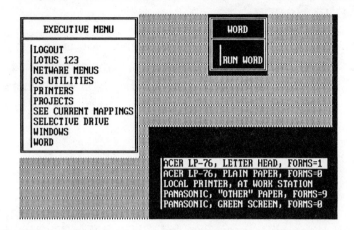

FIGURE 9-33.   Executive menu sample screen

The text file that creates these submenus (extracted from a much more complex customized menu) is shown here:

```
%EXECUTIVE MENU,2,9
WORD
  %WORD
SELECT PRINTER
  %PRINTERS
%WORD,2,45,4
RUN WORD
  WORD
  G:
PRINTERS
  %PRINTERS
%PRINTERS,30,45,4
ACER LP=76, PLAIN PAPER, FORMS=0
  CAPTURE Q=PRINTQ_1, TIMEOUT=10 FORMS=0 NB
ACER LP=76, LETTERHEAD, FORMS=1
  CAPTURE Q=PRINTQ_1, TIMEOUT=10 FORMS=1 NB
OKIDATA, GREEN SCREEN, FORMS=0
  CAPTURE, Q=PRINTQ_0, TIMEOUT=10 FORMS=0 NB
OKIDATA, "OTHER PAPER", TIMEOUT=10, FORMS=9
  CAPTURE, Q=PRINTQ_0, TIMEOUT=10, FORMS=9 NB
LOCAL PRINTER, AT WORK STATION
  ENDCAP
```

Is the Printer Ready?

Do not overlook the obvious when you are diagnosing network print job problems. For instance, is the printer to which a job is to be sent powered on? Is it loaded with paper? Is there a paper jam, or some other *printer* problem to be resolved? Before blaming the server, check the printer.

Multiple Jobs in a Queue

Users may be used to printing to a local printer where their print job receives immediate and sole attention. On a network, a server print queue may hold numerous jobs at once (including more than one from a single user workstation). These jobs are serviced in priority order; first in, first out of the print queue.

Sometimes users believe their job is not printing, when in practice it is just not yet their turn at the printer. Use the workstation PCONSOLE menu and the server print-specific Console commands to monitor print job status in a queue. This menu and these commands are previously discussed in this chapter.

Print Job Holds and Delays

A particularly large, complicated, or otherwise special print job may get in the way of other users accessing a printer. The problem is not a printing problem as such. A user's print job eventually gets printed. But from the user's perspective, a network printing problem exists.

You can help to get large, special, lower-priority print jobs out of the way in either of these ways:

• Place an indefinite hold on that print job.

• Delay printing of the job until a particular date and time.

Unless you are managing print jobs in a very centralized manner (which is not recommended—it is preferable to maintain the illusion of PC independence in the LAN environment), use of job hold and delay techniques will require that users understand both the CAPTURE command and the PCONSOLE menu, and have a willingness to cooperate with each other.

Multiple Print Queues And Print Queue Priority

More than one queue may service a single printer. Multiple queues can be useful if higher priority jobs need to be printed before lower-priority jobs. Each queue assigned to a printer is assigned at a specific service priority: 1st, 2nd, and so on. A user may not have his or her print job coming to the printer because there are jobs in a higher-priority print queue that are taking precedence over jobs in his or her lower-priority print queues.

If you map multiple queues to a printer, be sure that users have some understanding of the existence and consequence of print queue priorities. Monitor user satisfaction with the current configuration. Consider attaching an additional printer to the server or using other print job management techniques if users are too dissatisfied with the priority their jobs are receiving through the server.

Assigning Print Queues to a Printer

If you use multiple print queues for a single printer, you must assign each queue to the printer at a particular priority. Assignment is done through special server Console commands. Be aware of these problems:

- A user must issue these commands through the server keyboard. The commands cannot be issued from a workstation.

- The assign commands must be issued each time the server is powered on and NetWare is booted.

    Place Console command assignment statements in the server's AUTOEXEC.SYS file. This file, accessed through SYSCON, is executed each time the server is booted.

Special Print Job Management Problems

With all of the previously discussed problems resolved, you may still encounter these situations:

- A user is unable to use a particular printer because he or she has not been designated a user of the queue(s) servicing that printer. (Go to the PCONSOLE menu as SUPERVISOR and add the user, or a group of which he or she is a member, to the list of queue users.)

- The paper jams in a printer and the job has to be restarted. (See the Console REWIND command.)

- A user inadvertently places a print job in a queue multiple times (five, ten, or even more) and you waste reams of paper printing the same job over and over. (Teach users how to cancel print jobs.)

- The incorrect paper or form is mounted in a printer when a job prints. (See the Form= parameter for the CAPTURE command and the MOUNT FORM x Console printer command.)

- The person designated and set up to manage a network print queue and printer are sick, on vacation, move to another department, or leave the organization. (Have multiple backup people set up and trained as queue operators, or stay on call at all times.)

Summary

This chapter discussed network printing, including the following topics:

- Installing a server-attached printer to the NetWare operating system.

- Creating print queues into which jobs may be placed for servicing by network printers.

- Using NPRINT and CAPTURE to reroute print jobs from the local workstation to a network print queue.

- Using the PCONSOLE menu to view and manage print jobs, either as a user or as a queue operator.

- Issuing print-management commands through the server keyboard while in Console mode (Console print commands).

Gaining advantage of network print services will take some planning, practice, and education. But with the features and services provided through NetWare you will be well on your way to successful network printing. If you find NetWare print services insufficient, there are numerous third-party software packages available to expand on NetWare's basic features.

chapter **10**

NETWARE INSTALLATION AND MAINTENANCE

NetWare installation involves generating and loading onto the server the NetWare software operating system and generating workstation boot diskettes. The first task is accomplished through NetWare's NETGEN utility; the latter through the SHGEN utility.

This chapter introduces you to both NETGEN and SHGEN. The contents of this chapter are not intended to replace your Novell *SFT/ Advanced NetWare 286 Installation* or *SFT/ Advanced Net-Ware 286 Maintenance* manuals. It is hoped the discussion will help you better understand and follow the instructions contained in those manuals. Also discussed here is the purpose, creation, and use of a NetWare SHELL.CFG file.

Table 10-1 summarizes the basic NetWare installation process. Some phase activities are more fully delineated than others, and some of the activities are actually accomplished by NETGEN routines independent of operator control. The primary purpose of Table 10-1 is to give you some idea of where the discussion in this chapter is headed.

Here are some strongly made recommendations:

- Read this entire chapter before attempting to perform any server installation tasks.

- Read the NetWare manuals just mentioned before proceeding.

- Keep the NetWare manuals handy (along with this book).

- Plan the installation to occur over several time periods (possibly two or three days).

- Use NetWare default configuration routines and settings, if at all possible.

As Novell recommends, do not attempt a custom installation in your first installation efforts. The phases listed in Table 10-1 assume you will be performing a default server installation. A successful default installation is no small feat.

Phase	Activities
Set up computer hardware	Connect monitors to computers. Run server and workstation proprietary setup routines. Place network cabling.
Install configurable computer hardware	Set NIC addresses; install cards. Install uninterruptable power supply hardware in server/workstation. Install additional parallel (LPT) or serial (COM) device ports.
Make working backup copies of NetWare diskettes	All diskettes except GENDATA disk, which contains the NetWare serial number and is copy-protected.
NETGEN Phase I: Select Network Configuration	
a. Select server resources	Select NetWare configuration. Select LAN driver(s). Select internal disk drive(s). Select other device drivers.
b. Define NetWare server information	Specify network address. Specify communication buffers. Install NetWare serial number.
c. Review, record, and confirm server configuration	View configuration on the screen. Document configuration on paper. Approve configuration via NETGEN.
d. Generate the NetWare operating system	NET$OS.EX1 and NET$OS.EX2 created. Link disk utilities (COMPSURF, DISKED, INSTOVL, VREPAIR). Link additional, third-party utilities (for external disk drives). Write files to NetWare diskettes.

TABLE 10-1.   NetWare Installation Phases and Activities

Phase	Activities
Create workstation boot diskettes	Create bootable DOS diskette. Run SHGEN. Create SHELL.CFG file on diskette.
Boot server with DOS Run NETGEN to complete the NetWare installation on the server computer	To complete NETGEN activities.
a. Install external hard disks	Run disk setup. Select disk type and controller address.
b. Select installation options	Confirm attached drives information. Run COMPSURF, if necessary. Set up default partition table and install Hot Fix. Create mirror tables or duplexed pairs of hard disks (SFT Advanced NetWare only). Review (default) volume names. Fix master system table, as necessary. Name file server Other configuration parameters defined (custom configured, if SFT NetWare with TTS installed). Define network printers.
c. Install the NetWare OS on the server	Cold boot loader installed. Net$OS.EXE copied to SYSTEM directory. Create LOGIN, PUBLIC, and MAIL directory structure; NetWare files copied to each directory.
Exit NETGEN and reboot the server	Dedicated or nondedicated mode from prompt or hard disk boot files.

TABLE 10-1.   NetWare Installation Phases and Activities (*continued*)

SETTING UP COMPUTER HARDWARE AND INSTALLING CONFIGURABLE HARDWARE

Before you even concern yourself with NetWare software configuration issues, numerous hardware installation issues must be addressed. Where are the server and the workstations to be located? Who will uncrate and connect the basic hardware: central processing unit (with internal hard disk), monitor, printers, and surge protectors; and who will install the LAN cabling? And then there are the personal computer manufacturer's setup programs to be run, to configure each machine.

This chapter does not address the many issues surrounding the physical hardware installation process. The manuals that come with the server and workstation hardware and related peripheral devices provide specific instructions on accomplishing that task.

Some direction is given in Chapter 3 on network interface card (NIC) installation in workstations and the server. With NetWare and with your purchased NICs come additional instructions to inform your NIC installation. Similar instructions come with other *configurable* hardware you install: additional serial or parallel (COM or LPT) ports, uninterruptable power supply (UPS) or tape backup hardware devices, or additional hard disk controllers and external hard disk units.

One piece of advice you should heed is to record on paper each of the configurable hardware decisions you make (by commission or omission). Not knowing what interrupt and IRQ settings you used on a NIC, or not remembering what model of a manufacturer's tape backup system you physically installed on the server (or a workstation) may haunt you later.

Physical workstation design (ergonomics), layout (do we need a workstation connection in the conference room, and if so how many), and cable installation are also topics of considerable magnitude, each beyond the bounds of this book. If you are about to complete a costly, inflexible, or difficult LAN configuration, the services of a qualified *system integrator* may be worthwhile.

You will need to install at least your server NICs and any peripheral devices before running NETGEN. Get out those manuals and your screwdriver and open up that tin box (or have your NetWare installer perform this task for you).

GETTING READY TO CONFIGURE AND INSTALL NETWARE

After you remove your library of NetWare manuals from their shipping carton, the most important task at hand is not to build a bookshelf, though you might well think so. The next most important step is to record your NetWare serial number for later reference and to protect your software investment by write-protecting the NetWare software diskettes.

Recording the NetWare Serial Number

In the past, NetWare was copy-protected through a serial number installed in the NetWare operating system software and on a hardware device installed in the server called a *key card*. Moreover, you could not make a backup copy of the NetWare GENDATA diskette, on which the software serial number resided.

Key cards are no longer required (though if already installed they may be used for other purposes, such as uninterruptable power supply monitoring). A serial number is still embedded in the GENDATA diskette software, and it is this serial number that uniquely identifies your copy of NetWare. You can now make a backup copy of the GENDATA diskette, and the serial number installation process occurs automatically, through a NETGEN routine (to be described later).

The serial number is usually also printed on the outside of the box in which your NetWare diskettes arrived. You may need to refer to this serial number later, during installation or when contacting Novell. You should record your NetWare serial number on paper. (NetWare provides a series of forms for recording important information, blank copies of which are contained in the back of your *SFT/Advanced NetWare 286 Installation* manual. Make copies of these forms, retaining the originals in the manual.)

Even with a previously copy-protected GENDATA diskette, you can generate the operating system any number of times using that one GENDATA diskette. And you can install each generated version of NetWare on separate servers (since the key card is no longer required). However, *do not do this*. Possible is not legal. The GENDATA NetWare serial number identifies your copy of the NetWare programs. Installing that serial number on more than one server violates your software license.

Moreover, installing the same serial number on two different servers on an internetwork can cause difficulties. At the least, any user attempting to attach to another server with the same NetWare serial number will be presented a critical error message and will be disallowed access to that second server. This critical error will also be recorded in the server's error log. Try to connect to the wrong internetwork and you could be giving away that you installed your NetWare serial number on more than one server. (You could be testifying against yourself, before your trial.) From a practical standpoint, you want your server set up so that it can talk to each of the other servers. That requires installing different NetWare serial numbers (different copies of NetWare) on each server.

Write-Protecting and Copying
Your NetWare Diskettes

Either place a write-protect tab over the notch of each NetWare original diskette (if they are 5 1/4-inch diskettes) or slide the write-protect tab up, so you can see through the diskette casing (if you have 3 1/2-by-3 11/16-inch diskettes). To be sure you do not accidentally erase these diskettes, you should write-protect them before you attempt to copy them.

Your next task is to make a backup copy of the software, which is the copy you will use to perform your server NetWare software configuration and installation. You may need to invest in some diskettes (NetWare unconfigured is a very large bundle of software programs), but you do not need to format diskettes before making the backup copies. Novell recommends you use the DOS DISK-COPY command to perform your backup copy creation.

With DOS booted on your computer, and while pointing to your DOS directory, at the prompt type

DISKCOPY A: A:

Press (ENTER) to invoke the DOS DISKCOPY command.

You will be asked to place a *Source* diskette in drive A: and press any key. The Source diskette is any of your original NetWare software diskettes, which you have write protected. Place one of those diskettes in drive A: and press a key. DOS begins copying the contents of the original diskette to your computer's RAM.

At some point you will be asked to place a *Target* diskette into drive A:. This is the blank, non-write-protected diskette to which you wish the contents of the original NetWare diskette copied. Place the Target diskette in drive A: and press a key. DOS will format the Target diskette while it copies the contents of the Source diskette from your computer's RAM.

The entire contents of the Source diskette may not be copied to RAM, and from there to the Target diskette, in one pass. After writing to the Target diskette, DOS may again ask you to place the Source diskette into drive A:. If it does so, use the *same* write-protected NetWare diskette with which you began this DISKCOPY process. During this second Source diskette insertion, the remaining NetWare files will be copied into RAM, after which you are again asked to insert the Target diskette and press a key.

After all of the first Source diskette has been copied to RAM and then onto the first Target diskette, you are prompted as to whether you want to copy another diskette. You can type **Y** (for Yes), press (**ENTER**), and repeat the Source diskette, Target diskette cycle for each original NetWare diskettes.

 It is important to write-protect your original NetWare diskettes before performing DISKCOPY. If you accidentally place one of the originals into drive A: when you are asked for a Target diskette, you will end up reformatting an original diskette, and lose whatever files that diskette contained. Also be sure to label each backup diskette with the exact names used on the original, so you can find the correct backup diskette when needed.

NETWORK OPERATING SYSTEM GENERATION AND INSTALLATION

There are several modes of NetWare operating system generation you can use. To understand your options fully, it is helpful to know that some parts of the operating system generation and installation process can be performed on any personal computer running DOS, while other portions must be performed on the server to which the NetWare operating system is to be installed. Table 10-1 lists these two phases as NETGEN Phase I and NETGEN Phase II.

It is helpful to know of the several methods and two levels of NETGEN operation available to you. Accordingly, these topics are discussed before you begin a hands-on NETGEN operation.

NETGEN Methods

These are the methods by which you can run NETGEN:

- the standard floppy disk method

- the RAM disk method

- the hard disk method

- the network drive method

STANDARD FLOPPY DISK METHOD   If you use the standard floppy disk method of NetWare generation and installation, it is easier if you have at least two floppy disk drives (it can cut down substantially on the required disk swapping, though this is more important in the earlier than in the later phases of NETGEN).

If you use this approach, the NetWare NETGEN routines will write the NetWare operating system configuration you will be installing on the server directly to your NetWare backup diskettes.

RAM DISK METHOD   To avoid disk swapping and to speed the process of accessing NetWare configuration files, you can create on your computer a DOS RAM disk. You then copy the NetWare files from your backup diskettes to the RAM disk, and run NETGEN from the RAM disk. The disadvantage is that the RAM disk disappears when you turn off the power to your computer.

If you do not complete major chunks of the NetWare generation process all at once, you could spend as much time coping files to and from the RAM disk as it would take to use the floppy disk method. (If you use the RAM disk method on a computer that will not become the server, you will have to download these files at least once when you switch to Phase II of NetWare, which must occur on the server machine.)

HARD DISK METHOD   If you have a hard disk on a standalone computer other than the server, you can create a NetWare working directory on that hard disk. When you select this method of NETGEN, NETGEN uploads the files it needs from your backup installation diskettes to the local hard disk.

This method requires considerable free hard disk space (8 megabytes); you must be running DOS 3.0 or higher; and your DOS CONFIG.SYS file must set FILES = 20 and BUFFERS = 15 when you boot the computer.

NETWORK DRIVE METHOD   The network drive method is a variation on the standalone PC hard disk method. The hard disk used is that of a server on an existing internetwork. You again create a NetWare working directory, on the server hard disk (which must have at least 10 megabytes of free disk space). You must also log in to that server from the machine that will become the new server, used for now as a workstation on the internetwork. In this mode you will be able to complete the entire operating system generation and installation process from that workstation, without having to copy files temporarily to your backup diskettes.

If you use either hard disk approach (the standalone hard disk or network drive method) you can generate NetWare systems over and over. However, you must be sure to insert your own GENDATA diskette, the diskette with your NetWare serial number, when requested. Otherwise, the operating system installed on your server could include someone else's duplicate serial number.

Levels of NETGEN

NETGEN can be run to create a NetWare *default system configuration;* or you can run the NETGEN *custom system configuration* routines. The default system configuration is preferred if it works for you. Custom configurations require considerable hardware and software expertise. The admonitions in Chapter 3 to not unnecessarily change NIC IRQ or address settings are directed to allowing you to use the NETGEN default level system configuration.

You need to be careful not to run NETGEN as a *new* configuration. If you select **new**, NETGEN will ignore any previous configuration and you must begin your configuration from scratch. You will normally want to run NETGEN for a new configuration only once (preferably for a default system configuration).

NETGEN Quirks

More notes about NETGEN follow:

- It is a quirk of NETGEN that to accept or approve a particular operating system configuration you must sometimes press the (ESC) key, whereas to abandon the configuration and return to a previous menu level, you must either select from within a menu a **leave** or **abandon** choice, or attempt to complete the configuration and then tell NETGEN that the configuration is not correct.

- At times, NETGEN menus look and act like the menus discussed earlier in this book (including having submenus pop up when you either highlight a menu item and press (ENTER) or press (INSERT)).

At other times:

- You may not be able to press (ESC) to move back to a previous menu (because, as just noted, (ESC) is used to confirm acceptance of a configuration option and to continue installation).

- NETGEN menus will have additional choices added to them as you complete previous installation activities (and therefore will look different the second or third time you enter that menu through NETGEN).

In short, it is sometimes difficult to follow the menus. On the other hand, NETGEN does reliably move you through the choices you need to make. If you read the screen prompts carefully and forge ahead with making choices, the worst that can happen is that you will need to start over.

RUNNING NETGEN

The NETGEN method used here is the standard floppy disk method. A new, default system configuration is developed. Begin by booting DOS on your personal computer (one with disk drives that are consistent with the size and formatting of your backup diskettes).

To enter NETGEN, place your backup NETGEN diskette in drive A:, type **NETGEN**, and press (ENTER). You will be prompted to

Insert disk SUPPORT in any drive.
Strike a key when ready . . .

If possible, place your backup SUPPORT disk, with any write-protect tabs removed, in a B: drive, while keeping the NETGEN disk (also un-write-protected) in drive A:. (You can use a single drive, but must very frequently swap disks.) After NETGEN uploads the information it needs from the SYSTEM disk, a System Configuration Level menu, illustrated in Figure 10-1, is displayed on the screen. At this point you can easily terminate the NETGEN session by pressing the (ESC) key once, affirming that, **Yes**, you wish to exit NETGEN, and pressing (ENTER). However, it is suggested that you continue another step or two.

Keep the highlight bar over **Default Configuration** and press (ENTER). If you did not initiate NETGEN using available flags, you will see the NETGEN Run Options menu displayed, as illustrated in Figure 10-2. Highlight **Standard (floppy disks)** and press

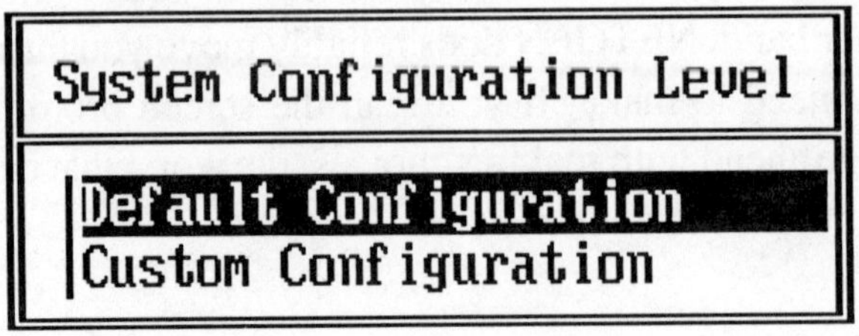

```
┌──────────────────────────────────────┐
│   System Configuration Level          │
├──────────────────────────────────────┤
│  Default Configuration                │
│  Custom Configuration                 │
└──────────────────────────────────────┘
```

FIGURE 10-1.   NETGEN System Configuration Level menu

(ENTER). A NetWare Generation Options menu is displayed (see Figure 10-3).

Through the Network Generation Options submenu you can do the following:

- Initiate the first, Select Network Configuration, phase of NETGEN during which you use an Available Topics submenu,

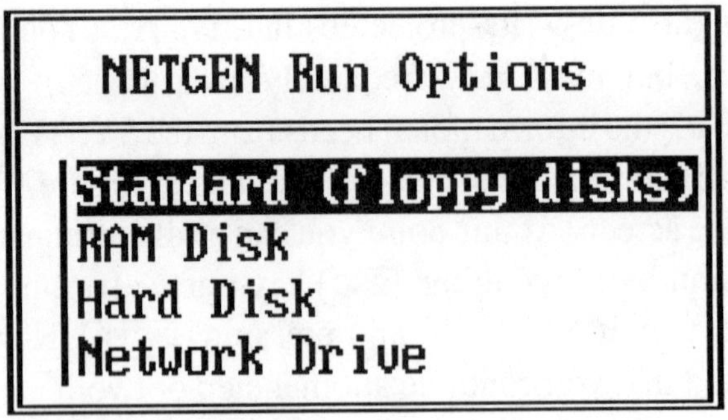

```
┌──────────────────────────────────────┐
│     NETGEN Run Options                │
├──────────────────────────────────────┤
│  Standard (floppy disks)              │
│  RAM Disk                             │
│  Hard Disk                            │
│  Network Drive                        │
└──────────────────────────────────────┘
```

FIGURE 10-2.   NETGEN Run Options menu

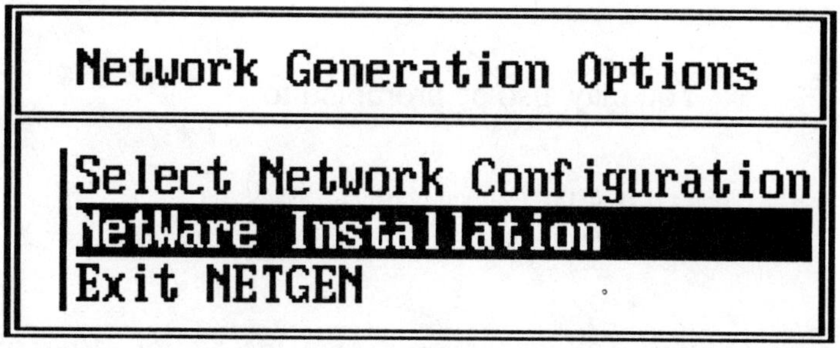

```
┌──────────────────────────────────────────────┐
│  Network Generation Options                    │
├──────────────────────────────────────────────┤
│ Select Network Configuration                   │
│ NetWare Installation                           │
│ Exit NETGEN                                    │
└──────────────────────────────────────────────┘
```

FIGURE 10-3.   NETGEN Network Generation Options menu

through which you select or input information NETGEN needs to customize NetWare to your network environment.

• Begin the second, NetWare Installation, phase of NetWare, which must be run on the server to which NetWare is to be installed.

If you have not yet read the rest of this chapter, and your Novell *SFT/Advanced NetWare 286 Installation* manual, you should highlight **Exit NETGEN** and press (ENTER). With a general feel for how NETGEN guides you, a reading of the Novell manuals and the remainder of this chapter is recommended.

SELECT NETWORK CONFIGURATION

When you are comfortable with the NETGEN process, re-enter NETGEN, advance to the Network Generation Options submenu (shown in Figure 10-3), highlight **Select Network Configuration**, and press (ENTER).

You will see the following message:

Loading Program Files. Please Wait.

You may also be prompted to

Insert disk AUXGEN in any drive.
Strike a key when ready . . .

Simply follow the on-screen instruction. Eventually, in a new, default installation, you will be rewarded with an Available Options menu, as illustrated in Figure 10-4.

Available Options

The Available Options menu guides you through numerous choices you must make to let NETGEN know what your server and network hardware setup looks like. Novell refers to this process as "selecting server resources." You begin with a very general but critical decision concerning which operating system options NETGEN must be informed about.

SET OPERATING SYSTEM OPTIONS   Keep the highlight bar over **Set Operating System Options** and press (ENTER). You will see one of two Set Operating System Options submenus.

The first screen, illustrated in Figure 10-5, is for Advanced NetWare 286, the 2.15 version that does *not* include advanced system fault tolerance features (disk duplexing, disk mirroring, and Transaction Tracking Services). The Advanced NetWare 286 operating system options are to install your server in either dedicated or nondedicated mode. If you are installing SFT Advanced Net-Ware 286, your choices will be these:

SFT NetWare Level-II+TTS
SFT NetWare Level-II

```
╔══════════════════════════════════════════════╗
║           Available Options                   ║
╠══════════════════════════════════════════════╣
║ ███████████████████████████████████████       ║
║ █Set Operating System Options█                ║
║ Select LAN Drivers                            ║
║ Select Disk Drivers                           ║
║ Select "Other" Drivers                        ║
║ Save Selections and Continue                  ║
╚══════════════════════════════════════════════╝
```

FIGURE 10-4.   NETGEN Select Network Configuration, Available Options submenu

Selecting the +TTS option will cause you to have to make extra decisions later in the installation process, but it is the recommended installation option if you are going to be running any database applications on your server (including an accounting package). TTS (Transaction Tracking Services) will allow you to flag data files with *TTS,* thereby taking advantage of automatic roll-back and other TTS services in the event of a system crash. If there is any chance you will be supporting a database (which is likely if you are investing in SFT NetWare), use the +TTS selection. As Novell points out in your *SFT/ Advanced NetWare 286 Installation*

```
╔══════════════════════════════════════════════╗
║         Set Operating System Options          ║
╠══════════════════════════════════════════════╣
║ Advanced NetWare 286 / Dedicated              ║
║ █Advanced NetWare 286 / Nondedicated█         ║
╚══════════════════════════════════════════════╝
```

FIGURE 10-5.   NETGEN Set Operating System Options for Advanced NetWare 286

manual, performance on nontransactional operations is not affected by having TTS installed. Installing TTS now makes it available when and if you ever need it.

SELECTING LAN, DISK, AND OTHER DRIVERS   Your next task is to define through NETGEN the drivers NetWare will need to communicate with your server-installed NICs, and with other hardware installed in or attached to your server.

Highlight **Select LAN Drivers** and press (ENTER.) You will see two menus and an instructions message box, as displayed in Figure 10-6. To arrive at this menu, you may have to place one or more NetWare backup diskettes in a disk drive when you are prompted to do so, at which time NETGEN uploads to RAM those driver files most commonly selected.

At the top of the screen (as illustrated in Figure 10-6) is a Select LAN Drivers submenu, which will initially be blank. In the middle of the screen is a LAN Driver Options submenu. And at the bottom of the screen are instructions for using the LAN Driver Options menu. Take a moment to read these instructions carefully. You will notice that pressing (ESC) does not take you back to the Available Options menu. This is one of those instances in NETGEN where (ESC) is used to save a selection to your backup diskettes and to take you to the next step in the resource selection process.

When you highlight **Select Loaded Item** and press (ENTER), a list of NICs for which drivers are already uploaded to RAM will be displayed (though you may have to insert the SUPPORT disk or other NetWare diskettes before the list appears). Simply move the cursor through the list until you see the name of your server-installed NIC. Highlight the item and press (ENTER). That name is placed in the Selected LAN Drivers submenu at the top of your screen. In Figure 10-6 a Standard Microsystems ARCNET/Pure Data V1.00 (880520) driver was selected.

If you have more than one NIC installed in your server, select a driver for each. If you have two NICs of the same type, the same

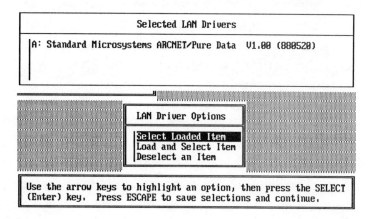

```
                    Selected LAN Drivers
┌────────────────────────────────────────────────────────────┐
│A: Standard Microsystems ARCNET/Pure Data   V1.00 (880520)    │
│                                                              │
│                                                              │
│                                                              │
└──────────────────────────┐                                  │
                           │  LAN Driver Options               │
                           │┌──────────────────────┐           │
                           ││Select Loaded Item    │           │
                           ││Load and Select Item  │           │
                           ││Deselect an Item      │           │
                           │└──────────────────────┘           │
─────────────────────────────────────────────────────────────
 Use the arrow keys to highlight an option, then press the SELECT
 (Enter) key.  Press ESCAPE to save selections and continue.
```

FIGURE 10-6.   NETGEN Select LAN Drivers submenus

driver will need to be selected twice, as each selection is associated
with a particular NIC (A, B, C, or D).

If you decide you selected an incorrect driver, in the LAN Driver
Options box place the cursor over **Deselect an Item** and press
(ENTER). (The Deselect an Item option does not appear in the LAN
Driver Options menu until after you have selected at least one NIC
driver.) You will then be allowed to remove a selection from the
Selected LAN Drivers list. You must deselect the item *before*
pressing (ESC.)

If you do not find a driver for one or another of your server NICs
listed, that driver may not as yet have been uploaded to RAM, but
may be included on another of your backup diskettes. To add that
driver to RAM (if it exists on a backup diskette), highlight **Load
and Select Item** and press (ENTER). Follow the instructions as to
which diskette to insert and how to select an alternate driver set.
The instructions are straightforward (but read them carefully from
your screen). All should go well, unless you select a LAN driver
that happens to be incompatible with another already selected LAN
driver, in which event the driver will not be added to the list of

available drivers. This would indicate a hardware conflict, which will have to be resolved either by using different hardware or, possibly, by altering IRQ or address settings on your hardware and reflecting this appropriately to NETGEN through Custom Configuration routines.

When you have completed selecting LAN Drivers (NIC drivers), press (ESC) to save these drivers to your NETGEN diskette. You will eventually be taken back to the Available Options menu (Figure 10-4).

The Select Disk Drivers option represents a choice of drivers for your server *internal* hard disks. The selection process is similar to that for LAN drivers, except that you must define a *hard disk channel* type appropriate for your hard disk. Channel types are numbered 0 through 4. Novell includes a diagram (Figure 4-3 on page 4-53 of the *SFT/Advanced NetWare 286 Installation* manual) to assist you in deciding which hard disk channel identifier (0 through 4) corresponds to the type of hard disk(s) installed internally or externally on your server. The documentation that came with your server should tell you what type of hard disk is installed. If you installed a controller board and one or more external hard disks, refer to the documentation that came with the board and hard disks you installed.

Highlight **Select Disk Drivers** and press (ENTER). When prompted to do so, type a channel number you believe is appropriate for your hard disk and press (ENTER). A window will appear, listing each disk driver type that can function with the specified channel (0 through 4) and that is compatible with any other hardware thus far selected through NETGEN.

If no disk driver types are listed, you may try selecting another channel number. But be aware that at each step of a configuration or maintenance process, NETGEN checks to see if any hardware conflicts exist, given the hardware thus far selected and the usual manufacturer's default settings for such hardware. If you have altered the manufacturer's default settings, you may need to run a Custom Configuration session of NETGEN. Or perhaps you should return the hardware settings to their original manufacturer's default settings.

When you have completed the hard disk driver selection process, press (ESC) to save your selections.

The **Select "Other" Drivers** option allows you to select drivers for hardware or software you may have purchased separately from your server, for which drivers must be installed before that hardware or software can communicate with your server—for example, a tape backup system. Having worked through the first two driver selection processes, you already understand how to proceed to select "other" drivers.

If you chose a driver that is configurable—meaning that you can define the IRQ interrupt or other settings installed on the hardware or software to which the driver applies—a Configure Drivers/Resources option will now appear in the Available Options menu. For most simple default installations, this option will not be relevant and will not be added to the Available Options menu. You can simply proceed.

SAVE SELECTIONS AND CONTINUE   When you have completed all of your driver selections, or all that you are prepared to complete installating at this time, highlight **Save Selections and Continue** and press (ENTER). You must continue on with the configuration process, and you will not be able to back up to the Available Options screen. However, if you later need to change or add to the selected drivers, you can do so through NETGEN maintenance routines. (Or you can always take all the diskettes out of your disk drives, shut down or reboot your computer, and then start NETGEN from scratch for a *new* installation configuration definition.)

Define NetWare Server Information

You have now entered another part of Phase I of the NETGEN process, one where you define to NETGEN information about your server. Some of this information you must specifically type in, while for other information you can accept the NETGEN default values (which is why you went into NETGEN in Default Configuration mode). NETGEN will display the necessary options and provide instructions on the screen.

DEFINING THE NETWORK ADDRESS   The first piece of information you must provide is a network address for each installed NIC and for the DOS partition to be set up on your server hard disk (if you are installing Advanced NetWare 286 and opted to install your server in nondedicated mode). For guidance, see Chapter 3, particularly Figure 3-2 and the section titled "The NIC Address."

If you have only one server and one NIC, the network addressing decision is quite simple. Select *any* positive hexadecimal numerical value (digits 0 through 9 and letters A through F) up to eight digits long. For instance, you could use 00000001 and 00000004; the first is associated with your single NIC and the latter for your hard disk DOS partition.

If you are on an internetwork, with internal or external bridges and gateways, additional rules for selecting network addresses apply. Again, refer to the discussion in Chapter 3 and to the instructions in your Novell installation and maintenance manuals.

SPECIFYING A COMMUNICATION BUFFERS NUMBER

Communication buffers are parts of the server's memory used to temporarily hold information coming from workstations, or being sent to or from the server's hard disks. NETGEN will suggest a default buffer size of 40, a minimum recommended figure. If you have only the minimum recommended RAM for your server (1 megabyte for a dedicated server, 1.5 megabytes for a nondedicated server, and an extra megabyte if hard disks of over 70 megabytes are attached), you may choose to leave the default buffer size at 40 and install that figure through NETGEN instructions you see on the screen.

Novell suggests you add one buffer for each workstation that may be simultaneously active on the server. Ten active workstations plus 40 buffers equal a recommended 50 buffer setting. If you have more or less than the required RAM, you can set buffers anywhere between 10 and 150.

 The sizes of NetWare blocks and buffers differ from DOS. If you think you need more or fewer buffers, be sure you are acting on NetWare experience, not irrelevant DOS experience.

INSTALLING THE NETWARE SERIAL NUMBER Your
NetWare serial number is installed at this stage of the NETGEN process. You will be prompted to place your GENDATA diskette into a disk drive. The serial number is read automatically from that disk and installed as part of your NetWare default configuration.

Reviewing, Recording, And Confirming Server Configuration

When you continue on to the next Default Configuration phase of the NETGEN process, you are asked to confirm the information you have thus far installed. This information is displayed in a Selected Configurations screen.

This screen provides an opportunity for you to accept or change the configuration you have selected. The screen also represents an opportunity to record the configuration information on the Net-Ware forms that come with your installation manual. Taking time to complete these forms may save considerable time later, for an installer or for the LAN manager who succeeds you (you are doing so well, and no doubt you are going to move on to bigger and better things).

When you have written down your current configuration, and if you are running the Default Configuration level of NETGEN using the standard floppy disk mode, press (ESC), select **Yes** (to accept the configuration), and press (ENTER). (For the custom level or for other modes, the procedures for exiting this phase of NETGEN may be different.)

NETGEN Linking and OS Generation

At this point NETGEN takes over and performs some generation and *linking* tasks, essentially putting together the pieces of the puzzle you have presented to it. Figure 10-7 illustrates what occurs. Two files are created, NET$OS.EX1 and NET$OS.EX2. These two parts of the NetWare operating system will be combined during the phase of NETGEN in which you install the operating system on the server.

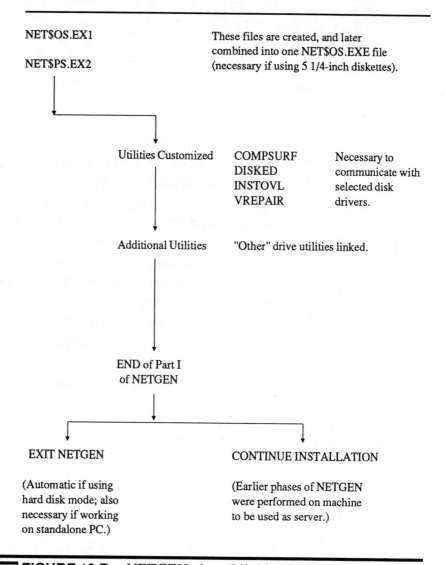

FIGURE 10-7.   NETGEN phase I linking and configuration activities

At this time several special utilities are customized for the operating system configuration you created earlier. These utilities are

- COMPSURF

- DISKED

- INSTOVL

- VREPAIR

To assist in this process, you will be asked to insert various NetWare (backup) diskettes, to which the customized and linked files are written. When this process is complete, you are returned to the Network Generation Options screen. If you have installed any disk coprocessor boards in your server and are attaching external hard disks, a Configuration Utilities option will be added to the Network Generation Options menu. Read on before attempting to do anything with those options.

You may either continue with NetWare Installation, if you are working already on the machine to which the NetWare operating system is to be installed, or you can highlight **Exit NETGEN** and press (ENTER) to leave the NETGEN process at your standalone PC.

NETWARE INSTALLATION THROUGH NETGEN

To complete the NetWare Installation phase of NETGEN you must be working on the machine on which the NetWare operating system is to be installed. You will have booted this server machine with DOS and will either be continuing the NETGEN default installation you originally initiated on this machine or re-enter NETGEN, up to the point where you see the Network Generation Options Screen (Figure 10-3).

It is assumed you will have installed all server hardware, including NICs and any external disk drives, before you continue the installation process. Highlight **NetWare Installation** and press (ENTER). If you took a break between the first and this second phase of NETGEN, you may chose to re-enter NETGEN in either the Default or Custom Configuration level. The discussion that follows assumes it is the Default Configuration level you are running. *Do not re-enter NETGEN with an N (new) command flag!*

Configuration Utilities

If you installed a disk coprocessor board (either a Novell disk coprocessor board or a third-party disk coprocessor board, you will need to run a disk coprocessor setup routine. Within the Network Generation Options menu, highlight **Configuration Utilities** and press (ENTER). A Configuration Utilities submenu will be displayed, listing the utility DISKSET (used to configure Novell disk coprocessor boards) or other third-party utilities installed earlier during the linking part of the first phase of NETGEN.

DISKSET stands for DISK coprocessor SETup utility. If you have a disk coprocessor board, highlight **DISKSET** (or an appropriate third-party utility) and press (ENTER). Follow the instructions found in your *SFT/Advanced NetWare 286 Installation* manual to complete this portion of NETGEN.

If you have only one internal hard disk on you server, the Configuration Utilities option will not be listed in the Network Generation Options menu and you can continue with NetWare Installation.

NetWare Installation

If you are running the default level of NETGEN, you will be cycled through the choices you must make, or the screens through which you must provide information.

Selecting the default level of installation, NETGEN will create a default *partition table* on your internal system hard disk. The partition table defines the entire storage capacity of the disk as one volume (SYS:), unless for nondedicated server operations you need a DOS partition (as indicated in your earlier setup decisions). Also installed automatically is the Hot Fix feature (discussed in Chapter 2 of this book).

REVIEWING DEFAULT VOLUME NAMES AND FIXING THE\ MASTER SYSTEM DRIVE TABLE   Some time may pass while NETGEN performs the disk setup tasks, but you will eventually be taken to a Reviewing the Default Volume Names screen, unless you are installing SFT Advanced NetWare 286 with disk mirroring or disk duplexing. In this latter event you are presented with a Mirroring Options submenu and asked to create mirror tables (Establish Mirror Pair). See your *SFT/ Advanced NetWare 286 Installation* manual for guidance.

Review the information displayed on the Reviewing the Default Volume Names screen. Remember that the hard disk to which your NetWare operating system files are to be stored must have a volume named SYS. You will not want to change that volume name. Other volume names are under your control, though you may choose to accept the default names.

On rare occasions you may have to go through a Fix Master System Table process, if this normally automatically created and maintained table needs correction or manual updating. For a new installation, which involves only one internal server hard disk and no disk mirroring or disk duplexing, this is an unlikely requirement.

NAMING YOUR FILE SERVER   After accepting the hard disk volume names, you are prompted to provide a name for your file server. The name can be between 2 and 45 characters. Having read the "NetWare Path Name Conventions" section of Chapter 1 of this book, you know you want your server name to be

- unique

- easy to remember

- not too long

Type a name of your choosing and press (ENTER).

VIEWING THE DEFAULT SYSTEM CONFIGURATION PARAMETERS
At this point you are shown default system configuration parameters. This is for information only, and is presented to allow you an opportunity to record the listed information in the NetWare Installation Parameters Worksheet, which is included in your Novell NetWare installation manual. Note that if you are installing SFT Advanced NetWare 286 with TTS, included among the default system configuration parameters will be a named Transaction Backout Volume and a Number of Transactions figure. If these (or any other parameters) are not to your liking, you can change them later through NetWare operating system maintenance procedures.

DEFINING THE NETWORK PRINTERS
The next step is to define to NetWare the existence of any network printers that are attached to the server. You must indicate to which port the printer is attached, and if the printer is attached to a serial (COM) port, you may need to redefine one of several serial communications parameters.

You can choose to install the NetWare operating system without any printers included in the installation at this time. You can later add or delete printers through NetWare operating system maintenance procedures. See Chapter 9 for further guidance on installing printers.

CONTINUE INSTALLATION   When you have completed the previous tasks, you are returned to the Installation Options sub-menu. Highlight **Continue Installation** and press (ENTER). You will see a prompt on screen asking if you wish to install the networking software on the server. Select **Yes** and press (ENTER) to continue with the final phase of installation.

NETGEN again takes control and begins its final installation operations. You will see a message telling you this process may take some time. As the message says, "Please Be Patient!"

If you are using the standard floppy disk method of installation, you will be prompted to insert numerous NetWare backup disk-ettes into a disk drive. Simply provide the named diskette and press any key to continue. If you insert an incorrect diskette, NETGEN will inform you of your error and give you a change to correct your mistake.

This is what NETGEN is doing during this time:

- Installing a cold boot loader program beginning at track 0 of your system hard disk (the disk on which the volume SYS is created).

- Creating the required NetWare directory structure (SYSTEM, PUBLIC, LOGIN, MAIL).

- Copying NetWare program files into the required directory structure (simultaneously creating any required subdirectory structure and creating the group EVERYONE and the users SUPERVISOR and GUEST).

All should go well, unless you are installing a server with several physical hard disks attached. In this case you could run out of available RAM, and NETGEN would hang up. In this unlikely event, Novell suggests either of the following:

- Using the Custom level of NETGEN installation.

- Running NETGEN to install the server with only one hard disk drive defined (that to which the NetWare operating system is to be created), and installing the other hard disks later.

 If you encounter problems, you can either start NETGEN from scratch and perform an all-new NETGEN installation, or you can (probably) re-enter NETGEN and update the operating system configuration.

If you have already created NetWare shells for your work-stations and for your server, you can skip forward in this chapter to "Booting Your Server." Otherwise, continue by reading about another NetWare special utility program: SHGEN.

RUNNING SHGEN AND CREATING A SHELL.CFG FILE

Having a server installed is half the battle to using NetWare. Equally as important is the ability to connect, boot, and log in a workstation to the server. This topic has been discussed at length elsewhere in this book. Two topics deserve some additional attention here:

- How to run the NetWare utility SHGEN to create the NetWare shell files necessary to use your LAN and to talk with NetWare on the server.

- How to create a SHELL.CFG file, which is particularly important if you are supporting multiple versions of DOS on your server for use by workstations.

SHGEN

SHGEN is short for SHell GENeration. As with NETGEN, SHGEN can be run at different levels (default, intermediate, and custom) and through different methods (floppy disk, hard disk, or network drive method). The discussion here assumes a Default Configuration level developed through a standard (floppy disk) method on a standalone PC. (Unlike NETGEN, the SHGEN process can take place on a standalone PC. However, you must be running DOS 3.0 or higher and have a minimum of 640K RAM in the workstation.)

FORMATTING A MASTER BOOT DISKETTE   You will be creating a NetWare master boot diskette, one master for each type of NIC used on your local area network and, possibly, one for each type of workstation connected to each LAN. These masters will then become backups for copies actually used at a workstation. (You can also program the EPROM chips installed in diskless workstations; refer to your NetWare installation manuals.)

To create a NetWare master boot diskette, first format a floppy disk with the DOS system files included. Use the DOS FORMAT command with an /S flag to accomplish this. At the prompt type

FORMAT A:/S

Press (ENTER) and when prompted to do so, place the floppy disk to be formatted into drive A: of your computer and press a key to initiate the formatting. Set the formatted floppy disk aside for later use.

STARTING SHGEN   Locate your backup copies of the following 5 1/4-inch diskettes:

- SHGEN_1

- SHGEN_2

- LAN_DRV_001

- LAN_DRV_002

(If you are using 3 1/2-inch diskettes, you will have only one SHGEN diskette, but will also use your AUXGEN diskette.)

Place the SHGEN_1 diskette into drive A:. If you have a drive B:, place the SHGEN_2 diskette in that drive. If a required diskette is not found, NetWare will inform you of this, at which point you can place an alternative appropriate diskette in a drive and press **R** to allow SHGEN to retry finding the diskette.

At the A:\ prompt, type **SHGEN** and press (**ENTER**). A menu like that shown in Figure 10-8 will be displayed.

A Default Configuration can involve as little work as selecting a correct NIC driver (LAN driver in NetWare terms) for your workstation. However, the Intermediate Configuration level will need to be used if you have changed the IRQ setting on an installed NIC from the manufacturer's default setting (something you might do in a particular workstation to avoid conflicts with other hardware installed at that workstation). The Custom Configuration level is required if you use a NIC that is not contained on the

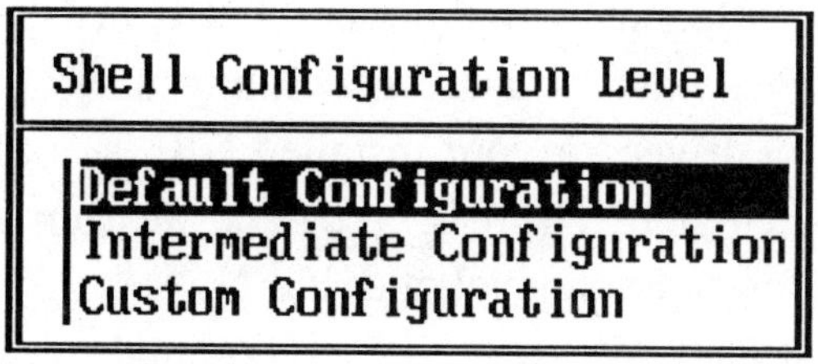

```
Shell Configuration Level

Default Configuration
Intermediate Configuration
Custom Configuration
```

FIGURE 10-8.   SHGEN Shell Configuration Level menu

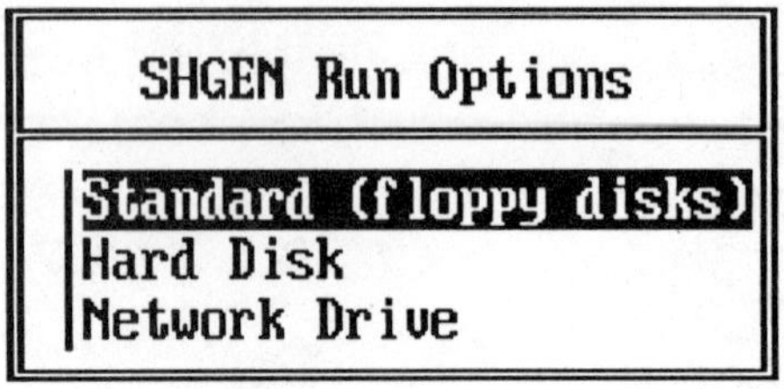

```
┌─────────────────────────────────────┐
│  SHGEN Run Options                   │
├─────────────────────────────────────┤
│ ┌─────────────────────────┐          │
│ │Standard (floppy disks)  │          │
│ │Hard Disk                │          │
│ │Network Drive            │          │
│ └─────────────────────────┘          │
└─────────────────────────────────────┘
```

FIGURE 10-9.   SHGEN Run Options menu

NetWare LAN_DRV_001 or LAN_DRV_002 diskettes. See your Novell *SFT/ Advanced NetWare 286 Installation* manual if you need to perform an Intermediate or Custom level configuration.

Within the Shell Configuration Level menu, highlight **Default Configuration** and press (ENTER). When you see the SHGEN Run Options menu (illustrated in Figure 10-9), highlight the method you wish to use to run SHGEN. In the example used here, you would highlight **Standard (floppy disks)** and press (ENTER).

SELECTING A LAN DRIVER   From your Default Configuration choice you will have displayed on screen a list of available LAN drivers developed for use with NetWare. The list includes all those drivers loaded into RAM when you started SHGEN. Use the (DOWN) arrow key to scroll through the list of drivers until you find one that corresponds with the type of NIC installed in the workstation(s) for which you are generating a NetWare shell boot diskette. If a driver for your installed NIC is not listed, you will have to exit SHGEN (press (ESC) and answer **Yes**) and run a Custom Configuration level of SHGEN.

With the name of your NIC highlighted, press (ENTER). The selected driver will be listed in a Selected Configurations menu at the top of your screen along with a "Continue Shell Generation

Using Selected Configuration?" prompt in the middle of your screen. Keep the highlight bar over **Yes** and press (ENTER).

SHGEN now calls up a linker routine to link the selected NIC driver with IPX.COM (discussed in Chapter 2 of this book). If you are working on a single floppy disk drive or have the incorrect disk in drive B:, you will receive a message asking you to place a correct, named disk in a drive. For instance:

Insert Disk LAN_DRV_001 in any drive.
Strike a key when ready . . .

Other disks may be requested as SHGEN goes about its linking activity. After providing SHGEN with the opportunity to upload all the files it requires, you will see a message like this:

Configuring SHGEN-1:IPX.

When IPX.COM has been configured, you will see a menu telling you to press (ESC) to continue. Press (ESC) and you are returned to the DOS prompt. IPX.COM on the SHGEN_1 diskette is now configured for use with the NIC you told SHGEN you have installed at a workstation.

COPYING THE SHELL FILES TO YOUR MASTER BOOT DISKETTE   Before you attempt to generate any new, alternative shell files, copy the configured IPX.COM file, along with the following files, to your master boot diskette:

- NET2.COM

- NET3.COM

- NETBIOS.EXE

- INT2F.COM

You will need the latter two files only if you are running NetWare's NetBIOS emulator, which is required for some NetBIOS-developed application packages.

When you have copied these files, do as follows:

- Place the name of the selected NIC driver on the label of the master boot diskette (Pure ARCnet, for instance).

- Write-protect the master boot diskette.

You may view your master boot diskette configuration information through use of the DOS TYPE command. Place the master boot diskette in a drive (A:\) and at the prompt type

TYPE CONFIG.DAT

When you press (ENTER), the existing configuration will be listed on your screen, including the LAN driver (NIC driver) name.

PLACING AN AUTOEXEC.BAT FILE ON YOUR BOOT DISKETTES   The addition of an AUTOEXEC.BAT file, such as described in Chapter 3, to each boot diskette almost completes the process of preparing NetWare shell boot diskettes for a workstation. The last step is to test out the diskette. If you can boot your workstation with the boot diskette in drive A:, you are home free. If not, you may have to create a new boot diskette, but always check other possibilities first: that cables are connected; that the server is booted; that power is turned on to any intermediate LAN devices (such as ARCnet active hubs).

Creating a SHELL.CFG File

The SHELL.CFG file is used to set NetWare shell options for IPX.COM or NETx.COM files. These include the parameter SPX

CONNECTIONS=*nn*, which sets the maximum number of SPX connections a workstation can use at the same time. This figure, an IPX.COM option, affects the number of server attachments allowed.

Another parameter, FILE HANDLES=*nn*, is a NET*x*.COM parameter that establishes the number of files a workstation can simultaneously have open on the network.

Defaults apply for most of these parameters, and changes to the defaults are seldom necessary. With the exception of the parameters to be discussed here, you are referred to "Appendix B: Shell Configuration File Options" of your Novell *Supervisor Reference* manual for further details.

One good use of a SHELL.CFG file is to define—for a workstation directory and subdirectory—names leading along a path to the version of DOS on the server required by that workstation. Use of the SHELL.CFG file for this purpose assumes the following:

- You are supporting more than one version of DOS from the server, and a workstation must be mapped to a correct version to function properly.

- You have included a mapping to DOS in the system login script using one or more of the replaceable parameters %MACHINE, %SMACHINE.

- Boot diskettes will not be passed around from workstation to workstation.

The last assumption needs to be valid, since the information contained in the SHELL.CFG file is customized for a workstation or type of workstation.

Just what you place in the SHELL.CFG file depends on what your directory structure pointing to DOS looks like. Figure 10-10 shows a directory structure for which you might use SHELL.CFG

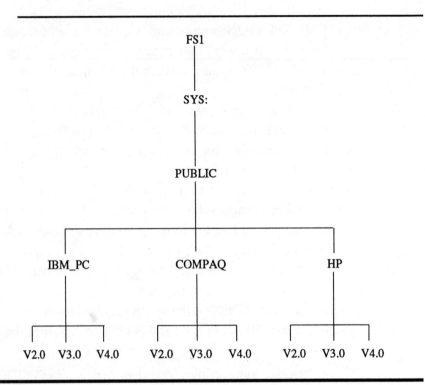

FIGURE 10-10.   Directory structure supporting multiple DOS
versions for multiple machine types

parameters to define subdirectories leading to DOS subdirectories
V2.0, V3.0, and V4.0.

The system login script mapping using replaceable parameters
would look like this:

```
MAP S16:=FS1/SYS:PUBLIC/%MACHINE/%OS_VERSION
```

In this instance, only one replaceable parameter is defined in the
SHELL.CFG file, a long machine name representing the type of
workstation equipment: IMB_PC, COMPAQ, for instance. The
NET*x*.COM file used at a workstation already contains a definition

for %OS_VERSION. Use the DOS COPYCON or EDLIN commands, or an ASCII text editor to place the following command in a file named SHELL.CFG.

LONG MACHINE TYPE=IBM_PC

For those boot diskettes that run on COMPAQ or HP machines, substitute those names in place of IBM_PC. When any user logs in at a workstation, having first called up a particular NETx.COM file (say, NET3.COM), the user is mapped to a version of DOS beneath the machine-specific subdirectory name.

Even if not included in your directory path to DOS, inclusion of a short machine name in a workstation's SHELL.CFG file may be advisable. For instance:

SHORT MACHINE TYPE=COMPAQ

Including a short machine name in a SHELL.CFG file helps ensure that a correct overlay file is loaded at the workstation. The overlay file (IMB$RUN.OVL or CMPQ$RUN.OVL, for instance) is used by the menuing utilities and will be needed if you run custom menus. (For a brief instruction on how to develop custom menus, see Appendix C.)

BOOTING YOUR SERVER

You begin by booting a server with DOS. For a nondedicated server, the command **NET$OS** is then issued. The NET$OS.EXE file is contained on your OSEXE-2 diskette. You may place that diskette in the A: drive of your server and issue NET$OS from the DOS prompt. Or you may copy NET$OS to a DOS boot diskette on which you have placed an AUTOEXEC.BAT file containing the NET$OS.EXE command.

You could also issue NET$OS.EXE from a workstation attached (not logged into) the server. More often than not you will simply boot the server from its hard disk when you power on the server.

For a nondedicated server, you will need to use the boot diskette approach, and in addition to NET$OS.EXE you will place an appropriate NETx.COM file on the boot diskette. The SHGEN-configured NETx.COM files are contained on the SHGEN-2 diskette (for 5 1/4-inch diskettes) and on the SHGEN-1 diskette (for 3 1/2-inch diskettes); or in a SHGEN-2 subdirectory beneath a NETWARE directory, if you ran SHGEN using the hard disk method.

SERVER INSTALLATION OUTSIDE OF NETGEN

Having completed installation of NetWare operating system files, you still have to install whatever application software packages you chose to support from your server. Additionally, there are two specialized applications that come with NetWare that you can choose to install. The first is a NetWare help information base (*infobase,* in NetWare's terms). The other is a server application (a Value Added Process, or VAP) that allows you to lock your server keyboard to prevent unauthorized use.

Installing the HELP Infobase

The HELP infobase is not automatically copied to your server when you install NetWare through NETGEN. The HELP infobase requires quite a few bytes of free hard disk space, and this may account for Novell's decision to exclude it from automatic installation through the NETGEN process. However, the program that allows you to access the HELP Infobase (or other infobases) is automatically installed. This is referred to as the FOLIO program.

FOLIO is a hypertext type program. You can purchase other FOLIO modules, a WordPerfect help infobase, for instance, and install them on your server. However, FOLIO represents one of those demonstration type programs Novell bundles with their software and is not a necessary part of the operating system.

To install the HELP Infobase, log in as the user SUPERVISOR. At the prompt type **HELP** and press (ENTER). You will see a FOLIO entry screen appear, divided left and right. On the right is the FOLIO introduction screen. On the left side of your screen are listed any currently installed infobases. On a new server, none will be listed.

Press (ENTER) once to enter the minimal infobase that has been installed with the FOLIO program. You will see a text type screen, with black squares (bullets) preceding what appear to be, and are, item choices. To learn how to install the HELP Infobase, you need to select **Infobase Installation Instructions**. Here is how you do that:

1. Place your blinking cursor directly beneath (or over) the black square (or rectangle) immediately to the left of the **Infobase Installation Instructions** words.

2. Press (ENTER).

If your cursor was over the black square (the "token"), instructions for installing infobases (of which HELP is one) will appear on your screen. Follow these instructions to install the HELP Infobase.

If your cursor was anywhere except over the token, you will see on screen another copy of the screen you already were in. Any difficulties you encounter in accessing the instructions for installing the HELP infobase are similar to the difficulties your users will encounter in using that infobase. Again, this feature is available, but not mandatory.

To exit the FOLIO program, press the (ESC) key until an Exit submenu appears on screen. Select **Yes** and press (ENTER).

Installing the Keyboard Lock VAP

Value Added Processes are server application programs which can be loaded when you boot your server. The Keyboard Lock VAP programs are contained on a disk separate from all your other NetWare disks.

To install Keyboard Lock, first log in as SUPERVISOR. Place the Keyboard Lock diskette in a workstation local drive (or on a nondedicated server, in the server's A: drive). Next, use the NCOPY command to copy a file named SETKPASS.EXE to the NetWare required directory PUBLIC. Then copy the file named LOCK.VAP to the NetWare required directory SYSTEM.

When you next boot your server, your boot process will be interrupted mid-stream. Do not panic. You will see on your server monitor a message indicating Value Added Processes are installed on your server, and asking whether you wish them to be loaded. At the server prompt, type **Y** and press (ENTER) (if you wish the Keyboard Lock VAP to be available). Or type **N** and press (ENTER) (if you wish to bypass loading the Keyboard Lock VAP). Regardless of which you answer, Yes or No, the server will continue with its normal boot process.

The Keyboard Lock VAP allows you to place a server lock on the server-connected keyboard. To use the server keyboard, a user has to issue an unlock command and provide a correct password. The keyboard can then be relocked when not in use.

This book does not discuss how to invoke the Keyboard Lock VAP or how to create a password. This is not something which should be done by just anyone. Once a password is set, one has to know it to use the console keyboard. Accordingly, the invoking of the Keyboard Lock VAP and the establishment of a password should be the responsibility of the network administrator. If you are a network administrator and wish to use this VAP, see the appendix "Installing and Using LOCK VAP" in your Novell *Console Reference* manual.

CONSOLE COMMANDS AND DOWNING YOUR SERVER

In Chapter 9, reference was made to server Console commands used to manage network printing. There are several other Console commands about which you very much need to be aware.

DOWN

This Console command should always be issued through the server keyboard (in Console mode) before turning off the power to your server. DOWN instructs the server to shut itself down normally, meaning jobs in print queues are saved to the hard disk, any changes to the RAM resident version of a directory entry table are written to its respective hard disk volume, and a check is made for any open files—files in use by users on the network.

If any files are open, the server will ask you whether you wish to continue with shutting down the server. If you answer Yes, you run some risk of open files being corrupted. Better to answer No and first be sure all users are off the network.

BROADCAST

The BROADCAST Console command allows you to send a message to all users on the network. For instance, you might send this message:

BROADCAST Server going down in 10 minutes. Please logout!

DISABLE LOGIN and ENABLE LOGIN

If you want to be sure users do not log in after you broadcast a message telling them to log out, issue the DISABLE LOGIN server command. Login will be enabled either

- when the server is re-booted

- when you issue an ENABLE LOGIN Console command

You may also want to use DISABLE LOGIN before performing a file backup or archiving session.

MONITOR

Typing **MONITOR** and pressing (ENTER) at the server keyboard displays a screen subdivided into sections, each section representing a logical workstation connection to the server. Through this screen you may monitor, in real time, a workstation's use of the network.

To see a specific range of logical connections, issue the MONITOR command with a number succeeding it, indicating the beginning connection about which you wish to view information. For instance, type **MONITOR 9** and press (ENTER).

CLEAR STATION

If when you try to down the server you receive a message that files are open, it may be that a user has neglected to log out of the server and has left his or her workstation running. You can disconnect that workstation from the server with the CLEAR STATION command. At the console prompt, simply type **CLEAR STATION** *nn* (where *nn* represents the workstation logical connection number) and press (ENTER). (The MONITOR command can help you identify the workstation number to be used with the CLEAR STATION command.)

CONFIG and VAP

The CONFIG Console command displays information about your current server configuration. Simply type **CONFIG** at the server prompt and press (ENTER).

To see a list of Value Added Processes installed on your server, type **VAP** and press (ENTER). If you copied the LOCK.VAP file to SYSTEM, NetWare will know of its existence when you issue the VAP command.

It is best to issue these commands and document on paper the displayed information. If you ever need to call Novell or your authorized reseller for assistance, it may be in a situation where the server does not boot.

Other Console commands are discussed in the Novell *Console Reference* manual.

Summary

This chapter introduced you to the NETGEN and SHGEN utilities used to generate and install the NetWare operating system on the server and to generate boot diskettes for workstations and for a nondedicated server. New to versions 2.1 of NetWare is the SHELL.CFG file. The SHELL.CFG file is placed on a boot diskette to help configure the IPX.COM or NETx.COM file for a particular workstation.

With NetWare installed; workstation boot diskettes in place; LAN cables and connections in place; a server directory and security structure established; and application packages appropriate to your LAN installed, you need only educate your users on LAN fundamentals to be in business.

BLANK FORMS FOR CHAPTER SIX

USER SECURITY PLANNING FORM

For Server: _____ By: _____ Date: __/__/199__ Page __ of __

Dir. Rights < >		<CDMOPRSW>	<CDMOPRSW>	<CDMOPRSW>	<CDMOPRSW>	<CDMOPRSW>	<CDMOPRSW>	<CDMOPRSW>
Trustee Assignment ( )								
Effective Rights [ ]								
GUEST	(TA)	( )	( )	( )	( )	( )	( )	( )
	[ER]	[ ]	[ ]	[ ]	[ ]	[ ]	[ ]	[ ]
	(TA)	( )	( )	( )	( )	( )	( )	( )
	[ER]	[ ]	[ ]	[ ]	[ ]	[ ]	[ ]	[ ]
	(TA)	( )	( )	( )	( )	( )	( )	( )
	[ER]	[ ]	[ ]	[ ]	[ ]	[ ]	[ ]	[ ]
	(TA)	( )	( )	( )	( )	( )	( )	( )
	[ER]	[ ]	[ ]	[ ]	[ ]	[ ]	[ ]	[ ]
	(TA)	( )	( )	( )	( )	( )	( )	( )
	[ER]	[ ]	[ ]	[ ]	[ ]	[ ]	[ ]	[ ]
	(TA)	( )	( )	( )	( )	( )	( )	( )
	[ER]	[ ]	[ ]	[ ]	[ ]	[ ]	[ ]	[ ]
	(TA)	( )	( )	( )	( )	( )	( )	( )
	[ER]	[ ]	[ ]	[ ]	[ ]	[ ]	[ ]	[ ]
	(TA)	( )	( )	( )	( )	( )	( )	( )
	[ER]	[ ]	[ ]	[ ]	[ ]	[ ]	[ ]	[ ]
	(TA)	( )	( )	( )	( )	( )	( )	( )
	[ER]	[ ]	[ ]	[ ]	[ ]	[ ]	[ ]	[ ]

GROUP SECURITY PLANNING FORM

For Server:_____   By: _____   Date: ___/___/199___   Page ___ of ___

Dir. Rights < >		<CDMOPRSW>	<CDMOPRSW>	<CDMOPRSW>	<CDMOPRSW>	<CDMOPRSW>	<CDMOPRSW>	<CDMOPRSW>
Trustee Assignment ( )								
Effective Rights [ ]								
EVERYONE	(TA)	( )	( )	( )	( )	( )	( )	( )
	[ER]	[ ]	[ ]	[ ]	[ ]	[ ]	[ ]	[ ]
	(TA)	( )	( )	( )	( )	( )	( )	( )
	[ER]	[ ]	[ ]	[ ]	[ ]	[ ]	[ ]	[ ]
	(TA)	( )	( )	( )	( )	( )	( )	( )
	[ER]	[ ]	[ ]	[ ]	[ ]	[ ]	[ ]	[ ]
	(TA)	( )	( )	( )	( )	( )	( )	( )
	[ER]	[ ]	[ ]	[ ]	[ ]	[ ]	[ ]	[ ]
	(TA)	( )	( )	( )	( )	( )	( )	( )
	[ER]	[ ]	[ ]	[ ]	[ ]	[ ]	[ ]	[ ]
	(TA)	( )	( )	( )	( )	( )	( )	( )
	[ER]	[ ]	[ ]	[ ]	[ ]	[ ]	[ ]	[ ]
	(TA)	( )	( )	( )	( )	( )	( )	( )
	[ER]	[ ]	[ ]	[ ]	[ ]	[ ]	[ ]	[ ]
	(TA)	( )	( )	( )	( )	( )	( )	( )
	[ER]	[ ]	[ ]	[ ]	[ ]	[ ]	[ ]	[ ]
	(TA)	( )	( )	( )	( )	( )	( )	( )
	[ER]	[ ]	[ ]	[ ]	[ ]	[ ]	[ ]	[ ]

GROUP TO USER CROSS-WALK FORM

For Server:_____ By:_____ Date:___/___/199_ Page__ of __

	EVERY-ONE						
GUEST							

SERVER TO USER CROSS-WALK FORM

By: _____   Date: ___/___/199__   Page __ of __

USER LIST	SERVER	SERVER	SERVER	SERVER	SERVER	SERVER	SERVER
GUEST							

SOLUTION TO
FIGURE 6-2

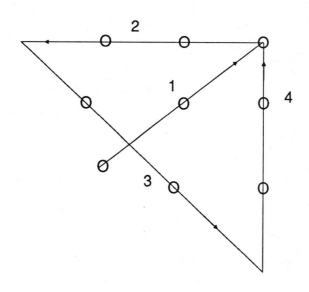

CREATING MENU
TEXT FILES

NetWare comes bundled with a menuing system, which allows you to develop custom menus for novice users. Several simple rules govern the creation of custom menus.

- The file must be an ASCII text file. If you use a word processor to develop the file, it must then be exported to ASCII format.

- The filename must use the extension .MNU. When placed in the PUBLIC directory, .MNU files are accessed by any user through the MENU command.

- Menu titles and menu choices begin flush with the left margin. Menu or submenu titles are preceded with a percent (%) sign.

- Any flush left items immediately below a menu or submenu title represent menu choices.

- Commands invoked when a menu choice is selected are placed immediately below the menu choice, but must be indented at least two spaces, to be distinguished from other menu choices.

- To call a submenu from any menu, place the submenu name with its percent sign (for example, %PRINTERS) indented at least two spaces from the left margin. Later in your file define that menu, being sure to use the exact same spelling for the submenu title.

- Menus and submenus may be located on the screen through row and column coordinates, which follow the menu or submenu titles at that point in the text file where the the menu or submenu is actually being created.

- A palette of colors may be selected through inclusion of a third parameter after the menu or submenu name.

Row, column, and color palette parameters must be separated by commas. For example, to select only a color palette for the main menu title EXECUTIVE MENU, you would type

%EXECUTIVE MENU,,3

The following listing provides an example of a menu text file with several submenus. The comments on the right are not part of the text file.

%EXECUTIVE MENU,2,2,9	The title for the main menu, with row, column, and color pallet selected.
SELECTIVE DRIVE	This choice takes the user to
%DRIVE POINTERS	a submenu named DRIVE POINTERS.
LOGOUT	When you select LOGOUT, a special
!LOGOUT	form of that command is issued.
LOTUS 123	This choice takes the user to
%123	the submenu 123.

WORD	This choice takes the user to
%WORD	the submenu WORD.
PROJECTS	This choice takes the user to
%PROJECTS	the submenu PROJECTS.
PRINTERS	This choice takes the user to
%PRINTERS	the submenu PRINTERS.
NETWARE MENUS	This choice takes the user to
%NETWARE MENUS	the submenu NETWARE MENUS.
OS UTILITIES	This choice takes the user to the
%OS UTILITIES	submenu OS UTILITIES.
SEE CURRENT MAPPINGS	This choice results in the MAP
MAP	command being issued from the
pause	primary EXECUTIVE MENU.
WINDOWS	This choice switches the user to
H:	drive H: (if it exists)
WIN	and calls up Windows, if a search
H:	drive mapping exists to Windows.
%123,2,45,4	This is the first defined submenu
RUN 123	beneath EXECUTIVE MENU.
123	
SELECT PRINTER	Notice that this submenu also
%PRINTERS	includes a goto PRINTERS choice.
CHANGE DIRECTORIES	
%DRIVE POINTERS	
%WORD,2,45,4	Another submenu beneath EXECUTIVE
RUN WORD	MENU. If the user selects RUN WORD,
MAP DEL S4:	the fourth search drive mapping is
MAP S4:=FS1/SYS:APPS/WORD	redefined, to allow the user to
WORD	always access the correct
H:	WORD help screen.
PRINTERS	
%PRINTERS	
%PROJECTS,2,45,4	This submenu also redefines the
RUN PROJECTS	fourth search drive, because
PROJECTS	PROJECTS and WORD use the same
MAP DEL S4:	filename to access help screens.
MAP S4:=FS1/SYS:APPS/PROJECTS	
P:	
PROJ.com	
H:	
MAP DEL S4:	
MAP S4:=FS1/SYS:APPS/WORD	
PRINTERS	Once again, you can call up the
%PRINTERS	PRINTERS submenu from this.

```
%NETWARE MENUS,2,45,0            A submenu with only some of the
SYSTEM CONFIGURATION            available NetWare menus included.
    SYSCON
SESSION
    SESSION
FILER
    FILER
PRINTER CONTROL
    PCONSOLE
%OS UTILITIES,2,45,7            This is an example of how you can
LOGIN                          create a submenu through which
LOGIN                          NetWare command-line commands can
HELP                           be issued.
    HELP
CASTOFF
    CASTOFF
CASTON
    CASTON
MAP
    MAP @1"ENTER MAP ASSIGNMENT"
    MAP
NPRINT
    NPRINT@1"Enter PATH/FILENAME [OPTIONS...]"
SALVAGE                        A very useful command, and
    SALVAGE                    the user does not have to
    PAUSE                      remember how to use it.
SLIST
    slist
    PAUSE
RIGHTS                         Another useful command.
    RIGHTS
    PAUSE
USERLIST
    USERLIST
    PAUSE
WhoAmi
    WHOAMI/A
    PAUSE
Copy Files, Network
    NCOPY@1"Enter the source" @2"Enter the destination"
    PAUSE
Copy Files, DOS(local)
    Echo Off
    cls
    Rem@2"Enter the destination"
    Rem@1"Enter the source"
```

```
        if not exist @1 go to no file
        Copy @1 @2
        go to done
        :no file
        Pause
        :done
SEE MAPPINGS
        MAP
        PAUSE
%DRIVE POINTERS
A:
        A:
B:
        B:
C:
        C:
D:
        D:
E:
        E:
F:
        F:
G:
        G:
H:
        H:
I:
        I:
J:
        J:
K:
        K:
L:
        L:
M:
        M:
N:
        N:
O:
        O:
P:
        P:
Q:
        Q:
R:
        R:
```

Rather than having to go back to the DOS prompt to switch drive pointers, this menu allows you to do so from a submenu (DRIVE POINTERS) accessed from the EXECUTIVE MENU (the SELECTIVE DIRECTORIES). (If you had meant the choice to read SELECT DIRECTORY within EXECUTIVE MENU, it would have to be spelled that way.)

```
T:
    T:
%PRINTERS,30,45,4                                  Finally, the PRINTERS
ACER LP-76, PLAIN PAPER, FORMS=0                   submenu, with
    capture q=printq_1 timeout=10 forms=0 nb       appropriate
ACER LP-76, LETTER HEAD, FORMS=1                   CAPTURE
    capture q=printq_1 timeout=10 forms=1 nb       commands
PANASONIC, GREEN SCREEN, FORMS=0                   issued
    capture q=printq_0 timeout=10 forms=0 nb       automatically,
PANASONIC, "OTHER" PAPER, FORMS=9                  including an
    capture q=printq_0 timeout=10 forms=9 nb       ENDCAP for when
LOCAL PRINTER, AT WORK STATION                     the user picks this
    ENDCAP                                         selection.
^Z                                                 Required CTRL-Z end-of-file
                                                   marker.
```

The main EXECUTIVE MENU created by this text file, along with the WORD and PRINTERS submenus, is shown in Figure 9-34 of Chapter 9. The NETWARE MENUS and OS UTILITIES submenus are shown in Figures C-1 and C-2.

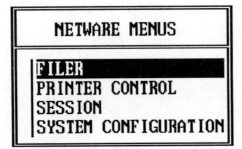

FIGURE C-1.   Customized NetWare menu's submenu as accessed from Executive menu

```
┌─────────────────────────┐
│      OS UTILITIES       │
├─────────────────────────┤
│ CASTOFF                 │
│ CASTON                  │
│ Copy Files, DOS(local)  │
│ Copy Files, Network     │
│ HELP                    │
│ LOGIN                   │
│ MAP                     │
│ NPRINT                  │
│ RIGHTS                  │
│ SALVAGE                 │
│ SEE MAPPINGS            │
│ SLIST                   │
│ USERLIST                │
│ WhoAmi                  │
└─────────────────────────┘
```

FIGURE C-2.   Customized OS Utilities submenu as accessed
from Executive menu

appendix D

NETWARE'S FCONSOLE MENU

NetWare provides a menu through which you can monitor server performance. Also, the user SUPERVISOR or a designated FCONSOLE operator can use this menu from a workstation for these purposes:

- to broadcast messages to users

- to disconnect a workstation from the LAN (and free up any files or resources the user has locked)

- to down the server

Console operators are created through the Supervisor Options portion of the SYSCON menu. Simply call up the Console Operators screen, and press (INSERT) to select from a list of server users those whom you wish to create as console operators, if any. You are not required to create console operators.

```
┌───────────────────────────────────┐
│         Available Options         │
│ ┌───────────────────────────────┐ │
│ │█Broadcast Console Message█    │ │
│ │ Change Current File Server    │ │
│ │ Connection Information        │ │
│ │ Down File Server              │ │
│ │ File/Lock Activity            │ │
│ │ LAN Driver Information        │ │
│ │ Purge All Salvageable Files   │ │
│ │ Statistics                    │ │
│ │ Status                        │ │
│ │ Version Information            │ │
│ └───────────────────────────────┘ │
└───────────────────────────────────┘
```

FIGURE D-1.   FCONSOLE Available Options main menu

To access the FCONSOLE menu, at the prompt type **FCONSOLE** and press (ENTER). You will see an Available Options menu like that shown in Figure D-1. Users who are not console

```
┌────────────────────────────────────────────────────────────┐
│                       Cache Statistics                      │
├────────────────────────────────────────────────────────────┤
│ File Server Up Time:   0 Days  3 Hours 23 Minutes 43 Seconds │
│ Number Of Cache Buffers:        314  Cache Buffer Size:  4,096│
│ Dirty Cache Buffers:              0                          │
│ Cache Read Requests:         23,059  Cache Write Requests: 1,054│
│ Cache Hits:                  23,173  Cache Misses:          998│
│ Physical Read Requests:         950  Physical Write Requests: 403│
│ Physical Read Errors:             0  Physical Write Errors:   0│
│ Cache Get Requests:          23,358                          │
│ Full Write Requests:            755  Partial Write Requests: 299│
│ Background Dirty Writes:         22  Background Aged Writes:  355│
│ Total Cache Writes:             379  Cache Allocations:      996│
│ Thrashing Count:                  0  LRU Block Was Dirty:      2│
│ Read Beyond Write:                0  Fragmented Writes:       24│
│ Hit On Unavailable Block:         2  Cache Blocks Scrapped:    0│
└────────────────────────────────────────────────────────────┘
```

FIGURE D-2.   FCONSOLE Cache Statistics screen

```
                         LAN I/O Statistics
 File Server Up Time:   0 Days  3 Hours 25 Minutes 52 Seconds
 Total Packets Received:              20,780  Packets Routed:              67
 File Service Packets:                20,428  NetBIOS Broadcasts:           0
 Packets With Invalid Slots:              0   Invalid Connections:          0
 Invalid Sequence Numbers:                0   Invalid Request Types:        0
 Detach With Invalid Slot:                0   Forged Detach Requests:       0
 New Request During Processing:           0
 New Attach During Processing:            0   Ignored Duplicate Attach:     0
 Reply Canceled By New Attach:            0
 Detach During Processing Ignored:        0
 Reexecuted Requests:                     0   Duplicate Replies Sent:       5
 Positive Acknowledges Sent:              0   File Service Used Route:      0
 Packets Discarded Because They Crossed More Than 16 Bridges:      0
 Packets Discarded Because Destination Network Is Unknown:         0
 Incoming Packets Lost Because Of No Available Buffers:            0
 Outgoing Packets Lost Because Of No Available Buffers:            0
```

FIGURE D-3.   FCONSOLE LAN I/O Statistics screen

operators will *not* be able to select Down File Server, Broadcast Console Message, Connection Information, or Purge All Salvage-able Files.

Included among the statistics that you can monitor are those

```
                         Physical Disk  0
 File Server Up Time:   0 Days  3 Hours 25 Minutes 20 Seconds
 Disk Type:  0. IBM AT Hard Disk "C"   type  018
 Non-Removable Drive
 Disk Channel:   0   Controller Number:   0   Drive Number: 0
 Controller Type: 0.
 Drive Size (less hot fix area): 57,610,240 bytes
 Drive Cylinders:    976  Drive Heads:   7   Sectors Per Track:  17
 IO Error Count:      0
 Hot Fix Table Start: 14,065        Hot Fix Enabled
 Hot Fix Table Size:  453 blocks    Hot Fix Remaining: 439 blocks
```

FIGURE D-4.   FCONSOLE Physical Disk screen, with
Physical Disk 0 information displayed

```
                         Volume Information
┌──────────────────────────────────────────────────────────────────┐
│File Server Up Time:   0 Days  3 Hours 26 Minutes 32 Seconds        │
│Volume Name:    SYS                  Volume Number:         0        │
│Volume Mounted:  Yes                 Volume Removable: No            │
│Volume Hashed:   Yes                 Volume Cached:    Yes           │
│Block Size:       4,096              Starting Block:      4          │
│Total Blocks:    14,061              Free Blocks:     1,923          │
│Maximum Directory Entries:       3,968                              │
│Peak Directory Entries Used:     1,410                              │
│Current Free Directory Entries:  2,673                              │
│Logical Drive Number:    0                                         │
│Volume Mirrored:        No                                         │
│Primary Disk Number:     0           Mirror Disk Number: N/A        │
└──────────────────────────────────────────────────────────────────┘
```

FIGURE D-5.   FCONSOLE Volume Information screen with
Volume SYS Information displayed

shown in Figures D-2 through D-5. The discussions in Chapter 2
and elsewhere in this book should help you understand some of
these statistics. Also refer to your Novell *Supervisor Reference*
manual for more precise definitions of each FCONSOLE menu
choice and displayed statistics.

TRADEMARKS

AppleTalk®	Apple Computer, Inc.
Arcnet®	Datapoint Corporation
dBASE IV®	Ashton-Tate
Compaq®	Compaq Computer Corp.
Ethernet®	Intel Corporation
HP LaserJet®	Hewlett-Packard
IBM®	International Business Machines Corporation
Lotus 1-2-3®	Lotus Development Corporation
Macintosh®	Apple Computer, Inc.
Microsoft®	Microsoft Corporation
Microsoft® Windows™	Microsoft Corporation
Microsoft® Word™	Microsoft Corporation
NetWare®	Novell Corporation
Norton Utilities®	Peter Norton Computing
Novell®	Novell Corporation
Okidata Microline®	Okidata Corporation
OS/2®	Microsoft Corporation
Paradox 3®	Borland International
Sidekick®	Borland International
Token-Ring®	International Business Machines Corporation
UNIX®	AT&T
WordPerfect®	WordPerfect Corporation
Xerox Network Services (XNS)®	Xerox Corporation

Index

D

E

FOLIO, 435
Function keys, in NetWare menus,
92

G

Groups
    adding member to, 106-108
    creating thru SYSCON,
      104-105
    deleting thru SYSCON,
      109-110
    EVERYONE, 88-89

H

Hard disks
    access speeds, 48-54
    partitioning, 42-44
    size, 5, 42-43
    storage, and resource
      accounting, 54
Help
    (F1), 91-92
    HELP command line
      command, 435
    help screen for menus, 92

I

IBM$RUN.OVL, 433
IBM PS/2, NIC node address
  setting, 68
Installation
    AUXGEN diskette, 410
    Help infobase, 434-436

Installation, *continued*
    Keyboard lock VAP, 436-437
    printers, 326
    NETGEN, 69, 395-400,
      403-425
    SHGEN, 395, 425-433
Inter-operability, 20, 195-197
INSTOVL, 420
INT2F.COM, 429
IPX (Inter-network Pack
  Exchange), 20
IPX.COM, 20, 72, 75, 228, 429,
  430, 431
IRQ (interrupt request) settings
    changing, 71
    default, 71

K

Keycard, 400

L

LAN management, reducing
  burden of, 378
LANs
    applications, using on,
      171-191
    bridging, 10, 11
    cabling and printing, 327
    components of, 7-8
    data integrity, 8
    data security, 9
    data sharing, 8
    diagram of, 7
    electronic mail and, 62